The Fly Fisher and the River

The Fly Fisher and the River

A Memoir

BY MAXINE ATHERTON

Edited by Catherine Varchaver

Skyhorse Publishing

Skyhorse Publishing books may be purchased in bulk at special discounts for
sales promotion, corporate gifts, fund-raising, or educational purposes. Special
editions can also be created to specifications. For details, contact the Special Sales
Department, Skyhorse Publishing, 307 West 36th Street, 11th Floor, New York,
NY 10018 or info@skyhorsepublishing.com.

Skyhorse® and Skyhorse Publishing® are registered trademarks of Skyhorse
Publishing, Inc.®, a Delaware corporation.

Visit our website at www.skyhorsepublishing.com.

10 9 8 7 6 5 4 3 2 1

Library of Congress Cataloging-in-Publication Data is available on file.

Cover design by Tom Lau
Cover photo credit: Maxine Atherton

Print ISBN: 978-1-63450-647-2
Ebook ISBN: 978-1-63450-648-9

Printed in China

On behalf of my grandmother, fearless fly fisher and pioneer, I dedicate these pages to Max's three greatest loves—her beloved husband and fishing partner, artist Jack Atherton, who left this world much too soon; her beautiful, ever creative daughter, Mary Atherton Varchaver; and perhaps most of all, to Nature's glorious rivers on which Max found joy and connection as a feminine force in a man's world.

Contents

Foreword

Catherine Varchaver

When I was growing up, most of my friends had grandmothers who baked pies and told stories, or slowly faded away in nursing homes. Some of my friends' grandmothers would venture on the occasional vacation cruise. My grandmother, Maxine Atherton, was different. She traveled to remote parts of the globe so she could wear waders and cast into fast-moving streams for hours, waiting to catch "a big one." She sent frequent, scrawled missives highlighting her latest adventures, complete with a grainy photograph of her standing next to a guide and the thirty-pound salmon she'd just caught. One year she sent us a giant side of smoked salmon from a catch which she had taken herself to a smokehouse.

Well into her eighties, my grandmother drove the 2,100 miles between New Brunswick, Canada and her then home in the Florida Keys. She had a constantly shifting array of houses and fishing camps, like the octogenarian equivalent of a carefree surfer chasing the next big wave. She would roll into town in her vehicle of the moment. Sometimes it was a Plymouth station wagon with '70s fake wood paneling, packed with fishing gear and her Springer Spaniel, Pete. One memorable year after a windfall, she pulled up to our house in a Cadillac

Sedan de Ville, gold and flashy on the outside, and more like an ad for Orvis on the inside. The very next year, she zipped into our suburban village in a two-seat Fiat Spider. It was red.

Not surprisingly, my grandmother always cringed at anything that suggested she was an old lady—like being called "Grandma"—and the last thing she wanted was a title. So everyone, including her grandchildren, was instructed to address her as Max. (She always detested the name Maxine.)

So, when I noticed the rubber band-wrapped roll of printed manuscript pages jammed into a crate of old journals, I was thrilled. And I had little idea of what lay ahead. It was summer and I had just bought a small house so my teenage son, Sasha, and I could stay in the town he'd always called home—Takoma Park, Maryland, on the border of Washington, DC. Once I started reading the manuscript, I was hooked like a hungry salmon to a fly. Max's adventures as a wanderer and fly fisher came to life in her collection of remembrances, organized around fishing rivers. I savored the brief family history before watching her tie together the major elements of her life with a string of stories that revolved around fishing, and the rivers and characters she admired along the way. It had always been my grandmother's intention to add her memoirs to the annals of fly fishing literary history.

My mother had given me the manuscript for safekeeping fifteen years earlier, following my return from two years in Central Asia, only a few months before Sasha came into the world and just weeks after my grandmother Max left it. So Max's manuscript disappeared in the frenzy of a move across the globe and the excitement of becoming a parent, only to resurface as I completed yet another move. Holding the rolled pages, the unfinished memoir felt especially weighty. I could hear Max's voice telling me, with her lilting laugh, that her dream was in my hands now. It felt right that I, as her sole granddaughter, would be the one to edit Max's manuscript and find a publisher for her book—to carry her literary baton over the finish line.

In the last fifteen or so years before 1996 when Max died, just seven years shy of a century, she made it clear to all who would listen that she had tales to tell about fishing, the art scene, and the extraordinary people who passed through her life—including several quite celebrated ones. Max came close to fulfilling her dream, but old age finally overcame her unflinching will—a will exerted honorably over decades of learned patience and natural determination while fishing on dozens of trout streams and salmon rivers, as a woman engaging and excelling in a man's world. Anyone who knew her outside of the fishing scene would be surprised to hear the word "patience" and "Max" in the same sentence; but as a fly fisher on a river, my grandmother shifted into another way of being, depending on skills honed out of necessity as battles with salmon or trout cannot be won through rash action or impatient maneuvers.

With a perpetual, mischievous glint in her eye, my grandmother's less meditative side delighted in scandalizing people. At one big dinner with friends and family when she was well into her eighties, Max interrupted a conversation about mundane matters to loudly proclaim that she favored premarital sex.

Somehow, Max never got around to teaching her grandchildren how to fly fish. She was probably too busy to educate us on the art of casting and choosing flies. My only sustained experience of fishing was fishing for bass from a row boat in the wilds of Ontario with my best friend, Valerie, and her parents, "Uncle Vincent" and "Aunt Betty-Jean." A veteran first violinist in the New York Metropolitan orchestra, Uncle Vincent's obsessions were opera, Volkswagens, and fishing. For several summers in the 1970s, Val and I would pile into his Bug or Aunt Betty-Jean's Rabbit and make the two-day trek north from Hastings-on-Hudson, New York. We looked forward to fishing and swimming at "the Island," where we happily went weeks without electricity, phones, or running water. It was an hour's motorboat ride across Lake Penage, not far from Whitefish, to the tiny pine-covered island where their two-room cabin sat at the top of a hill. Uncle Vincent taught us how to squeeze live worms over sharp hooks and assured me that they felt no pain. When we got tired of sitting, Val and I would jump into the lake to swim in its silky, pristine waters and Uncle Vincent would light up a Kent and put away the fishing gear, resigned to our restless energy. I didn't understand what he was looking for when he'd row up to a good fishing pool, but there was always magic in the air as we wondered if we'd catch enough for a supper of pan-fried bass with boiled potatoes and canned peas. While I loved my one and only extended experience of ordinary fishing, I was more of a small-town-near-the-big-city kind of girl.

My brothers, Nicholas and Peter, and I were all born in a suburb outside of Paris, and moved to the States when I was six. We grew up in a small town on the Hudson River, a forty-minute train ride from Grand Central Station in Manhattan. The three of us always looked forward to the Christmas, Easter, and summer vacations when we were likely to see Max. Her visits were an event. While she did not make us the center of her life the way other grandparents did, there was never any doubt that she adored us, as any waiter who ever served us could tell you. "These are my grandchildren," she would loudly announce as someone would walk over to take our order. "Aren't they wonderful?!" My brothers and I would slink down in our seats or lift menus to shield our reddening faces.

When our family took a road trip to visit Max at her house or "camp" of the moment, she spoiled us as any grandmother would, with homemade meals of roast chicken, mashed potatoes, seasonal vegetables, often from her garden, and green salad; or with homemade deserts of coconut or chocolate cake served with generous spoonfuls of Cool Whip, an attempt at calorie consciousness. Cool Whip aside, Max encouraged us to eat plenty of vegetables and take vitamins for this and that, in an era when wellness products were not yet a multi-billion dollar industry. I always assumed her obsession with vitamins was just one of her newfound quirks; but in getting to know Max through her memoirs, I have come to see that her interest in nutrition and health was first inspired by her longtime friend, fly fishing legend Edward Hewitt, who was chemist by training. Hewitt was one of the first to isolate the value of nutrients and to preach supplementation, to improve the health of fish and animals, as well as people.

As easy as it was to appreciate her eccentric, quirky qualities, there was also an elusive air about Max that made it difficult to feel that we truly knew her, perhaps because she seemed to be in constant motion, always on her way to or from some place. Reading her stories helps fill in some of the missing pieces. And looking back at Max's adult life, it is impossible not to notice the mid-life line that divided her years with her beloved husband, Jack, and her years without him. Recognized as a serious artist, John Atherton was admired for his magical realism and abstract paintings. Early in his career and marriage to Max, a painting from his first one-man show in New York, *The Black Horse*, won a $4,000 prize from among 14,000 entries. It became part of the permanent collection at the Metropolitan Museum of Art. My grandfather's "bread and butter" work was as an illustrator in the advertising industry and then as a magazine cover artist. Between 1942 and 1951 he created more than forty-five *Saturday Evening Post* covers alongside artist friends Norman Rockwell, Mead Schaeffer, and others, as well as a few covers for *Fortune* (which, coincidentally, is where my brother Nick works today). With my grandfather's career secure, he and my grandmother were free to manage their newly empty-nest years with longer fishing expeditions.

The turning point in Max's life came in September 1952 when my grandparents traveled to New Brunswick for some late-summer fly fishing. Jack was only fifty-two years old when he collapsed of a heart attack on the shores of the Miramichi River, doing what he loved most: fishing. He had just caught an enormous salmon and was beside himself with joy. Perhaps the excitement was too much. In any case that terrible day Max lost the love of her life and her most devoted fishing partner—just two weeks before her forty-nineth birthday. Twenty-six years had passed since she and Jack met in art school. Once married a year or so later, Max focused on being the wife of a successful artist by supporting local causes, taking an occasional literature or poetry class, and happily raising their daughter, Mary (with help from a housekeeper), and, as often as possible, fly fishing. Once my grandfather was gone, Max wondered if she knew who she was apart from her husband. And her only child was living on her own, finishing college at Bennington—something Max never accomplished herself, much to her regret.

With help from many, especially longtime Arlington, Vermont friends and neighbors Norman and Mary Rockwell, Max found the courage to face the devastating turn her life had taken. Fly fishing and the desire to write gave Max a reason to get up every day and re-engage in life, as did raising awareness about the growing environmental degradation of streams and rivers and the health of salmon. She applied her energies and funds to the causes about which she cared deeply, supporting institutions that included the American Museum of Fly Fishing in Manchester, Vermont, major art galleries and museums that were honored to acquire her husband's paintings, community hospitals, environmental organizations, and universities.

Not long after Jack's death, Max began exploring her long-time interest in writing and participated in a writer's conference at Middlebury College, part of the famous Bread Loaf Writer's Conference program. There she connected with a handful of struggling writers with whom she became fast friends, including Shane Stevens, who eventually gained respect as a crime novelist. Max created the Bread Loaf John Atherton Scholarship so that talented writers could follow their hearts even when their pocketbooks were empty. She always had a soft spot for the underdog, for anyone she thought deserved a chance to be saved or propelled forward in life. In fact, one of the stories Max produced as a result of a Bread Loaf retreat relayed a dramatic real-life account of coming upon a young woman and her abusive husband in the midst of a violent rage. While camping and fishing in the Sierras with her father as a child, Max had learned that when faced with a bear who feels threatened, angry or hungry, it's better to stand one's ground calmly rather than to run. This lesson served Max throughout her life, and in turn served the young couple whose drama she entered and helped redirect, and then recounted.

In keeping with what she eventually realized was her fearless, independent nature, Max followed the advice of fishing friends after

Jack's death: She traveled by ship across the Atlantic to fly fish in remote parts of France and Spain. There adventures abounded and she encountered all kinds of people, including armed guards serving the Spanish dictator, General Franco. As a widow on her own in the 1950s, taking off to travel the world and trudge into fishing streams with strangers—inevitably men—Max was undoubtedly viewed as unusual, if not eccentric. And given the slow, demanding modes of travel, limited means of communication, and frequent dearth of lodging options near the best fly fishing venues, her travels as a woman alone in foreign lands (and waters) are all the more remarkable.

Also notable is the fact that Max was already a published author before starting work on her memoir. *Every Sportsman's Cookbook* was produced by Macmillan in 1962, and her straightforward, practical style reads like a Julia Child-like inspiration for fishers and hunters. Fortunately for the angling world (and those with an interest in post-World War II American artists), Max decided to capture her fly fishing experiences on paper. An early version of this manuscript made the rounds among a few publishers about a dozen years before my grandmother's death. In 1981, Max sent a draft to her fly fishing acquaintance and successful publisher-author, Nick Lyons. He liked the stories but advised her that the book needed a strong editor's hand and he was too busy to do it himself. Discouraged but determined, Max reworked parts of the book and over the next few years some chapters appeared as essays in the *Atlantic Salmon Journal* and various fly fishing magazines.

In giving us this memoir, my grandmother wanted readers to feel the love she had for fishing, and for preserving the natural world. She reveled in the rivers around which her life revolved as she waited for her chance to duel with one worthy, stream-dwelling opponent after another. Salmon proved to be as much a friend as a foe because the beauty of fly fishing was not merely about the catch, but about playing the game with elegance and strength—and about gaining the respect and admiration of her fishing companions, and perhaps even the respect of the salmon who got away! Max's expansive imagination, to which she makes reference numerous times, took her to beautiful places whenever she wanted. On a river, away from urban noise and distractions, her imagination blossomed and transported her to another realm, even as she remained aware of the subtle activity all around her as any outdoor sportsperson would.

In a conversation one snowy Christmas at her house in Fairfax, Vermont (when she was still living with her second husband, Watson Wyckoff, another avid angler and a character in his own right), Max reminded me that life was fairly bleak for many years when World Wars raged overseas and the Depression was at home. I was ten or eleven, listening to her talk of the old days. She explained that fly fishing had been, and still was, a wonderful escape from the depressing and sometimes horrific news of the day, especially when she and Jack found themselves raising my mother during the early Depression years. My grandfather's profession as an artist was a challenging one. But his hard work and recognized talent—and some measure of luck—meant that he and his family lived comfortably. Max told me that although Jack did well and they struggled very little compared to many, they also never knew if the bottom was about to fall out from under them, especially during the thirties. A sensitive soul, painfully aware of all the suffering around her and around the world, Max could tolerate these tragic visions for only so long. She was blessed with the freedom to escape, financial privilege, and a mindset that sought out the joys in life, rather than obsessing on the deep wrongs and downsides.

Max was aware of her good fortune as a woman born at the tail end of the Victorian era. In spite of her mother's more conventional views, Max grew up believing she could have her own ideas and act on her own behalf. Her marriage with Jack provided as much space for freedom as it did love and security, and she would not have tolerated limits on her choices. This attitude carried her forward after Jack's death and during the rest of her days. Only in her eighties, when fighting a river's current and reeling in a weighty salmon had become taxing for her petite frame, did she feel the need to begin adapting to some of the realities of age. At that point, her Miramichi fishing camp neighbor and fellow fly fisher, baseball legend Ted Williams, designed a lightweight graphite rod for Max to use, which she gratefully accepted; although I imagine it never compared to her beloved first Powell rod (or borrowed Hewitt reel, whose misadventures are recounted here). A few years later when she felt her legs were no longer able to resist strong river currents, Max sold the New Brunswick fishing camp and shifted her focus away from fishing and exclusively to writing.

The chapters of this book are generally, but not completely, chronological. Like fast moving currents, these fishing tales move us through a selection of Max's experiences within the rivers' waters, as well as at their outer edges. They remind us that alongside the (then) radical environmentalist-explorer part of her, there was a playful joie de vivre, one that appreciated the company of good-looking, intelligent outdoorsmen. Even before Jack Atherton's death, Max clearly enjoyed the attention she got as a fisherwoman—especially from men. While she cherished her friendships with a few women, she felt they did not generally engage their minds as much as they could and tended to settle for less in their lives than she was willing to. Men—educated and with leisure time to fish—had more freedom and could have adventures and talk about ideas, politics, and the intricacies of fly fishing. This refined form of angling provided an escape from the mundane and Max enjoyed the adrenaline rush of fishing and camping in the great outdoors as much as the meditative quiet of time in Nature. Her expertise provided the entrée she needed to thrive in a man's world, and Max always longed to write about the joys of casting her lines into one river after another.

With the blessing of my mother (Max's closest living relative), I stepped into my role as editor, determined to honor my grandmother's dream. The process of absorbing and working with Max's words reeled me into a profound journey that tightened my connection to both my grandmother, and my mother who helped provide context and some of the missing pieces to the puzzle that was Maxine Atherton. It took more than two years to complete the editing process, as I spent time getting to know the fascinating characters in Max's life while simultaneously juggling a demanding full-time job and life as a single parent. I not only reconnected with my family history, but felt the disparate pieces of my life fitting together, in rough parallel with my grand-mother's. My own adventures—living and working around the world, writing and editing stateside over the years for a variety of non-profits, practicing as a holistic nutrition counselor, and finally, promoting conservation programs at World Wildlife Fund—resurfaced as these threads pulled me closer to the journey Max relays here.

Fans of my grandfather's classic, *The Fly and the Fish,* may find Max's *The Fly Fisher and The River* to be the yin to his yang. It's easy to see how their shared passion for art and fly fishing, and for the smallest wonders of the natural world, would make for an enduring and fulfill-ing marriage. Working on this book, I have come to appreciate the richness of the camaraderie that fly fishers enjoy. And I see the impor-tance of giving time to the full experience of casting as an art and fishing as an opportunity for meditative reflections and for being in the "now," away from the distractions of daily routines and demands. There's a reason fishing is so often used as a metaphor for life as a jour-ney to be relished rather than a goal to be reached.

The Fly Fisher and the River will, I hope, speak to fly fishers eve-rywhere who share my grandmother's obsession for this elegant, yet earthy sport and to anyone with an appreciation for nature and an interest in conserving its future. Max thrived on the expansive quiet of being in Nature as much as the concentrated interruptions of adrena-line at the sudden bowing of the fly rod. Through her stories one can feel the trained fisher's presence to the details of reels and flies that seems to give way to an intuitive awareness of the river's ripples, and the flies' telling dances above the surface, while below majestic salmon or trout wisely lurk. Like countless anglers before and since, my grand-mother was happily addicted to the inevitable tension between the chaser and the chased, and ultimately, the joy of engaging in respectful battle with a strong and savvy adversary.

In the end, Max not only expresses her lifelong love of fly fish-ing and the need to conserve the biodiversity and magic of both the planet's rivers and all of Nature, but also of her eternal love for the man who helped her realize her passion for angling. Jack Atherton was

Max sitting with a friend's dog on a skiing outing. Bromley Mountain, c. late 1940s.

Max's granddaughter, Catherine Varchaver, Ontario. c. 1970.

proud of his accomplished fly fisher wife. In Jack's book *The Fly and the Fish*, we feel this sense of pride as he concludes a chapter about angling on the Neversink River with their dear friend Edward Hewitt:

> *To Max, particularly, he [Hewitt] imparted a practical knowledge of streamcraft, casting and fishing with a patience and interest equaled only by her appreciation. How much he contributed toward making her an angler of prowess neither a big brown trout nor I realized until one day when I tried fruitlessly for an hour to deceive him. He looked over my fly a few times but each time turned it down with a nonchalance which was irritating to an already sorely tried angler*
>
> *When I finally decided to give up, Max, who had been waiting on the bank, waded out to try for him. Secure in the knowledge that if I could not get him after such a long effort, she could not, I started off up the stream. I had gone but a few steps when I heard her reel screech and turned to see the fish slash madly across the pool. He had taken her second cast and thus two more males had underestimated the power of a woman.*

Many men (and women) before and since that time have made the mistake of underestimating my grandmother, but most learned quickly that Maxine Atherton was a force to be reckoned with. Through this book, Max gives us a glimpse into the woman behind the force, into the fly fisher and the river.

CHAPTER ONE

Heritage

Said the river: Imagine everything you can imagine, then keep on going.

—Mary Oliver

While scientists may try to grasp the mysteries of humankind's genetic origins, almost all of us are fascinated by our own family heritage. Mine is undoubtedly much the same as thousands of other Americans. My sister, Petey, and I came into the world during the end of the Industrial Age and beginning of the Mechanical Age. Our American forefathers came to the New World to escape wars and the binding social and religious restrictions of the Old World. What I know about our genealogical heritage, I learned from the stories told by my parents and elderly relatives.

The early American ancestors on both sides of my family tree came from the British Isles and settled in New England. My father's last name was Breese, and his first known ancestor was French and fought alongside William the Conqueror when he invaded England. According to the famous eleventh edition of the *Encyclopedia Britannica*,[1] William the Conqueror was a conscious conservationist in the elev-

---

1. The eleventh edition of the *Encyclopedia Britannica* is noted for having been published when Swift, Shaw, Freud, and other renowned writers, scientists and historians authored the text. My grandmother's suede-bound set remains today at the home of my mother, Mary Atherton Varchaver, in Hastings-on-Hudson, New York, where my brothers and I spent the bulk of our childhood years.

enth century. As King, he forced British land owners to plant trees to replace those they cut down.

My father's French ancestors remained in the British Isles and settled in Wales. Gradually over many generations, the original surname of Brise (French for breeze) was changed to Breese. Later, one of the descendants came to North America and settled in New England. (Today several Breese families have made their homes around Bennington, Vermont.) Generations later, a branch of that family moved somewhere near Washington, DC.

My father's family was closely allied with the Marquis de Lafayette, noted for his triumphal tour of the United States between 1824 and 1825, and about that time in the early history of the United States a Mrs. Breese boosted the family name up the social ladder by leading an inaugural ball in the nation's capital to celebrate John Quincy Adams's election as president.

A son of that Breese family migrated to Michigan, then a sparsely settled state rich in rivers and lakes. One of his sons, my grandfather, moved to the town of Three Rivers and married a beautiful young woman, Polly Anna Foote, originally from New England. (Some will be surprised to learn that my legal first name is in fact Polly, which I despised from a young age; so I became known by my middle name, Maxine. However, since I have never been fond of the name Maxine, either, most of my friends and family know me as *Max*.)

My paternal grandparents had only one child, and with that marriage our heritage began its descent back down the social ladder once Polly Breese committed the outrageous sin of divorcing her husband and taking their small son to California. I have no idea what happened to my grandfather Breese afterwards, but I would like to think that the rest of his life he enjoyed the wonderful fishing and hunting that the state of Michigan had to offer a sportsman at that time. As for my grandmother, Polly, I feel sure that if she were alive today, she would be an active member of the women's liberation movement.

Polly's son, Frederic Fenimor Breese, was my father. He was born in 1862, the year before the Emancipation Proclamation. Father was seven when his mother and he traveled to California on the new Transcontinental Railway, the first railway across North America, completed in 1869. They rode in one of the first Pullman Palace cars, luxurious sleeping cars draped in Victorian elegance with seating and walls covered of red plush and gold trim. They left the train at Colfax, a booming railroad town north of San Francisco, and boarded a narrow-gauge train that traveled to Nevada City, their destination.

That storybook train was still running when I was a child living in Nevada City in the early 1900s. I remember lying in bed and listening to its whistle, a nostalgic decrescendo of fading tones that would slip into the distance of long ago dreams. Occasionally, Mother took my big sister, Petey, and me to San Francisco and we reveled in our rides on that little train. Father said it was the first narrow-gauge in the West, and I remember the fancy coal-burning potbelly stove that kept the passenger coach cozy and warm in the wintertime.

In Colfax we changed to a big Union Pacific train, on its way to San Francisco from the East. When the train reached San Francisco Bay, it was dismantled and the sections were loaded on an enormous ferryboat that carried the train and all of us across the Bay to San Francisco. That train was enormously important if only because it brought my father across North America when he was a child.

My father, Frederic, and his mother, Polly, moved to Nevada City about twenty years after the Gold Rush.[2] Upon arriving, the lovely young lady from Michigan took her young son to the area's only respectable lodging, the National Hotel. The next day she set out to look for a house to rent, a daunting task given that a large part of the population of that frontier mining town lived in tents, and there were no houses to rent. That did not stop her. My grandmother had a house built, made the downstairs into a dress shop and used the upstairs as living quarters. Later, Polly employed thirteen seamstresses

---

2. Since the great California Gold Rush began in 1948 and ended about ten years later in 1858, it's not clear whether Max meant that Frederic and his mother moved to Nevada City in 1868 or 1878. See http://ocp.hul.harvard.edu/immigration/goldrush.html. for more information.

to make the clothes she designed for the wives and mistresses of men who "struck it rich" in the gold fields around Nevada City and Grass Valley, another mining town four miles from Nevada City.

The two largest gold mines in California—the North Start and Empire mines—were connected by a little street car resembling the Toonerville Trolley in the old comic strip.[3] A very important trolley indeed, running through Grass Valley. All of the assay offices for the area were based in Nevada City, also the capital of Nevada County.

In Nevada City, my enterprising grandmother Polly became quite successful. She had another house built, collected rent from it, and her dress shop developed into a thriving business. A photograph of her at that time has her seated in an open fringe-topped carriage pulled by a pair of beautifully matched horses, black and sleek. Two Dalmatian dogs followed side by side behind and the driver, sitting in his seat above wore a stovepipe hat and held the reins as though his carriage were carrying a queen. I can't help but wonder how pedigreed dogs and pure bred horses got to that wilderness mining town. Perhaps the man she later married in Nevada City gave them to her. He owned a livery stable, a lucrative business at that time.

Unfortunately, Polly had little time for her son. She boarded him with a childless couple living on a farm outside the rowdy mining town, and from there he made the five-mile walk to school in Nevada City. Needless to say, his formal education was sketchy, but his mother, well educated, tutored him in reading, writing and good manners, and he wrote in the most beautiful script I had ever seen.

Father had another tutor during his childhood, an old Native American who took him to the best hunting grounds in the Sierras around Nevada City and taught him how to hunt and fish. During summer vacations as a teenager, Father worked in mines, picked up a string of swear words from rough miners, and adopted them as part of his vocabulary. His swearing embarrassed me, a self-conscious teenager, but now I recall it as a quirk that added a spark of zest to this dialogue.

---

3.   Visit http://www.kenpiercebooks.com/toonerville.html. for more information.

When Father moved to San Francisco, a growing metropolis, he was nineteen. I wish I knew more about his life there. He seldom talked about his past. I think he worked on the McCall Building, the first tall building in San Francisco, six stories high. Other than that, I know almost nothing about what my father did until the late 1800s when, driven by the wanderlust and spirit of adventure inherited from a long line of restless ancestors going back to the time of William the Conqueror, he sailed up the Pacific coast in a freighter to the Klondike.

There he found no gold, and so crossed over to Alaska on foot and by dogsled. In Alaska, Father found a wealth of fishing and hunting, and remained for several years living among the Eskimos, now known more respectfully as the Inuit, hunting and fishing with them. "The happiest and sanest people on Earth," he would tell me. I loved hearing his stories about the Inuit. The hunting and fishing were marvelous, of course. In the meantime, the United States had fought and won the Spanish-American War, but Father knew nothing about that war until he returned to San Francisco.

It was there he met my mother, and as I write this, I am now admiring a photograph of him. Wearing a formal cutaway jacket and ascot tie, he held a gold-topped cane. It is difficult to reconcile that handsome, dashing man to the father I remember in the Sierras. I suppose the photograph was taken the day he and Mother were married. His first known ancestor was a Celtic Frenchman from the South of France in a region between the Seine and Charonne rivers. Father had dark brown hair and eyes, his height was less than average, and his temperament was more stereotypically Celtic—cheerful, bright, adventurous, easily moved to extremes of enthusiasm and depression. That is exactly how I remember him.

And so my father, Frederic Breese, and my mother, Mary Frances Rogers, were married in San Francisco in the year 1900. He was nine years older and I never heard him address Mother by any name but *Sweetheart*. He spoke of her as "the kid," and I never heard him quarrel with her or saw him get angry, although Mother said that he had been known to lose his temper with people now and again.

My parents moved to Nevada City a couple of years before the earthquake of 1906 that almost demolished San Francisco, when I was one year old. I wish I could say they lived happily ever after, but while Nevada City had become more respectable by that time, life was far from easy. Father had inherited some mining property from his mother's estate, but with the falling gold standard, it had little value. He was not meant to be a miner, and there was no place for his athletic abilities in Nevada City. He decided to run a hardware and plumbing business and while everything he did he did well, he lacked his mother's natural gift and drive to succeed in business.

Father's potential was never realized. Neither was Mother's, and she complained constantly. She was quite beautiful and as a young woman dreamed of becoming an actress, but her father insisted that the theater was no place for nice young ladies. And in that strict Victorian Era, young women obeyed the wishes of their parents. She had a talent for art, too. Our house was filled with her work. The oil paintings she reproduced of famous paintings in San Francisco museums showed impressive skills, but in Nevada City, she was a slave to her family and the big house Father had inherited, with no time to devote to her artistic gifts. Her existence in a small town became stultifying, her talent and beauty sadly wasted. And yet she managed in her own way to adjust to the rugged West.

My maternal grandmother, Elizabeth Jane Hare, was proud of the fact that her father was born in England and graduated from Oxford University. She was been raised in the South and tutored by him, later marrying Nathaniel Petite Rogers. Rogers's ancestors had settled in Pennsylvania, and some later migrated to Columbus, Ohio. Nathaniel and Elizabeth Rogers ended up in Des Moines, Iowa where she gave birth to five children, all born within seven years at home with the help of a midwife—and the ordeal of childbirth ruined the delicate young mother's health.

From Iowa, the family migrated to California, but the long journey by train with five children was too much of a strain for the ailing mother. She remained an invalid the rest of her life and died in San Francisco in her mid-years. Grandmother Rogers was only one of many women from the East who ventured west, but she could never tolerate its hardships and culture. Her pride would not allow her to adjust. She claimed a heritage stemming from the Earl of Bolton, but Grandfather Rogers advised her not to brag about that since the Earl had been disowned by his family when he eloped with his mother's chambermaid and brought her to America.

In my research I learned a bit about the early Bolton family in England. It seems that "the first duke . . . [became the] Duke of Bolton in April 1689 . . . An eccentric man hostile to Halifax and afterwards to Marlborough, he is said to have traveled during 1687 with four coaches and one hundred horsemen, sleeping during the day and giving entertainment at night. He died February 1699 and was succeeded by his eldest son . . . whose third wife was Henrietta, a natural daughter of James, Duke of Monmouth."[4]

If the heritage of all Boltons in America stemmed from the Earl of Bolton and his mother's chambermaid, I would say it was a good, healthy heritage. I believe my Grandmother Rogers came from a town called Bolton in North Carolina. Mother also told me that her mother, Elizabeth Jane Hare, had been a southern belle from a plantation noted for breeding thoroughbred horses.

Grandfather Rogers loved fly fishing, and before he died, when he could not get to a trout river, he fished in San Francisco Bay with bait. In the final moments before his death, the last words he uttered were, "Oh, what a big fish."

---

4. *Encyclopedia Brittanica*, 11th Edition.

CHAPTER TWO
Eastern Sierra Trout Stream, California

The song of the river ends not at her banks but in the hearts of those who have loved her.

—Buffalo Joe

I was a blue-eyed little girl with brown curls and a dreamy gaze in my eyes. On my bed, I held a large conch to an ear. Mesmerized by the inner flowing of a faraway sea, I escaped by way of an active imagination from the rough chinks and sharp-edged fluting of the outer world into a smooth creamy pink world that Nature had designed for an entirely different creature. Day after day, hour after hour, I sailed off to a fairyland that turned me into the Cinderella of my dreams; and always in that rosy land of make-believe, my enemies, friends, schoolmates, everyone—particularly my sister, Petey—eyed me with envy.

Everyone, that is, but my Father, who one sunny day came into my room, insisted I should play outdoors more and asked if I would like to go fishing with him next Sunday. The brown curls on my head shook a decided no. He had interrupted a very important flight of fancy. Besides, I had been fishing once before and had no desire to repeat my fishpond experience.

Mother had taken me to a church fair and given a lady twenty-five cents for a ticket to the fishpond. When I gave my ticket to the lady,

9

she handed me a long bamboo fishing pole with a length of string tied to the tip and a safety pin tied to the string. I cast the safety pin into a fishpond walled in bed sheets and caught a small porcelain-headed doll with a lumpy body stuffed with (now wet) sawdust.

Some member of the church guild had devoted hours to making a dress for the doll. Mother thought it was beautiful and said now I had someone very pretty to play with. Shoving it into her hand, I promised myself that no hardheaded doll would ever take the place of Jip, a soft, warm, cuddly dog who never did anything to hurt my feelings or make me feel stupid, as did my sister and playmates at school. Inevitably, Jip's never-ending display of love gave me great happiness, while his adoring eyes told me I was the most important person in the whole world.

We were living in the foothills of the Sierras, about ninety miles north of San Francisco, where fish and game were plentiful. Father had two hunting dogs: Pete, an Irish Setter, and Jip, who was an Irish Water Spaniel, sometimes called an Irish rat-tailed spaniel. Jip had been delegated to me because he preferred chasing butterflies and dreams to hunting birds and human commands. He had a curly coat that Father described as liver colored. I called it brown, but never mind.

One day when I accompanied Father to go hunting with both dogs, Jip ran off to chase butterflies while Pete diligently hunted quail. I was starting to dream about the dinner Mother might prepare for us later and suddenly Pete froze on point. Father moved up, flushed the bird, shot it, and gave Pete the command to retrieve it. Proudly, he ran out, picked up the quail and started back toward his master. Father looked pleased until, out from nowhere, Jip shot out from the trees, raced up to Pete, deftly lifted the bird from his mouth, and delivered it with not a feather out of place to Father.

Jumping up and down, I clapped my hands. Both Jip and Pete had given me a perfect demonstration of what Father meant when he said that a bird dog must have a light mouth so as not to crush the bird. But now Father surprised me by taking the bird from Jip, pushing him aside, petting Pete and telling him that he was a good dog.

My father never whipped his dogs, but that day the punishment was much worse. Jip was banished from hunting. When I announced that I would not go fishing unless Jip could go, too, Father eventually relented. Mother and Petey were not with us. They preferred the comforts of home to the bugs and snakes in the woods, and Pete was not with us because I had not invited him.

Reluctantly, I left the security of my conch shell on a table in my room, and now Father, Jip and I were riding in his Ford around the Sierra foothills. Father drove several miles to the bottom of Bear Mountain and parked the Ford, modeled after a horse-drawn carriage, in the shade of a pine forest. He called his elderly Ford *Lizzy*,[5] affectionately.

Father led me along a trail traversing back and forth up the mountain, and since we had started out early that morning, my eyes and legs felt heavy with sleep. I lagged behind Father until we came to a forest in which early morning rays of warming sunshine, pouring through open spaces in the high canopy of pine boughs, came splashing down over the steaming ground. Suddenly, the moist air saturated with the spicy essence of pine activated my legs and spirits. Dashing past Father, I ran up the mountain trail.

He called me back to him, "Follow right behind me and don't run. Keep a little bend in your knees, like this, the way Indians do. We'll see more wild animals that way and you'll get less tired."

Slight and sinewy, Father moved along the trail as lightly as a deer; and following close behind, I was delighted to discover that walking with a slight bend in the knees put springs in my legs. Jip raced ahead of us with his nose to the ground, stopped suddenly and, wiggling from head to the tail, circled the ground around the path. Father, noting that Jip was on the trail of something or other, stopped, motioned to the muddy path and mouthed, "Bear tracks."

Creeping up next to Father, I stopped and asked in a whisper, "Are you afraid of bears?" His head shook a no. "In all my travels through

---

5.   Model T Fords were known as "Tin Lizzies." For more information, visit http://www.history.com/topics/model-t.

the Sierras, I've never come across a mean bear." But he advised me to never try to pet and kiss one as I did Jip, and told me I should never turn tail and run. Ever. A natural instinct made wild animals chase what runs, he said, and if I faced it calmly, chances were it would turn away from me. He also warned me against doing anything to provoke a mother bear with her cub because she would fight ferociously to protect her baby. "Wild animals aren't naturally mean. Animals in the wild kill only for food while there are some foolish, misguided men who like to kill everything in sight."

It was the first time I had heard anyone defend wildlife. I loved animals and as I knelt on the ground and examined a bear track, like a man's large hand, I told myself that if Father wasn't afraid, neither was I. I looked up, "If we meet a bear, I will stand very still and look him straight in the eye until he goes away."

Smiling, Father added, "Bears hate the smell of humans so you get out of their way as fast as they can without turning your back on them. I wouldn't be surprised if this bear has gotten our scent and is far away by now." Father went on to explain that the wind was behind us, that bears had very sensitive noses and could pick up a scent miles away if the wind was blowing it up his smeller.

We continued along the deeply wooded trail and Jip, with his nose to the ground, wiggling with excitement, kept hunting. He never caught up with the bear, though, and lost interest when Father turned onto a narrow trail running along the side of the mountain. The trail led us to the bottom of a small waterfall, a wispy white spray falling over a cliff to the ground where it turned into a stream of clear, pale green water and wound through a mountain meadow dotted with lavender wild flowers.

We followed the stream for a while and then Father stopped at what he said was a trout pool. Resting his backpack on the ground at a turn in the stream, he explained that the force of the water running down the slope had dug a comfortable place in the riverbed for trout where there were good places for them to hide, such as under the overhanging bank.

Father always talked to me and treated me as he would an adult. Although half of the time I had no idea what he was talking about, he made me feel very important. Standing close to him, I watched while he fished until the sound of pounding hoofs drew our attention to the far end of the mountain valley. I was surprised to see a small pack of horses galloping across the meadow and asked Father how they got way up there.

Father spoke is a low voice as he cast a fly into the trout pool. "Ranchers drive cattle and horses into the mountains to graze in the wild meadows during the summertime. Sometimes a horse wanders off and doesn't come back; and if it survives the winter in the mountains, it generally returns to a wild state, a maverick, free to wander." And then Father mumbled, "That would be a good life."

I didn't know much about these horses that escaped to be free, but I knew about cowboys driving cattle up to mountain meadows to feed during the summer months. Every summer on their way up, a parade of cows and cowboys would appear out of a cloud of dust as they drove their cattle herds past our house in Nevada City. The exciting parade of tinkling cow bells and pounding hooves like drums in a marching band caused my heart to beat wildly. I looked forward to the great event each year, but not Mother. Since only the two main streets in Nevada City were paved, the organized stampede filled our house with dust from the dirt road. But I loved watching those handsome cowboys, wide-brimmed hats tilted back at a jaunty slant, and chaps trimmed with sterling silver pieces. Just the thought of cowboys waving to me sent me into a girlish tizzy.

Father interrupted my reverie by suggesting that I go down to the meadow and pick wild flowers. "You'll be safe—nothing down there to hurt you. We're as free as mavericks in this paradise." I asked Jip to go with me, but he refused to budge. He loved to fish. He fished with his eyes. His eyes never left the fly on the water and he never left Father when he was fishing. So, I went off by myself.

The wild horses were gone, but the magic was still there in the mountain meadow, pale green in its cover of new grass, studded with bright flowers and fragrant sweet grass, all aglow in brilliant sunlight. On that stunning natural stage, the sun's spotlight followed me as I was transformed into a beautiful ballerina, dancing and leaping over clumps of buttercups and daisies growing like a soft yellow blanket on the meadow floor with its cushion of lush grass.

Toward the end of the morning I stopped to pick a bouquet of flowers and then circled back to father. "Haven't caught any fish," he announced. The idea of fishing and catching nothing seemed silly. I asked him why he was smiling, but he and Jip were too busy watching the fly to answer, so I dropped down on the ground and wove myself a crown of flowers.

Handling each dainty Johnny-jump-up, each Mariposa lily the color of coffee and cream, each gleaming white daisy centered with gold, handling each flower as though it was a precious gem, I wove it into a crown a sweet grass and worked diligently until Father called to me. He had a trout! Plunking the crown on my head, I ran over to see.

Father handed me a trout net. "Hold it under the water and don't scoop up until I say to." Kneeling on the ground at the edge of the bank, I waited. When a big rainbow trout jumped out of the water, the spirit of the chase took over and made me jump into the river. I scooped up the trout, but it hit the rim of the net and splashed back into the river. Jip jumped in and barked hysterically as I tried again and again to scoop up the slippery trout. Finally, I got it inside the net and not until then did I hear my Father's voice. "Come here at once—I said, come here at once!"

Clutching the large trout in the net to my chest, I stumbled over to him. He pulled me up to the bank and, although he said nothing, the expression on his face told me that he was far from pleased. Jip jumped up to the bank, shook, and sat on the ground beside me.

Suddenly, Father began to laugh. Drenched from head to toe, I stood before him with my face and gingham dress soaked and smeared with mud. The crown of wild flowers had slipped down over one eye and the trout flopping in the net against me required every bit of composure I could muster in an attempt to maintain a posture of regret and shame for what I had done—while Jip, the most woebegone-looking dog imaginable, squatted beside me, waiting for his scolding. But there was none. As Father laughed, Jip's long tail began pounding the ground happily.

Taking the trout from me, Father hit it on the head with a rock. "If you hit a fish right here on the head it will die without any pain or time to realize what's happened." Jip and I watched him clean the trout and I felt no qualms whatsoever about the gory operation because he worked quickly, deftly, and in a matter-of-fact manner. Father wrapped the trout in ferns and put it in his fishing basket under a tree in the shade.

Watching my father rinse the blood from his hands, I asked when we were going to eat. Chuckling, Father went after the package of lunch. And in that fairyland of a valley, we sat on the grass in the shade of a tall pine and feasted on chicken sandwiches made with yeasty homemade bread, and on peaches and large slices of chocolate cake. And Jip was happy because Mother had included a chicken sandwich for him, too.

After lunch, when we returned to the trout stream, Father seemed surprised to find the trout pool covered with dimples. It was smiling, he said, because trout were feeding on insects just below the surface. I had never seen him so excited, and that afternoon he caught a basketful of trout, not only in that pool but farther down where the stream made an abrupt turn at the end of the meadow.

Following Father's instructions carefully, I netted every fish success-fully while Jip sat dutifully on the bank and behaved himself. With the exception of the first large trout, the others averaged from nine to ten inches in length, and Father said they were just right for eating. If there were any limits to trout caught then, I had never heard of them.

We fished until dusk and decided to start for home; but Lizzy, an early model that had to be cranked by hand, refused to start. Poor Father, after cranking and cranking until he'd worked himself into a lather, suddenly let go of the crank, shook his fist at Lizzy and called out, "Son of a bitch!"

"What's a bitch?" I asked.

Glancing at me sheepishly, Father mumbled something about a bitch being another dog and then quickly began cranking again. The idea of Lizzy being the son of a dog made no sense to me, but I sensed Father was in no mood to explain so I kept my questions to myself.

Finally, the engine seemed to sputter, choked and groaned, and then stopped dead. That time, Father called Lizzy a stubborn old mule; and when he began cranking again, Lizzy decided to start her engine at once, so Father ran around to the front seat and pulled down the gasoline lever. Lizzy began choking from the large dose of gasoline, but she settled down when Father pushed up on the lever a bit. Quickly, he released the handbrake, pushed a foot down on the clutch pedal, and released it—but too fast. Lizzy, belching and hiccupping, shot forward in jerks and stops. Yanking down the gasoline lever once again, Father told Lizzy to get going and that time, she did, sounding an indignant roar and throwing dirt and gravel in all directions. We shot down the road at the shocking speed of forty miles per hour. Stunned by the conflicting sensations of rapture and fright, I squeezed my eyes shut and clung to the front seat with all my little might.

The instant Lizzy pulled up in front of our house, I grabbed the basket of fish, leapt from the running board to the door and rushed in to present the trout to Mother, as proudly as if I had caught them myself.

Pushing his head between us, Jip wiggled his share of pride, too, and we stood beside mother and drooled while she sautéed the firm trout in butter until it was golden brown, crisp on the outside and melting on the inside. She placed the trout on a hot platter, poured the bubbling hot browned butter with herbs over all, and surrounded the fish with lemon slices and sprigs of parsley.

At the dinner table that evening the whole family agreed that the trout was sensational. Jip agreed with a wiggle but swallowed his fish whole. Father congratulated Mother on her cooking, said she had cooked them just right, not too long. Then to my great delight he remarked, "Well, I couldn't have done it without my little girl.

You were an excellent fishing companion. I guess I don't need a son after all!"

Thankful he did not mention the fiasco of the first netting, I strutted around the dining room, proud and happy for taking the place of the son my father had always wanted (and never had).

That night when I held the conch shell to an ear, nothing happened. Even the roar of a faraway sea seemed dull. I suppose I had no more need for a shell Nature had designed for an entirely different creature. Jumping out of bed, I marched down the hall to Petey's room and presented the prize possession to my big sister.

"Why?" she asked, glancing at me suspiciously.

CHAPTER THREE
Lake Tahoe, California

In rivers, the water that you touch is the last of what has passed and the first of that which comes; so with present time.

—Leonardo da Vinci

Father and I were going to Lake Tahoe. Mother was not with us because the last time she had gone camping Father had taken her on a lake in a rowboat and while they were out on the water, a three-foot snake slithered out of a large pocket in Father's hunting jacket and slid over his lap toward her. Father had left his jacket outside the tent overnight and the snake crawled into one of his pockets to keep warm. It was harmless, he said, and threw it overboard. Mother had remained adamant and refused to go to Lake Tahoe or any other lake, and Petey gladly elected to stay home with her.

I was ten and it was my first camping trip. Our first night out Father stopped Lizzy, the Ford, at a camping area along the gravel highway from Colfax to Tahoe and we slept there. I can't recall any inns or hotels along the main highway at that time, and there was very little traffic—almost no automobiles, not many wagons and no gasoline stations. Father carried gas in a large can and refilled it at hardware stores along the way.

Late in the morning of our second day, we stopped at a lookout station at the top of a mountain. Father suggested we get out of the car and stretch our legs. I followed him to the edge of the cliff and stood next to him, my small hand wrapped in his large palm. Awed into silence, I gazed toward the horizon. Father motioned toward the east. "Over there you can see Nevada. Way over there are the eastern states, where your early American relatives came from; and even further over there, your European ancestors sailed across the Atlantic to the New World," Father explained as he pointed towards various parts of the horizon. Inspired by the mystic mountain tops rising above the ethereal blue haze in the distance, I felt an overwhelming urge to explore the beyond and began flapping my arms up and down in the air. Alarmed, Father pulled me from the edge of the cliff and back to the safety of Lizzy's leather lap.

That afternoon as Lizzy sped down the gravel highway and main road to Tahoe, she kicked up rocks in all directions. "Cars, like horses, drink water, too," Father said. So we stopped at a large watering trough on the side of the road. He filled Lizzy's radiator and we were on our way again. Later that day, we arrived at Lake Tahoe, a vast body of clear water whose glassy surface reflected the surrounding evergreen forest—a forest still virtually untouched by loggers. Father explained that Lake Tahoe was twenty miles long and filled with snow water so icy cold I wouldn't want to swim in it.

Finally, he turned Lizzy onto a dirt road that followed the west shore. We passed no buildings and could see none in the quiet wilderness surrounding the lake. There were a few cabins, Father said, but they were hidden by dense brush and trees. We passed no traffic. Automobiles were rare in the high Sierras in 1913 and toward the end of the day Father turned the Ford onto another dirt road, one so rutted it almost bounced me off the front seat. After winding through deep woods, we arrived at our destination.

The instant the car stopped, I jumped from the running board to the ground, ran down to a sandy shore and slid to an abrupt stop, mesmerized by the beauty of Lake Tahoe's Emerald Bay. Father, at my side, took in the magnificence of the vast Sierra wilderness and exclaimed, "Okay, Maxie, now we're in paradise, with no sign of civilization!"

I began taking in deep breaths of air laced with essence of pine as though I could not get enough of it. Father said it was the resin that smelled good and that I reacted to it like a cat to catnip. My head shook an emphatic no while I insisted the air smelled like holy incense in a church. Kneeling on the shore, Father began washing red dust from his hands and face. Imagining I was a beautiful goddess like Venus in my storybook of myths, I knelt beside him but had no desire to do anything as mundane as washing my face. Instead, I performed a sacred rite by bathing my face and hands in a bay of holy water sparkling with precious emeralds.

Standing up, Father said, "Time to help me make our camp." I jumped up, grabbed his hand and pulled him over to the car. He had loaded all supplies into the back seat and, feeling very important, I helped unload them and then, to the best of my little girl ability, helped him pitch the tent. He set the tent toward Emerald Bay so we could see it as we woke up. We would sleep outside if it didn't rain, he said, and use the tent for a dressing room and storage space.

Just outside the tent we made the beds. But first, Father cut balsam boughs in the forest behind our campsite and I helped him drag the boughs over to the tent. Next, he stuck the sharp ends into the ground, layer upon layer of sweet-smelling balsam, and over the top we placed the soft feathery ends of the branches. Over each springy mat I spread a bedroll, while Father placed a prickly hemp rope around the beds. To discourage a rattlesnake from crawling into bed with us, he said.

Terrified, I backed away from him, but he assured me that no snake would crawl over a prickly rope. "Rattlesnakes avoid people. They are gentlemen. They'll rattle a warning before they decide to strike. We're in rattlesnake country so be very careful when you climb up a rock ledge. Never, ever, put your hands where you cannot see because rattlesnakes like to lie out of sight on ledges." He also advised me to always stay alert along the trails and wear boots. Glancing down at my feet, he smiled and nodded his approval. Mother had dressed me in a short khaki skirt and blouse, long brown stockings, and high-laced shoes.

Still not entirely convinced, I asked if rattlesnakes killed people. "Never heard of anyone dying from a rattlesnake bite, but if one does bite you when you're alone, you'll need to suck the area around the bite and spit out the venom, and keep doing that until you can get help." Father's quiet, casual composure eased alarm, as it always did, and working with him on our camp made me feel grown up. It was more fun than playing house. It was real.

Handing me a few nails, he asked me to help him make a cup-board. Then he nailed an orange crate to a tree trunk, and placed it low enough for me to reach. "That's your cupboard," he told me. In it I put the tin plates, flatware, and other items on one shelf, and canned goods on the bottom shelf.

Father stored the flour, sugar, cooking oil, and all the other foods relished in a large tin and placed it inside the tent. Next, he dug a hole in the ground, in the shade near a spring, and when a little icy water had seeped in, he put a pail of meat, butter, and all perishables in the hole and covered it with a board and evergreen boughs. That was our icebox.

Someone else had camped in the same place and left us a log table with benches and a fireplace—a half-circle of rocks over which Father placed an iron grate. He built a fire while I swept our kitchen floor with a broom I had made myself, a branch with a bushy cluster of long pine needles. When we were finished, Father picked up a shovel and said there was one more chore. We had to make a privy.

I followed him behind our camp where he carefully chose a spot from which he could see the beautiful bay through an open space between the trees. There, he dug a deep hole in the soft ground. On each side of the hole he built up a pile of rocks and across the top, he placed a three-foot plank in which he had cut a hole before leaving home. Next, he put a can of lye on one end of the seat, a roll of toilet paper on the other end, and when finished, he sat down on the seat and admired the view of Emerald Bay. It was a great ball of magenta sun resting on the top of a mountain to the west, covering the bay with a glowing sheath of reddish-gold *lamé*.

That evening, we cooked what Father said was a feast fit for the gods, and he showed me how to bake potatoes under the glowing coals in the fireplace, and how to broil two T-bone steaks on the grill over the open fire. Steaming with melted butter, the potatoes had a wonderful woodsy flavor and so did the tender, juicy steaks. For dessert, we had slices of cake with lemon custard filling and vanilla frosting covered with shredded coconut, made especially for us.[6] We finished the feast in the light of our campfire and that balmy night Father had no trouble getting me to go to bed since I had eaten myself into a stupor.

Inside the tent, the carbide lamp, smelling like rotten eggs, forced me to change into my pajamas quickly and rush outside. Snuggling down in my bedroll, I stretched out on the soft springy mattress of fragrant balsam boughs and gazed up at the galaxy of diamonds on the black velvet sky until a romantic bullfrog, singing his repetitive love song with a honking voice like a bass horn, interrupted my flight of fancy and sent me into a fit of giggles.

I yearned to stay awake that magical night, but the proverbial sandman came along and shut my eyes. At once I was a great pelican, flying high in the soft black sky, soaring up to the North Star, a brilliant wonderland planet. I slid down the Milky Way, stopped, and perched on the handle of the bejeweled Big Dipper, and watched it pour an endless stream of happy dreams into the magic night. Scooping up happy dreams with my pelican beak, I flew them down to slumberland and snuggling against a soft cloud of balsam-scented perfume, settled onto my silk princess bed.

The next morning I awoke to delicious wafts of bacon and eggs. I usually hated getting out of bed in the morning, but my taste buds were awake and I jumped up to greet the enchanting view of Emerald Bay. I dressed quickly, ran to the shore and rinsed my face and hands in holy water before devouring a huge breakfast for such a very little girl.

---

6.   This is a cake I associate with Max—she would make this to celebrate my mother's birthday, or just because her grandchildren were visiting and she wanted to spoil us.

Father said he wanted to acquaint me with the forest so he was going to take me for a walk before going fishing. First, though, he put out the fire and as he squelched it with buckets of water and drenched the ground around the fire pit. He instructed me never to go off in the woods and leave a fire burning. And soaking the ground around the fire was important because sometimes fire burns the dry humus underground and doesn't break out in the open until everyone has left camp. "Too many forest fires get started that way," he told me.

Having seen the devastation caused to great forests in California, I understood what he was talking about. Finally, we started on our walk through a Sierra forest scented with fragrant conifer, aroma scent that always aroused my imagination, turning the open spaces within the forest into large rooms, cool, quiet and carpeted with fallen needles that hushed our footsteps.

There were no trails, but Father blazed a tree now and then, and he was careful to keep the bay in sight. I followed beside him until he stopped at a Ponderosa, a great pyramid of feathery green plumes. It was the queen of the forest, reigning supreme amid the other pines. The only ponderosa pine around, it had sucked up so much nourishment and water from the ground that no other large tree could grow there to encroach on her domain. Father explained, "This is one of Nature's clever methods for keeping the forest floor clean of weeds and scrub brush." Father had a way of bringing everything in the forest to life. "Queen Ponderosa, towering over all the other trees, is going to be our guide," he announced. Reaching out and stroking one of her soft, delicate plumes trailing the ground, I told her she had a pretty name and smelled nice.

Father led me into another forest, and I followed close behind on the wooded trail until we came to a log cabin at the edge of Emerald Bay. The cabin, surrounded by fascinating driftwood creatures with buttons for eyes, faced the Bay, and over the front door an owl perched—a wise-looking owl with large mother of pearl buttons as eyes. Driftwood squirrels scampering around the cabin window had button eyes, too, and on the ground a bear cub carved from a tree stump squatted on his haunches, guarding the front door, while drift-wood birds perched in trees around the cabin. An old hermit lived there. He had picked up these wonderful pieces of driftwood and with his hunting knife, made a few finishing touches, adding button eyes, and creating a menagerie of friendly companions.

Father knocked on the cabin door but no one was home. So we made our way down to the Bay where a large alligator, made from a scaly log, sprawled over the ground. Frogs and lizards with shoe button eyes lay scattered along the shore. And in the Bay I saw driftwood fish of all shapes and sizes -- silvery fish scoured by the waves, bleached by the sun and tied to the bottom, all swaying in rhythm with the Bay's gentle waves in the clearest water imaginable.

Father had trouble getting me to leave that Sierra wonderland. He succeeded only by asking if I would be his guide and lead him back to camp. Proud, I ran ahead on the trail, making a game of following the trees he had blazed, and took direction from the Queen Ponderosa's crown of green plumes as they waved to me in the distance and led us back to camp without any trouble whatsoever.

For lunch, I watched Father make sandwiches of Mother's delicious homemade bread and American cheese which he toasted in a buttered iron skillet over the fire until they were hot, crisp, dripping with melted cheese and absolutely divine. Our friends the chipmunks joined us for lunch, and a singing thrush in a nearby tree furnished the background music. One old-timer chipmunk amused me by driving all the other chipmunks away and then scrambling up a table leg and boldly snatching pieces of a sandwich from my plate.

I helped Father wash our dishes in the Bay and put them on the table for the sun to dry. Then I learned how to scour the skillet with sand and gravel until it was clean as new. Finally, we put out the fire and soaked the ground around it. Ready to go fishing, Father put his two-piece trout rod together. For me, he tied a few feet of fishing line to the tip of a willow branch and on it secured a short length of gut leader with a barbed hook on the end. Then he squeezed a huge worm securely to the hook.

Handing the fish pole to me, he announced, "I'll be upstream fishing for trout—do you want to come along, or would you rather stay on your own?" I hesitated. Was I afraid to stay in the woods alone? Glancing at Emerald Bay, I asked, "Is it alright if I fish here and then play in the forest for a bit?" "I don't see why not—you'll be safer here alone than on the street in San Francisco. Remember to follow the blazed trees and blaze some for yourself," Father advised as he belted a small hunting knife around my waist.

I waited until he disappeared around the bend in the trail and, pole in hand, ran down to the Bay, clambered up on a large boulder at the shore's edge, and dangled the worm in water so very clear that I could see every grain of sand but no fish. Time passed, and passed some more. So, quoting one of Father's pet expressions, I told myself that seeing was believing and jumped down to the shore. Attaching the worm and hook to the butt of the pole as Father had instructed, I swung it over one shoulder and skipped into the forest.

Carefully following the blazed trees, I soon came to Queen Ponderosa, stopped, curtsied, and asked permission to go on a treasure hunt in her forest. The green plumes on her crown nodded a yes, so waiving my fish pole, now a wand, I turned myself into a princess and began dancing through the open spaces, now great halls in the forest architecture, in my beautiful forest castle. I followed the blazed trees until a ray of sunlight splashing onto the ground in the distance threw me off course. I found no treasure there, but went on as all kinds of fascinating illusions drew me farther and farther away from the blazed trees. Even so, I remembered to blaze a few trees with my hunting knife.

On and on, I ran through the roomy forest interior of tapering tree trunk columns that held up the ceiling of evergreen plumes. Suddenly, I flushed a mountain quail! Its topknot and whirring wings stirred my imagination and made my heart flutter. I ran after him, the handsome prince, mounted on a winged steed. Suddenly, the steep leapt through an open window in the forest ceiling and took my prince away with him.

Undaunted, and bent on finding treasure, I blazed another tree and then continued through the forest until a beautiful flower stopped me. Its orange petals covered with black polka-dots were curving back so its soft red tongues could lick up sunbeams. It was a Turk's cap, and I recalled Father saying that they were rare in the Sierras and shouldn't be picked, so I pulled my hand away, blew the beautiful flower a kiss, and continued my search for treasure.

This time, a huge spider stopped me. It had horns on its back and was lurking in the center of a web that covered the entire entrance to a trail through a tunnel of thick brush. Scared, I was about to run back to camp before I noticed a blaze of light at the end of the tunnel. A treasure! Looking the devil spider straight in the eye, I exclaimed that my father had said no wild creature would hurt me if I didn't bother it, so I would go around.

Careful not to disturb the web, I crawled under the branches at the side, stood up, raced through the tunnel and came out into the light. I froze. There in front of me was what amounted to a graveyard of dead trees, filling a black bog and emanating a ghastly effluvium of moldy decay at the edge of Emerald Bay. Over a period of many years, the lake had slowly crept up the slope and killed a stand of trees. Stripped of foliage, they had fallen one by one into the bog and were lying, crisscrossed on top of each other.

They reminded me of a funeral pyre I had seen in my storybook about ancient humans. Dotted around the gloomy bog were rotten tree stumps like headstone markers, and along the shore stood a row of young fir trees, dead, stripped of foliage and bleached a ghostly white, all standing upright like a fence of skeletons. I wanted to run back to Father, but my feet, rooted in the ground, wouldn't budge—until a large wake cutting across the bog's glassy black water unlocked my legs and sent me flying down the slope.

Falling to my knees in the mud, I held a willow branch, now my fishing pole, over the water and waited. Like a cat staring into a fishbowl, I stared without batting an eye. Meanwhile, I had a chance to survey the bog and was surprised to discover that it wasn't really black. The dark humus on the bottom made the clear water seem black.

Finally, the fish ventured out from under a log lying in the bog and, holding my breath as it swam toward me, I was ready, kneeling in position, holding the pole over the water. But the spirit of the chase took over and suddenly I dropped the worm on the fish which shot back to the protection of the submerged log. I had seen the fish. It had a rolypoly body the color of the bog, with a large round head and little spear at the top, held forward, ready to do battle. It had long whiskers, too, and that moment I wanted to catch the fish more than anything else in the world.

The fish came up again. I was ready and waiting, but again instinct got ahead of me and I plunked the worm down and drove the fish away. Again and again the fish ventured out, but each time the spirit of the chase sent it back to the log. Time passed, but I had eyes only for the fish and noticed nothing else, not even the cramps in my legs from having kneeled in the mud without moving for goodness knows how long. When dusk came, I didn't see the fish, but I heard my stomach growl.

Just once more I thought, I must have that fish, I'll get it this time, I told my complaining stomach. Discouraged but still determined, I held the worm over the water, waiting and wondering why the fish was so persistent. It seemed to have some urgent business in the spot under my knees. Leaning over the bank, I inspected the place in question and . . . there it was! Its home was nothing more than a hole in the muddy bank, just big enough for a fish.

This time, when it returned and hovered in the bog, I managed to wrestle control of my instincts. Remaining motionless on my knees, I left the worm lying at the bottom of the bog and watched as the fish swam up, stopped to investigate the work, nosed it gingerly, and returned to the log again. As still as a cat stalking a bird, I waited and plotted my strategy with cool calculation. At last, I began to use the two cerebral hemispheres Nature had planted on the instinct-driven brain of one of my ancestors millions of years earlier.

I lowered the worm to the bottom of the bog again and left it on the doorstep of the fish's den. It seemed desperate and I felt sure it would take the worm, but it didn't. It hesitated and then turned away. Exasperated, I retrieved the worm, grabbed the leader, yanked the bedraggled worm from the barbed hook and lowered the bare hook so that it was resting right in the fish's doorway. This time, when the fish emerged, I waited until its head passed over the hook and then yanked the line, jumped up, let out a wild whoop, and with a wildly flopping fish and beating heart, I used to rock to hit it over the head as I'd seen Father do and raced back towards camp as fast as my little legs would carry me.

Careful to follow the blazed trees and keep the lake in sight, I had no trouble finding the way back. Father was there, waiting, and when I presented my catch, the worried look on his face spread into a broad smile. Holding up the fish admiringly, he announced, "This is a catfish! I am very proud of you, princess." I was thrilled.

It felt like the happiest moment of my decade-long life, and that evening Father sautéed the fish in plenty of butter. "Never in my whole life," I told him, "have I ever tasted any fish as fine as this catfish!"

CHAPTER FOUR

Little River, Deep in the Sierras

Salmon are incredibly driven to spawn. They will not give up. This gives me hope.

—Kathleen Dean Moore and Jonathan W. Moore, "The Gift of Salmon," *Discover Magazine*, May 2003

Father and I were riding in his new Ford touring car, Lizzy II. The canvas top was folded down and he was praising the Ford's improvements: an electric windshield wiper, the gas throttle on the floorboard, the stick shift and, best of all, the electric starter on the dashboard. "No more cranking," he remarked.

We were on our way to do some fishing. Sulking on the front seat beside him, I was feeling sorry for myself. We would be away a whole weekend and were now speeding farther and farther away from my beau, my first great love, whom I had left to the wiles of competitors lovelier that I.

Unfortunately, at the age of seventeen, all that had enchanted me in the Sierras during my early years had given way to a competitive and vapid social life, and with it my sense of joy. Nevertheless, all of my peers—denizens of the Jazz Age—and I pretended to be hilariously happy. I had consented to go fishing with Father because I felt sorry for him. No one else would go, and I knew he was beset with worries. I had overheard him telling Mother that he needed to get away from it all.

And now, as we drove along a dirt road around the Sierra foothills, Lizzy II was blanketing all of his worries in voluminous clouds of red dust and he was happy again. Father began singing his favorite song, "In the Shade of the Old Apple Tree." We were going to stay with a friend, Mr. Flint, at his mine deep in the Sierras. I asked what river we were going to fish. Father didn't think it had a name, but the miners had dubbed it Little River. I was going to fish with artificial flies for the first time, and I pulled one out of a box lying on my lap, held it up and asked, "What do you call this one?" "That's a Speckled Brown—it's made of duck feathers."

A Scotsman, an old gentleman with a halo of pure white hair and benign smile, had tied the flies. They looked like tiny jewels. He'd ordered everything from Scotland, special hooks, colorful feathers, tinsel—all the materials that go into the delicate art of tying beautiful flies. He had introduced Father to fly fishing and, as I recall, at that time in 1920 he and Father were the only two fishermen using flies in that part of the West.

The Scotsman had left his homeland to seek a fortune in the gold fields of California when he was a young man, but had found no gold. Instead, he discovered a wealth of trout streams in the Sierras. We were nearing the top of a mountain. Closing the fly box lid, I turned my attention to the narrow one-way dirt road that ran along the top of a deep canyon at the bottom of which we could see the surreal remains of wrecked wagons, wheels, an old automobile, and various debris strewn over the bottom of the gorge. All reminders of past disasters.

"It's impossible to get wrecks out of that hell hole," Father told me. I wondered what would happen if we met another automobile on that terrifying road. I learned there was an unwritten law that the auto driving down the grade must stop and back up to the last turnout to let the driver going up the grade pass. Just the thought of it made me shudder.

We were on the only road to Washington, a small mining town of bygone days (now a ghost town) deep in the Sierras. As we waited on a turnout for Lizzy II's brakes to cool, Father relayed the story of one of the bloodiest hold-ups in the West. It happened at a time when stagecoaches carried large mounds of gold from Washington to the assay offices in Nevada City and were therefore valuable prey for bandits. The bandits rode their horses in packs, as they did in Western movies, and one day when a stagecoach stopped at the very turnout on which we were resting, a group of bandits galloped out of the woods and held it up. All hell broke loose as the driver turned the team of four horses down the steep grade. The bandits followed, opened fire, and the guards on top of the coach fired back. After several bandits were killed, the others gave up and hightailed it back into the woods for cover. The stagecoach didn't stop until the horses pulled up in Washington. Once there, the driver fell to the ground, dead with a bullet in his chest, and the guards died later. All for what? Gold. "That pretty metal that drives men crazy," Father lamented.

By the time Lizzy II pulled up in Washington State, I had become engrossed in Western lore to the point of imagining forty-niners wandering in and out of the saloon's swinging half-doors. I envisioned a row of feet in high-heeled boots lining the veranda railing as their owners, sitting in saloon chairs tipped back against the outside wall, spit brown streams of chewing tobacco out toward the hitching posts where their horses waited.

Father parked Lizzy II beside a huge watering trough. Its old wooden frame was leaking and filled with moss. Washington was not completely dead, though. Across the street, the only street and a continuation of the rutted road, a couple lived over their store. The bandits had disappeared with the fallen gold standard, but the solid iron shutters that barred the store's doors and windows remained as a reminder of that era's hopes and dreams.

Inside, the storekeeper and his wife greeted Father as a long lost friend. My father seemed to know everyone everywhere in the Sierras, and as the grown-ups reminisced about the good old days, I explored the store's interior. Dank and gloomy, light entered via two small windows. Crowded into one corner was a cubicle, a United States Post Office, still serving the almost-deserted mining country around

Washington. On the counter stood a wooden tub of butter and on the shelves, a few sparsely placed cans of food could be found. Sacks of beans, flour and sugar were stacked along the wall, and a very important pot-bellied stove sat in the store's center.

That was when I began drawing in deep, happy breaths of the aroma emanating from the wood floor which had been preserved with countless coats of pine tar. The storekeeper's wife, staring and tugging at Father's sleeve, asked what was wrong with his daughter. Chuckling, Father explained that I liked the smell of her floor. Dumbfounded, she glared at me. Furious with Father, I marched out of the store and climbed into the Ford.

A few minutes later, Father joined me. Silent but smiling, he drove Lizzy II down a road that was nothing more than a wide path cut through the woods. Having grown up during the horse and buggy days, Father drove carefully when the road climbed almost perpendicularly, or dropped down what seemed like a precipice; but over the flat stretches, he drove Lizzy as though she were a team of runaway horses, over fallen logs, deep cross-ruts, and even large rocks. Indeed, he seemed to think Lizzy could go any place a horse could go. Suddenly, a flat tire stopped us. Father considered a flat tire a normal part of any trip, so he always took along patching material, a jack, and a hand pump. It didn't take long before he had the inner tube patched, pumped up, and back in the tire on the wheel.

On our way again, I learned that the mine we were going to was a small one and Mr. Flint had willed it to Princeton, the university from which he'd graduated in the East. Sometimes, during summer vacations, Princeton students studying to be mining engineers would come to have an experience of working in a mine. Mr. Flint was retired from business and spent each summer at his mine, but had to close it during the wintertime because snow and freezing weather made getting in and out impossible.

It was late afternoon when we arrived. Mr. Flint, a tall, attractive, grey-haired man, greeted us in front of his lodge, a two-story building of peeled logs. He seemed happy we were there and led us into a charming living room. The whole interior of smooth logs had turned a honey color. The sofa and upholstered chairs were covered in colorful flowered chintz, and the burning logs in the large fireplace of filed stones cast a cheerful atmosphere throughout the room. I had not expected to find such luxury in that isolated wilderness. Mr. Flint, noting the look of surprise on my face, explained that his late wife had decorated the lodge.

He led us upstairs to a most elegant guest room in which the bed and windows were draped in lovely chintz; and at the back of the room, French doors opened out to a small balcony with a view of Little River, running down a narrow valley walled in by mountain slopes.

This was to be my room. I was thrilled. Father's room was elegant, too, but more masculine. There was a bathroom, with a tub, shower, basin, hot and cold water, and a toilet—all very modern. And pictures on the walls. The basement room was even more exciting because Little River ran right through it! Having been directed through a channel in the cement foundation, its job was to turn a great wheel which in turn ran a dynamo.

Mr. Flint explained, "The stream supplies electricity for the whole camp. Its job is to keep the wheel running and in good condition." Father commented that everything was as polished and immaculate as the engine room of a big ship. Smiling, our host led us to the other end of the room where carpeting covered the floor, and on it stood a rocking chair, side table and bookcase filled with books. All the furnishings had been brought in by horses and wagons, and his wife had filled the basement with comfortable furniture because he spent so much time there. Taking me by the arm, Mr. Flint announced, "We'll be eating supper tonight with the miners, so why don't you go upstairs and get ready."

I enjoyed the luxury of a hot shower in the wilderness and luckily had brought a long divided skirt of navy blue corduroy and a red silk blouse. I tied my curls on top of my head with a red ribbon and joined Mr. Flint and Father in the living room. From there we walked the short distance to the cook house.

The bunkhouse and a set of small buildings, all covered in tar paper, were grouped together on the bank of Little River. A chill in the high mountain air sent us hurriedly inside the cookhouse, where savory fumes and welcome warmth greeted us. The kitchen was separated from the long dining room by a peeled log wall, reaching halfway up to the beamed ceiling. Two long tables covered with red and white checkered oilcloths were set for dinner, and down at the far end of the room, a line of miners were standing before mirrors hanging over a long shelf that held a line of enamel washbowls.

Mr. Flint, glancing at Father, remarked, "Well, I don't think I've ever seen these miners feeling so particular about their appearance, but I'm not surprised. They haven't seen a young lady for some time, especially such a beautiful one." My face probably turned the color of my bright red blouse. Ah, woe to the agonies of a teenager! Bowing my head and staring at the floor, I followed my host to one of the long tables. There, he introduced me to the superintendent of the mine at the head of the table. Leaving me in his care, Mr. Flint joined Father at the other table.

The superintendent pulled out a chair, bowed with a long sweep of his arm, and said, "Howdy, beautiful."

Verging on panic, I dropped down on the chair and stared at my plate. Every eye in the dining room seemed fastened on my burning face. Sensing my embarrassment, the superintendent sat down beside me and began talking to the miner sitting at his right. That gave me a chance to study my dinner partner, which I did out of the corner of my eye.

A large, burly man wearing a red and black checkered shirt, pink ribbon sleeve-garters, a green vest, tight striped trousers and high-heeled boots, his long black hair at the back of the head was combed over a bald spot with dashing flourish; and a jet black mustache, very luxurious, was curled at each side of his generous mouth. His dark eyes already sparkling with mischief suddenly caught me staring and, wishing I could fall through the floor, I stared at my plate until a sudden hush of voices turned everyone's attention toward the cook. Greatly relieved, I looked up.

The cook, the most important personage at the mine, was a jolly plump man dressed in voluminous white trousers, a pristine white apron, and a tall white cook's cap. He entered the room carrying large bowls of fragrant venison stew, cooked with red wine and onions, along with bowls of baked beans, steaming hot vegetables, canned fruit, crusty homemade bread, still warm and yeasty, and platters with huge slices of homemade chocolate cake.

Presto, the food began to disappear as if by magic, but the long arm of the superintendent came to my rescue and he heaped food onto my plate. Then he turned his attention to his plate and I watched, fascinated, as he lined, in one deft swoop, a knife blade along the beans, and dropped them into his mouth all at once without cutting his throat or disturbing a single hair in his silky mustache.

Unhindered by my stare, he looked me straight in the eye and said, "I bet you can't do it!" Rather than admit defeat, I meticulously lined beans on the blade of a knife, threw back my head, opened my mouth wide, and shoved the blade inside. Every single bean fell on my lap and a blast of guffaws exploded throughout the dining room. That broke the ice and I joined the ruckus, enjoying the rest of the evening immensely.

After dinner, the miners helped clear the tables and push them against the wall. Mr. Flint brought out a gramophone, one of the early models with a loudspeaker shaped like a horn, and the superintendent claimed the first dance with me.

Father and Mr. Flint sat on the sideline and talked while we danced. Some of the miners danced together and each in turn danced with me. We danced to the music of "Alexander's Ragtime Band" and "The Maple Leaf Rag" and, my favorite, "The St. Louis Blues." After I had had a turn with every miner and the cook, a student from Princeton invited me to dance and refused to let me go. I was thrilled, of course, and we danced until Cook took away the gramophone, saying he had to set the tables for breakfast.

Father and I walked back to the lodge with Mr. Flint, and that night Little River's liquid music outside the open French doors lulled me to sleep. Not once did I think or dream of the beau I had left back in Nevada City.

The next morning, after a hearty breakfast prepared by Mr. Flint in his own little kitchen, Father and I gathered up our fishing rods and flies and followed our host up the mountain. From the lodge we climbed a hundred wooden steps and then walked across a ridge to the mine's entrance. Out of this large hole in the side of the mountain ran a line of small tramcars on narrow tracks, loaded with dirt and rocks, that rolled slowly out of the mountain and along the ridge to dump refuse down the slope.

The superintendent stood at the entrance waiting for us and Mr. Flint, needing to get back to the dynamo, left us in his care. Handing us hardtop hats, we followed as the superintendent led us into the mine. Attached to each hat was a small carbide lamp that smelled of rotten eggs but helped us find our way in the dark, in the gloomy mountain tunnels, dripping with water and eerie in the light cast by the blue flames of the carbide lamps. Some tunnels had been closed off due to cave-ins and, liking none of it, I couldn't help but pity the poor miners.

In one tunnel we stopped to watch miners chipping away at quartz. They greeted us cheerfully, but there was so much grime on their faces, I failed to recognize them as the men who had danced with me the night before. In another tunnel, the superintendent chipped out a piece of quartz and gave it to me. The salmon-pink crystal covered with veins and flecks of gold was pretty, but I felt hugely relieved when he led us out of that claustrophobic man-made cave.

We thanked our host and I followed Father up the slope to a flume. Walking on a narrow plank over running water had once been a frightening experience, but I had said nothing because Father could be a strict taskmaster and I wanted only to please him.

Now, I felt no fear. The flume, about six feet above ground, had been built along the side of the mountain. We walked on the plank a quarter mile or so, jumped to the ground, slid down a slope slippery and fragrant with fallen pine needles, and then followed a deer trail to an overhanging ledge of rock.

We stopped to admire the spectacular view of Little River, now far down in a mountain ravine, following a fold in the mountain, running busily to the mine where it supplied the miners with fresh cold water and turned the great wheel to create electricity. "We're going to fish the headwaters of Little River," Father announced. "And the best way to get down the steep hill is to slide down on our bottoms." Luckily, I had put on a divided khaki skirt which was just right for such antics.

At the foot of the slope we followed Little River to a small pool full of trout. Most of them were lined up at the head of the pool, fanning their fins in the clear water and waiting for Little River to deliver their lunch. "The trout like it here," Father said. The force of the strong current rushing down a mountain sloe and then squeezing through the narrow space between boulders at the head of the pool generated large amounts of oxygen; and since the swift current had dug out gravel in the riverbed, and the large rocks at one end had slowed down the current, it made for an ideal trout pool.

They were not large trout. They averaged nine to ten inches in length and Father said they wouldn't get much bigger because there were too many for Little River to feed properly. However, through the clear water we could see one fourteen-incher lying in the shade of the overhanging bank across the river in a section about twelve feet wide.

Father assembled our trout rods and on my fishing line put a sturdy leader of 2X gut and on it a wet fly, more specifically a Speckled Brown that the Scotsman had tied for me. Father handed the rod to me and disappeared around a bend in the river before I realized he was gone. Father believed experience was the best teacher—that I knew, but I felt annoyed. He had gone off and left me alone, and I knew almost nothing about fishing with an artificial fly. That he had deliberately left a pool full of trout for me to catch never entered my teenage head. Nor did I appreciate the fact that he had given me one of his precious trout rods to use, one of the two secondhand Hardy rods he had bought from the Scotsman.

Grumbling to myself, I fished for a half an hour and had no action in the pool whatsoever. And no wonder. Every time I cast out the fly, it fell on the water in a heap of leader. I never did reach the big one across the river. Trying again and again, I cast the fly into the water the best I could, but could not place the fly well enough to suit those uncooperative trout. When the wet fly settled on the pool, the strong current picked it up and yanked it down to the tail of the pool where it hung lifelessly. Not one single ornery fish looked at my fly. Infuriated, I lashed line down on the pool and drove all the trout asunder. Finally, I reeled in the line and stomped downriver.

A feeder stream, running into Little River, stopped me. It was too wide to jump across, and I didn't want to get my shoes wet, so I decided to go up the stream and fish from its bank. That was no fun. I had to fight my way through a thick growth of alder bushes as tough as iron. Too tired to go another step, I dropped down on a large flat boulder.

The water in the brook was opaque. I groaned. No doubt, there had been a storm at its source high up the mountain. I was about to go back to Little River when dimples spreading over the smooth surface of a backwater stopped me. Recalling that Father had said dimples indicated trout were feeding on insects just beneath the surface, I stood up and began stripping line from the reel.

Without realizing it, I had stopped at a small trout pool. Half of the large flat boulder on which I was standing extended into the brook and was pushing the current to one side. Rushing through the narrow channel between the boulder and the other rocky bank, the swift current had dug out the riverbed to form the trout pool.

Soon, more dimples covered the quiet surface. Quickly, I began casting a wet fly into the water, but over the next hour I spent most of my time climbing trees or pushing my way through dense brush to retrieve my fly. Luckily, Father had tied it to a heavy leader. Finally, exhausted, I sat down on the boulder and watched, spellbound, as the dimples over the pool turned into splashes! I jumped up and started fishing again, but once again, the trout ignored my fly. Terribly discouraged, I reeled in the line.

I sat on the boulder, brooding. I glanced down toward the tail of the pool and saw a live fly with gauzy wings like tiny sails pop up on top of the water out of nowhere. Too stunned by such magic to move, I watched one dainty fly after another pop up on the surface film and bob down with the current; and when a fly sailed past the submerged rock and disappeared in a s-l-u-r-r-r-p, I couldn't believe what I was seeing.

The telltale rise of a Big One! Father always said that big trout were wise and cautious old fish and, unlike small trout, generally sucked in a fly without splashing for it. The water had begun to clear and so had my head. I began plotting my course of action. I had been standing too close to the pool, almost on top of the fish. Of course, that was why I couldn't get a good swing on the line.

Holding the rod over my head, I moved off the boulder, pushing my way through the brush along the bank, scrambling over large boulders, and got well below the half-submerged rock. I waded, shoes and all, out to the middle of the brook and began to cast out line. I had no trouble with the backcast—while stripping line from the reel, I cast it back and forth in the open space over the brook, let the fly drop a foot or so above the rise, and started stripping in line. Perched on surface film, my fly sailed past the boulder, the rod jerked into a deep arch, the tip almost touched the butt and, clutching the line tight to the rod, I reached out with my left hand, grabbed the leader and dragged the heavy trout to shore.

Once there, the wildly flopping fish got away from me. Falling down on top of it, I stayed there until it quieted down. Then I hit it on the head with a rock, to put it out of its misery, and then hooked it onto a forked stick and walked back to the pool where Father had left me.

He was there, fishing, and after giving me due praise, he asked, "Do you know what it is?" "It's a trout, isn't it!?" "Yes, but it's a special one, a *rainbow* trout."

What a gorgeous fish! Streamlined, its small pointed head and silvery fat body tapered into a slim wrist at the tail, and down each side ran streaks of color—all the hues of the rainbow, seemingly painted on the body with watercolors.

That was indeed a red letter day for me. Simply by chance I had discovered for myself, after drying the wet fly while casting it back and forth in the air, the technique and joy of dry fly fishing.

Had Father caught any trout? Yes, a basket full for our host. Smiling, he motioned across the river. "The big one is still there. Too smart to get caught," he said.

CHAPTER FIVE

Muir Woods Trout Stream, Northern California

~~~~~~

To trace the history of a river or a raindrop . . . is also to trace the history of the soul, the history of the mind descending and arising in the body. In both, we constantly seek and stumble upon divinity, which like feeding the lake, and the spring becoming a waterfall, feeds, spills, falls, and feeds itself all over again.

—Gretel Ehrlich, *Islands, The Universe, Home*

My father and I never fished together again. In San Francisco, Mother enrolled me in the California School of Fine Arts (affiliated with the University of California in Berkeley) and, as a maverick who enjoyed the freedom and happiness found only in Nature, I unwittingly chose a path through life that soon transformed me into a restless wanderer, forever searching for I knew not what.

Shortly after moving to San Francisco, I made my debut into the melee of the Jazz Age. To my poor mother's dismay, I had my curls cut off, the hair shaved up the back of my neck like a boy's, flattened my bust with excruciatingly tights bras, and donned a tight, short sheath flapping with fringe, a long necklace of beads bouncing below the hemline, and long earrings dangling at my bony shoulder blades. In that regalia, I sallied forth, batting mascara-darkened eyelashes, night after night. As a result, I arrived each morning at the art school unprepared and bleary-eyed.

I shared an apartment near the art school with my sister Petey, who was studying voice with a retired opera singer, and with two other girls who were students at the University of California. It wasn't long before I'd become a true flapper—a miserable one, never happy with my college boy escorts, and they were not so happy with me either. I expected too much from them and gave too little, since no one could possibly measure up to my secret love, Rudolph Valentino.

Hollywood's glamorous films had played an important part in forming my teenage character, as they had those of my peers. The late Deems Taylor has left, in his book *A Pictorial History of the Movies*, an amusing but true characterization of that phenomenon of modern society when he wrote that

> Within the year Valentino was on the screen again in an adaptation of another best seller, *The Sheik*. Concerning the literary merits of this effusion, it is kindest to be silent. Nevertheless, it gave the American moviegoer—particularly the flapper, spinster and housewife—what she yearned for: romance, mystery, fear, the spell of the tropics, the lure of the desert, and the perfect lover.

Since my behavior was based on pretense, I felt miserable most of the time, although I could not admit it to anyone, including myself. I hated cocktails and highballs, had trouble swallowing them, but forced them down because more than anything I wanted to be popular.

Sometimes my married friends invited me to cocktail parties and served a sickly sweet concoction, sticky pink with grenadine, canned grapefruit juice, and bathtub gin, said to be so named because it was made in bathtubs by bootleggers who smuggled it across the border stuffed in their high boots. Hating the thought of swilling the stuff, I held the glass in my hand until the cocktail became lukewarm and then mustered every bit of willpower I could to swallow it. Ugh! I smoked cigarettes, too, because I thought it was a must to become a popular flapper like the sophisticated movie actresses, all of whom smoked.

My teenage years were the most miserable and boring of my life. However, the California School of Fine Arts was an unusually progressive school for the times, with policies resembling John Dewey's theories of empirical education: learning by doing, by experience, by experimenting, by Nature's methods. The School saved me from a fate that destroyed too many of my peers whose lives unraveled the way they did in F. Scott Fitzgerald's novels.

I loved the art school. The building sprawled over the ruins of the Mark Hopkins estate on top of San Francisco's Knob Hill. The property had been donated by Mark Hopkins after the 1906 earthquake and fire had demolished his mansion. A patron of the arts, he had donated the property for the purpose of making San Francisco the art center of the West; and when I was there the School was less than twenty years old. In its place today stands the Mark Hopkins Hotel.

Leigh Randolph, a local artist, was director of the school. The faculty was remarkable. Each was a talented artist and teacher, and avoided negative criticism, looking instead for the potential and talent in each student and making a special effort to encourage students to develop their gifts. No report cards were sent to parents or students. Each student was expected to judge his or her own progress, or lack of progress, and act accordingly. We were treated as adults and expected to behave as adults. Students were free to come and go as they pleased—no one reprimanded us if we cut classes and went to a movie in the afternoon—but if a student's work fell below standard, that student was asked to leave to make room for someone on the waiting list.

At first, I had problems adjusting to such liberal policies, but during my second year I was lucky to meet a small group of young World War I veterans who had come to the art school with scholarships thanks to the GI Bill. Older and more mature than most students, they earned a reputation as the California School of Fine Arts's avant-garde.

My association with these artist-veterans opened up a whole new world for me. They usually met outside on a terrace during lunch, and from their discussions I first heard about Sigmund Freud, whose work and theories as a psychoanalyst had only recently been published. What I learned inspired me to read everything I could and Freud's essays on the sibling problems and the inferiority complex interested me particularly. Having grown up with an older sister who I considered more talented and intellectually gifted, someone who excelled in almost everything she did, I had little self-confidence and become easily discouraged.

After reading Freud's essays, I began to understand one of my deepest, personal challenges. I was too ashamed to admit to any of it until one afternoon at the movies I watched a documentary film that illustrated a similar dynamic in the context of a competition between two white rats from the same litter—and that simple but profound laboratory experiment opened the door, gradually, to a vast vista over my perceptions and self esteem.

I will call these female lab rats Sister Fast and Sister Slow. They had been placed behind a trapdoor on a narrow runway, standing about six feet above the floor and just wide enough for one rat to pass the other. A piece of cheese had been put at the end. The trapdoor opened automatically and both rats raced down the runway and Sister Fast reached the cheese first.

The experiment was repeated several times and each time, Sister Fast got the cheese; and each time Sister Slow moved more slowly until finally, a dejected, forlorn little ball of white fur, made no attempt to move from the starting line. A more pathetic creature I had never seen, but that was not the end.

Phase 2 had the same two rats in separate cages. A piece of cheese was strung up to the ceiling of each cage, and the other end of the string attached to a pulley spring anchored on the cage floor. Sister Slow had revived and each rat was running around her cage, sniffing, head held high. Suddenly, Sister Slow accidently stepped on the pulley string, the cheese dropped to the floor, and she gobbled it up.

More cheese was put in the ceiling and Sister Slow began racing around her cage again, once again accidentally stepped on the spring, snatched up the cheese and continued looking for more. The next time, after the cheese was positioned in the ceiling, Sister Slow rushed to the spring and deliberately stepped on it. In a burst of empathy, I clapped my hands and the rest of the audience in the theater joined in the applause.

In the meantime, Sister Fast had been running all over her cage and had spent all her energy and strength failing to get at the cheese in her ceiling, and had fallen in to a heap of despair and exhaustion. Did I feel sorry for her? Not in the least, and right there and then I saw my own inferiority complex and dug it out of what Freud called the subconscious, took a hard look, disliked what I saw, and vowed to get rid of it. It took time, a lifetime in fact, but I still give credit to those little white rats for helping me understand my own lack of confidence and the shameful and counterproductive resentment of others' success I could sometimes feel.

During my last year at the California School of Fine Arts, my sister and I lived across the San Francisco Bay with Mother, who had rented a house not far from the University of California. Father was still in Nevada City, but visited us whenever possible.

There were no bridges across the Bay back then. I commuted back and forth to the art school in ferryboats, gleaming white and resembling the romantic river boats of Mark Twain's tales. Each morning, when the skies were clear and sunny, I stood at the back of the boat and let my imagination follow the stream of foam churned up by the great propeller. And each time, that stream took me on a different adventure, out past the rolling hills behind Berkeley and Oakland, out beyond the horizon and the hidden dreamland in which romantic dreams always offered happy endings.

I loved the foggy mornings, too, soft and mysterious in the quiet of the dense fog—a silence broken by rhythmic wails of mournful foghorns, warning boats to steer clear and avoid a deadly accident. Sometimes a second boat, sounding quick sharp toots of alarm, would suddenly appear through the curtain of fog. Instantly, our ferryboat would answer with frantic blasts as we would rush to the railing to witness a collision. The voice on the other end of the ferry loudspeaker would plead with us to get back inside and redistribute our weight before we upset the boat. Having no intention of missing the excitement of a collision, we mostly ignored the voice and told each other that a ferryboat had yet to tip over in San Francisco Bay since they always traveled at a snail's pace when there was fog. If there was a collision, the damage would be slight.

The ferryboats docked at San Francisco's Ferry Building (which exists to this day), a large white Victorian building capped with an impressive tower at the foot of Market Street where a great web of streetcar tracks that led all over the city began and terminated. Upon their return to Market Street, the little cable cars were pushed around on a turntable by the cable man and conductor so they could travel back uptown again.

Each school morning one of those storybook trolley cars carried me up California Street—a steep stretch of cobblestone—and delivered me to the California School of Fine Arts at the top of Nob Hill. The art school's white clapboard building stood out amid the ruins of

Mark Hopkins mansion, c. 1880.

the once-elegant Mark Hopkins estate in one of San Francisco's most fashionable residential districts.

Sometimes I walked across California Street to a terrace at the Fairmont Hotel that gave me a sweeping view of San Francisco Bay and its mountain top islands (before they were covered with buildings), great mounds of rock sculpted and modeled by weather and erosion, beautiful rounded breasts of slopes, brown and bare during the winter and adorned with carpets of golden poppies and purple lupine in the summer—before Alcatraz prison marred the landscape visually and otherwise.

The view of San Francisco from the school's back terrace was wonderful, too. What an exquisite location! Verdant San Francisco, a city of gardens and trees, spread over a great peninsula of undulating hills, reaching beaches of beige-sand brilliance, out to sheer rock cliffs and dropping into the deep blue Pacific. Out beyond the dramatic shoreline was the entrance to San Francisco Harbor, the Golden Gate, which was protected on all sides from wind and weather and always the favorite of ancient and modern mariners alike.

The mansion and weathered gardens created the most romantic setting for our art school. The underground stables and tunnels leading to them were still there. Each time I stood on the back terrace the underground structures and the old ruins spoke to me of San Francisco's fabled past, as it had been when my mother and father lived there, when they and San Francisco were young and alive with great expectations for the future.

During my last year at the art school, I still joined the young war veterans whenever I could on the terrace. They had become an important part of my education, particularly in subjects other than art. I felt more at ease with them and it was from one of their discussions that I learned about John Scopes, who was on trial for teaching evolution in a Tennessee high school. Outraged, I expressed my fury in no uncertain terms. Surely Darwin's theory of evolution made more sense than what I had been taught by the church. My friends, better known as the "angry young men," agreed, and when I questioned the validity of the church's denial of Darwin's views on evolution, one young veteran began singing the hymn, "Onward Christian Soldiers, marching into war . . . ' "

Another student commented that Monarchianism was the only religion that that made any sense. Having never heard of Monarchianism, I kept my mouth shut; but the minute I returned home that afternoon, I retired to my room with a dictionary that explained, "Monarchianism is any of the several anti-Trinitarian doctrines current in the church of the second and third centuries, the common principle of which is that God is one in person as well as Nature."

Excited by what I'd read and panting for a good debate, I ran downstairs to convert my mother who was an Episcopalian (as was I technically since I was confirmed in her church). But she disappointed me by smiling condescendingly and changing the subject.

The next time I joined my friends at the art school, they introduced me to a new student. His name was John Atherton. He had come from the College of the Pacific on a government scholarship. I soon learned that John was not one of the angry young men. He had never come into direct contact with any of the horrors of that futile war. Having lied about his age, he enlisted in the navy at the age of seventeen (the minimum age for US soldiers in World War I was nineteen) and the navy, recognizing both his youth and his talent, assigned him to paint posters and signs on battleships in port.

Born in 1900, John was twenty-five when we met. I was attracted to him at once, but had no intention of falling in love with him because although I had shed the shell of a flapper, I was still secretly in love with Rudolph Valentino, and appraised every prospective suitor according to how closely they matched his qualities. John Atherton was the scholarly type, an intellectual, and not for me, I told myself. But as time passed and he showed no signs of being aware of

John Atherton, c. 1919.

my existence, I changed my mind. The slight stirred me into action and I went out of my way to make my existence known to the fascinating young man.

John showed the promise of unusual talent and even genius, and he soon became one of the top students at the art school. He was known as Jack to his friends and soon I, too, used that name. I learned that he was also an excellent athlete, had a delightful sense of the ridiculous and a zest for life in general. Jack was a wonderful musician, to boot. His mother, a concert pianist, had given him piano lessons and a background in classical music when he was growing up. He played the banjo when I met him and had offers to join big jazz bands as far east as New York, but Jack had no desire to become a professional musician. Nevertheless, he supplemented his income from the GI Bill by joining a very sophisticated and sought-after band that played for private parties and events around the Bay area. That gave him more cash than the average student had to spend on amusement and he spent the better part of it on concerts or the opera.

Jack took me with him and we grew closer sharing the experience of these wonderful performances. He gave me an education in the best of music, and in the joy of deep listening—a pleasure I might never have experienced otherwise. By the year 1923, San Francisco was on its way to becoming the cultural center of the West and had its own symphony orchestra and new opera house. Almost all of the operas came out of New York, and Puccini's *Madame Butterfly* was my favorite. We went to the Russian Ballet, too, and saw the famous ballerina, Anna Pavlova. She danced the lead in *The Dying Swan*, the ballet for which Mikhail Fokine had composed music especially for her. Jack and I also attended a performance by Yehuda Menuhin, then only nine years old, when he played violin with the San Francisco Symphony Orchestra. And we listened, enraptured, when Geraldine Farr came to town and sang in the romantic opera, *Carmen*.

Jack also made sure we attended every important art exhibition in San Francisco, and I can remember one from France that Leigh Randolph managed to get on loan (a great feat) and hang in our art school galleries. It consisted of paintings by impressionists and post-impressionists, artists of a school noted for painting subjective and sensory impressions. The exhibit included pictures by Picasso, Van Gogh, Gauguin, Cezanne, Monet, Manet, Degas, and others. A very special event for San Francisco, it was somewhat of a shock to see these works. Having been brought up to appreciate more conventional art, I had simply never seen anything like it.

It was years before I fully understood why the paintings were so exciting to Jack. Actually, I learned why by looking at works of art through his eyes, and he helped me with my school work as well. Sometimes on a Sunday I would pack a picnic lunch and we would sketch around the Bay area. We traveled by streetcar and ferryboat, and one Sunday, while Jack and I were sketching San Francisco Bay, I glanced at his canvas and threw my paint brush to the ground, groaning. Bewildered, he asked, "What's wrong?!"

"How is it that you can paint so well, so fast, with so little effort? It isn't fair!" Without waiting for his answer, I went on, "I can't paint with you anymore because every time I look at your canvas, I become completely discouraged."

Jack shook his head and said, "My sketches are too facile, and that's something I have to guard against." I had no idea what he meant, but I knew what he was talking about when he said my painting had a primitive quality he liked. That I understood because it was in fact a quality I had been fighting, to no avail. It showed up in every drawing and painting I produced.

I failed to finish the sketch of San Francisco Bay that day, but later, at the art school, I followed his advice and began giving full vent to the naive quality he admired. And I began to enjoy my work and paint with greater confidence.

As time passed, I became more interested in Jack. Never before had I met a more intriguing individual—or a more complex personality. He was a prodigious reader of the best literature and I remember the day he gave me James Joyce's *A Portrait of an Artist as a Young Man*. I found it difficult going, but struggled through as I realized that

John was very much like Stephen, the protagonist. By the time I finished the book, I had become more tolerant of Jack's temperamental outbursts. Yes, Jack Atherton was a temperamental artist, but a very lovable one.

He was a perfectionist, tormented by a craving for absoluteness. If he made a mistake or thought he had failed, his seething wrath was directed inwardly, although he never realized he was the victim of his own critical anger. Outwardly, he directed his outbursts at inanimate objects, never at a person or animal.

The first time I witnessed one of his emotional outbursts he was in an empty classroom. I walked in just as he had grabbed his drawing from an easel, tore it into shreds, threw everything onto the floor, and stamped all over the shreds. He shot past me and out of the room. Sometimes, his explosive moods struck me as funny, and if I laughed he came out of the rage laughing with me. But not always. There were times when I sensed that the problem was too serious to be laughed away and then I knew the only way I could help was to remain concerned and sympathetic. He truly seemed to embody all the stereotypical qualities of a genius and I must say, there was never a dull moment around him. Jack was a kind, tender and sensitive man. His sense of humor delighted me and everyone else around him. My first impressions had been superficial and absolutely wrong.

I was very pleased one day when Jack asked if I would go with him the following weekend to visit his sister, Lucile Atherton Harger, a popular radio singer (in the days before television). She lived in San Rafael, and on Saturday we traveled across San Francisco Bay to Sausalito by ferryboat, and from there went by train to San Rafael. I liked Lucile the instant we met and felt at ease with her and with her husband.

On a Sunday morning, Jack borrowed her car and drove me to Muir Woods, the magnificent protected redwood grove only a short distance from Lucile's house. We parked outside the grove and walked along a path into Muir Woods until we came to a brook. Having been away from the Sierras too long, I dropped down on my knees, splashed the cool clear water over my face, dug my hands deep into the rich moist earth, squeezing it between my fingers, and squealed with joy at being alive. The look of surprise on Jack's face brought me to my feet. "You probably think I'm crazy, don't you," I commented. Smiling down, he replied, "I think you are the most natural girl I've ever known."

Walking hand in hand, we continued along the path until Jack, stopping beside a giant sequoia, picked up one of its cones and from it shook minute seeds over the palm of my hand. It seemed incredible, he said, that this great tree, over three hundred feet tall, had started from a seed no larger than a pin head before the birth of Christ. Reaching out, I ran my hand along the sequoia's trunk, a great column of soft, cinnamon-red bark, deeply furrowed, and asked, "If Nature could make a tree live that long, why couldn't people live longer?" Jack let that question sit in the air a moment and then noted, "There is no resin in the redwood's bark, which makes these trees naturally more fire resistant, so they live long. Not sure what Nature could create to make the human body more age resistant!" That had us laughing, just two happy hearts surrounded by great trees and not another soul around.

A sacred silence settled over the grove and I strolled beside Jack, silent, taking it all in. Speaking might sound a sacrilegious note in that twilight-green forest sanctuary. Neither of us made a sound until the loud chatter of a squirrel, scolding us for intruding in his domain, broke the quiet and shook us out of our reverie.

Laughing some more, we continued along the wooded trail until we reached a small stream. Jack expressed great excitement as he discovered a steelhead in the shallow water. "It must have come up from the Bay," he remarked, adding "I'm surprised to see a steelhead in Muir Woods." I had never heard of a steelhead, but was fascinated by it and its perfect example of protective coloration. I did not see the big fish until Jack gently poked it with a stick. "A steelhead is a rainbow trout that spawns in a river and goes to sea to feed," he told me. And this one was almost dead because it had spawned. Jack went on to relate the life cycle of anadromous fish and all the obstacles they had to surmount during their migration back to the spawning grounds in their parent rivers.[7]

By the time he had finished, I was almost in tears over that poor steelhead, dying before our very eyes; but then Jack distracted me by saying that he had fished for steelhead in the state of Washington, had fished with flies, and that he tied his own flies. He had started tying flies when he was seventeen.

I thought Jack would never stop talking about fly fishing and when he did, he looked down at me, smiled, and apologized for boring me. I told him I knew something about fishing with artificial flies and that I had fished with my father in the Sierras and caught a large rainbow trout with a fly.

He seemed thunderstruck. Holding me at arm's length, he asked, "Why haven't you ever told me you like to fish?!"

"You never asked," I replied, "and besides, I didn't know you were such a fanatic!"

Pulling me closer, Jack asked if I would like to spend the rest of my life with him. "I would love to," I answered, without even a fleeting thought of my once great love, Rudolph Valentino.

Jack Atherton and I were married in Berkeley, California the following November of 1926.

---

7. An anadromous fish, born in fresh water, spends most of its life in the sea and returns to fresh water to spawn. For more information, please visit www.nefsc.noaa.gov/faq/fishfaq1a.html.

CHAPTER SIX

The Neversink River, New York

I stand by the river and I know that it has been here yesterday and will be here tomorrow and that therefore, since I am
part of its pattern today, I also belong to all its yesterdays and
will be a part of all its tomorrows. This is a kind of earthly
immortality, a kinship with rivers and hills and rocks, with
all things and all creatures that have ever lived or ever will
live or have their being on the earth. It is my assurance of an
orderly continuity in the great design of the universe.

—Virginia Eifert

During the 1920s an optimistic mood prevailed across the United
States until the Stock Market Crash of 1929. Having arrived at the end
of the prosperous Industrial Age and the beginning of the Machine
Age, Americans viewed the future through a rosy haze of euphoria.

In San Francisco, the period of the Roaring Twenties—an offspring of the Jazz Age—was in full swing. The Era's youth had gone on
a rampage with a vengeance, rebelling against society's conventions,
against cultural restrictions handed down by our Puritan ancestors and
the restricting tentacles of Queen Victoria's strict social mores. This
movement reached across the Atlantic to America's shores and as far
west as San Francisco. That is when a more sophisticated and destructive expression of revolt emerged.

In the meantime, the younger generation's more serious thinkers, such as the war veterans at the art school, waged an intellectual revolution against the military factions responsible for sending them and the rest of our strongest and healthiest young Americans to help fight World War I in Europe.

Somehow, though, I was unaware of what was happening outside of my own little world. My entire life revolved around my husband, who had no need for revolutions of any kind. For our honeymoon he borrowed a friend's jazzy Ford Runabout, sporting a rumble seat in back, and we drove down the Pacific Coast to Carmel, then a quaint little village and art center.

It was the most wonderful place in the world for a honeymoon. Only a few tourists visited Carmel at that time of the year, and the November weather was kind to us. We stayed at a hotel overlooking the Pacific, played golf at Pebble Beach, and rode horseback out to gorgeous Point Lobos every day.

Back in San Francisco, where we had rented a small apartment, Jack went to work for an advertising agency. Within a couple of years he earned recognition as one of the top commercial artists in San Francisco and, at the same time, gained recognition in the field of fine art. Fine art was what Jack really cared about and he planned to earn enough in commercial art to be able to devote more time to painting and drawing.

Jack entered a drawing in an exhibition at a San Francisco art museum and won an award of three thousand dollars (quite a windfall at that time). He was delighted about the award but astonished by the controversy and publicity the drawing had generated. The subject was a nude woman and that shocked the museum's more Victorian-minded trustees, who voted to remove the drawing from their walls and hang it in the museum's basement, out of easy public view.

Immediately, the irate avant-garde art judges posted notice of the award in the empty space upstairs, thereby causing an overflow of curious visitors who made their way downstairs to see the immoral drawing. The press had a field day with the story and the incident gave Jack some valuable publicity. Yes, indeed, San Francisco was fast becoming the art center of the West, despite trustees who could not agree on what constituted art and what was immoral.

Jack put the prize money into a savings account, added to it now and then, and when the balance increased to four thousand dollars, we decided to move to New York City, the art center of America. In the summer of 1929, we said goodbye to our families and friends and started for New York. We traveled up the Pacific coast by boat to Vancouver, and from there traveled to New York by train. The long tiresome journey across North America was alleviated by the spectacular scenery in the Canadian Rockies, and by stopovers at Banff Lake, Emerald Lake, and Lake Louise. There, we rode horseback up to mountain meadows at the foot of the great glacier. As there were no other tourists around, we had all of that beauty to ourselves. From Lake Louise, we traveled by train to Montréal and then down the Atlantic coast to New York. Staring at the celestial sphere of twinkling stars that made up Grand Central Station's ethereal ceiling, we entered our new life in New York appropriately starry-eyed.

It was August 1929, and a few months later in October that prosperous decade crashed to the bottom of its paper mountain in Wall Street's New York Stock Exchange, subsequently spreading across the country and pulling the American economy down with it. As luck would have it, we hadn't had enough cash to invest in stocks, and we'd spent our savings to travel to New York, so we were not encumbered by luxurious possessions requiring costly upkeep. We owed no bills and Jack's gift for commercial art was earning twice as much as it had in San Francisco.

I thought we had escaped the effects of the stock market crash but gradually, as New York newspapers and radio reported one suicide after another by desperate men whose fortunes had been lost, I realized that no one in New York could escape being hurt in one way or another. Seeing once-successful business men peddling apples on the streets of Manhattan symbolized the depths of this Depression and hit me hard emotionally.

The contrast of poverty and filth in New York's slums lay only blocks from the affluence and elegance of our apartment on East 75th Street between Park and Fifth Avenues. All of it depressed me. Living in the eye-burning foul atmosphere gnawed at me. And the noise—the thunderous roar of elevated subways, the nerve-wrangling, earsplitting pneumatic drills almost continuously tearing up asphalt, the piercing shrieks of sirens from police cars, ambulances or fire trucks, and the traffic with constant honking from hundreds of cars driven by ill-tempered drivers had gradually tempered my mood so that I could think of very little else. I yearned to return to my family and the quiet beauty of the Sierras. For the first time in my life I experienced, amid all of New York's excitement and splendor, that lonely aching feeling of homesickness.

Jack, enjoying his work and inspired by all New York had to offer an artist, was not affected by the gloomier side of the City. He took me to all the performances of Wagner's Ring of the Nibelungen, and to a ballet I can recall vividly. It was a special performance of Stravinsky's *Le Sacre du Printemps* at the Metropolitan Opera House. I loved the earthy stage sets, the primitive costumes made of burlap, both designed by a great contemporary artist, Rorach. I loved Stravinsky's syncopated music, the primitive dancing, and the choreography, all recounting early man's worship of Nature and his cruel rite: the sacrifice of the most beautiful of all maidens.

In particularly good spirits at that time, Jack joined the Anglers' Club of New York which is where he met our soon-to-be dear friend, Edward Hewitt. Mr. Hewitt,[8] known as the dean of fly fishers in the East, invited Jack to fish with him at the Neversink River up north in New York's Catskill Mountains.

Everyone at the Anglers' Club, except a few old friends, called that charming elderly gentleman Mr. Hewitt, out of respect for his age.

---

8. Edward Ringwood Hewitt (1867–1957), son of iron mogul Abram Hewitt, was a famous fly fisherman and conservationist who wrote (and illustrated) several notable books on fishing and conservation. Please see www.bigbluegill.com/profiles/blogs/edward-ringwood-hewitt for more information.

Jack and I never called him anything other than Mr. Hewitt. He was much older than Jack, but they had interests in common and soon became close friends. I was invited, too, to stay at his camp, an old farmhouse near the river.

For the most part we had the fishing all to ourselves. Mr. Hewitt fished with us, but we seldom fished together in one pool. There was no need. He owned more than five miles of the river and the riparian rights to both sides. His water had good natural runs and pools, and he created a series of excellent pools by putting up low dams made of logs.

Each weekend we fished until dark. Afterwards, I cooked a late supper on the old wood-burning stove while my host and husband sat in the kitchen talking about fish, fish, fish—nothing but fish and fly fishing until I thought they were daft. Nevertheless, I loved them dearly and shall be forever grateful for what they taught me about fly fishing and the habits of trout, especially the erudite Brown trout.

Mr. Hewitt taught me about releasing fish for the purpose of conservation. At first I begrudged having to release the fish I caught. But I learned to appreciate the value of this approach. Now, since more and more trout streams have been "fished out," I believe the return of trout to the river is absolutely vital.

I had so much to learn, and sometimes I learned by sitting on the bank and watching Jack and Mr. Hewitt as they fished. One day I stopped along the river and settled to watch Mr. Hewitt fish one of the pools he had made. The low log dam formed two terraced pools, with one above and one below. Mr. Hewitt waded knee-deep into the middle of the upper pool, a long flat one, and casted a dry fly to the opposite side of the river where the current had carved a channel close to the shore and where big brownies liked to rest under the bank's edge, in the shade of overhanging branches.

To lure out a trout, Mr. Hewitt had chosen a Spider, an artificial fly made of exceptionally long and stiff hackles. It looked like a water spider, as described in Jack's book, *The Fly and the Fish*,[9] and to place the fly beneath the branches, Mr. Hewitt used the roll cast, dropping his fly on the water close to the bank, below his stance. The instant the fly touched the water, he lifted the rod's tip a bit, twitched it slightly to set the hackles on edge, started strip in the line while jerking the rod so that the fly skipped in darts and stops across the surface, just like a live skater.

At once, a huge brown trout splattered water in all directions and as it dove down on the fly, Mr. Hewitt lifted the rod, struck, played the trout until it tired, and then scooped the fish into a net and released it while holding the net beneath the surface.

"This Spider fly seems to drive big fish crazy," he said. Mr. Hewitt joined me on the shore and was holding the trout out for me to examine. "It's important to keep the fly light." He wound the long stiff hackles around a tiny hook; but the long hackles made it easy for a fish to spit out, and he recommended that I use it only to locate large trout and never let a fish feel the hook. If it did, I should change quickly to a different kind of dry fly (perhaps a variant) and should not give up until the trout got mad enough to take a swat at it. "That could take you a hundred casts or more," he told me.

Then Mr. Hewitt led me down to the lower pool, a small area in which the water pouring over the dam had dug an ideal place for trout to hide under the dam base. He added three feet of 4X tippet to my nine-foot gut leader (nylon leaders and floating lines had not yet come onto the market), and then he tied on a Quill Gordon, the artificial fly that matched the natural ones in the air over the water.

Advising that I stand well back, Mr. Hewitt instructed me, "Strip out the amount of line you'll need to reach the dam, cast only once,

9. *The Fly and The Fish* by John Atherton was originally published in 1951 (Freshet Press), reprinted in 1971, and in paperback in 2006 (Macmillan). The latest edition, with a special color insert and new foreword by flyfishing expert Mike Valla, is set to be published by Skyhorse Publishing in early 2016.

and get the fly as close to the base as you can." Somehow, with one cast I managed to get the rod to drop a dry fly right at the foot of the dam. I stated quickly stripping in line but, suddenly, a brilliant flash in the dazzling dark, clear green depth was my undoing. I yanked the fly away before what looked like a whale had a chance to get its mouth around the hook.

Mr. Hewitt patted me on the shoulder, wished me better luck next time, and went off upriver. Of course he knew that smart brownie would not come up again, but I did not . . . until a couple of hours and an aching arm later. After casting a hundred or more times, I understood exactly what Jack meant when he said catching brown trout required more skill than catching any other fish.

I learned from another expert at the Neversink, too—Richard Hunt, then president of the Anglers' Club of New York and editor of its bulletin. Jack liked to say that Dick Hunt cast a fly better than anyone he knew, so one day while he was fishing on the Neversink, I sat on the bank to watch. Dick was using a dry fly, casting upriver using only about thirty feet of line and only once each time. Somehow (Jack explains how in *The Fly and the Fish*), he cast a curve in the leader so the fly settled on the water and floated down the current ahead of the line. It all looked easy, but when I went to another pool to give it a try, I discovered there was nothing easy about it. Indeed, it seemed impossible.

Still, I was learning. Both Jack and Mr. Hewitt helped me see that there was more to enjoy around a river than catching fish. Trout pools and the habits of trout turned out to be fascinating. When Mr. Hewitt was not fishing, he could usually be found in his hatchery, working on experiments or improving his formula for a trout diet rich in protein, lecithin, amino acids, vitamins, and everything else Nature, as part of her plan for the survival of the species, used to make fish and the humans who ate that fish healthy. I had never heard of vitamins but learned later that Mr. Hewitt graduated from Princeton as a chemist and he applied what he'd learned to good use in his trout hatchery.

The hatchery was a magical place. Located in back of the camp at the bottom of a slope, Mr. Hewitt piped water from a lively spring brook that flowed down the hillside right into the hatchery building, through two long table troughs, and then outside into small rearing ponds. Indoors, the troughs were filled with trout fry and fingerlings which had been hatched from eggs spawned and fertilized by the largest and healthiest of the trout in the rearing ponds outside.

One of those small ponds held six or seven Brook trout, averaging four to five pounds each. Mr. Hewitt explained that they grew large because he fed them lights—a mixture of ground liver, gizzards, hearts, and so on—a gourmet delight on the trout menu.

One day, after I had fished the camp pool all morning and failed to catch or even raise a trout, I returned at lunchtime and announced to Jack and our host that there were no fish in the camp pool that day. Mr. Hewitt, who was very sensitive to derogatory remarks about his pools, said nothing, but marched out to the hatchery and returned to the kitchen with a pail of lights. He invited me to follow him and when we arrived at the pool, he scattered the lights over the water.

The pool exploded in trout! They were there all right, but having been caught and released more than once, they were not likely to take an artificial fly readily, Mr. Hewitt explained. Embarrassed, I bowed my head and followed him back to camp, quiet, with the humbling thought that he and Jack had very little trouble catching wise old brownies in that pool.

Jack could make anything happen with a flyrod and I learned about dry fly fishing from him. He insisted that I fish with a short line and advised me to hold loops of line in my left hand and release them on the forward cast, and then said I should never let go of the line entirely since holding onto it would give me better control when a fish took the fly.

Watching Jack fish, I noticed that if trees or brush interfered with his backcast, he somehow changed the direction of the cast in midair so that the line shot out behind him into the open space over the river, and then he somehow directed the forward cast to the opposite shore and let the fly drop a foot above the rising trout, a feat I never mastered. Mr. Hewitt said Jack had perfect timing and arm-eye coordination. And I observed that Jack's movements were as graceful as a ballet dancer.

One day Mr. Hewitt took me to the river, greased my silk line and then tied on a heavy gut leader with a strong 2X gut tippet. He tied a Neversink Streamer onto it, his own pattern, explaining that "This is meant to represent a minnow." He waded into the river and stopped at the head of a run.

I followed and stood beside him as he demonstrated. First, he showed me how to shoot line through the rod guides. "You don't want to cast it back and forth over your head. That will scare off the trout." Holding several large loops of line in his left hand, he cast them on the water, upstream, where there was no sign of a trout. When he had enough line to reach the opposite bank, he picked up the line and cast the streamer into the current—to get a pull on the line—and then he cast the line to the opposite bank, a bit above his stance. At the same time, he created slack in the line by jerking the rod tip backward a bit at the end of the forward cast. The instant the streamer touched the water, he lifted the rod tip and tossed the loop of slack line upstream.

He was using Arthur Wood's greased line technique and mended the line so the streamer would have a chance to sink a bit and swim underwater, down past the overhanging bank before the current dragged it in a way no real minnow would ever behave. His purpose was to show the streamer, before it swung around in the current, to any trout that might be resting under the overhanging bank.

Mr. Hewitt handed the rod to me. "I'd try fishing down at the end of the run, if I were you, by the boulder jutting out just over the water." Reminding me to release any trout I caught and wishing me luck, Mr. Hewitt also urged me to be careful around the big rock and then left me to my own devices.

I had a terrible time at first. The streamer was heavier than any fly I had ever cast. It simply would not move the way it had for Mr. Hewitt. Even so, the six huge Brook trout he had planted from the

Jack Atherton c. 1940.

hatchery near the big rock were very gullible. Each one hooked itself securely when the streamer swung around in the current a couple of inches under the surface near the partly submerged boulder; so I caught and released every single one, six trout averaging four to five pounds each!

When it was time for lunch, I returned to camp victorious, elated, irrepressible, and as I described my adventures play by play, articulating how I had outwitted each trout, my astonished husband turned to our host wide-eyed, asking for an explanation.

Mr. Hewitt nodded, smiling knowingly, and said he had planted them in the river before I was out of bed and that he took me there to fish so I could teach them to be more cautious the next time they saw a minnow with a hook on its bottom.

Later in the season, Mr. Hewitt showed me how to fish a nymph by using the greased line method, and I was delighted to discover that when trout were feeding on them under the surface, fishing with a nymph could be as much fun as dry fly fishing. Jack and I went to the Neversink every fishing season until 1944. Soon after, Mr. Hewitt's section of the river, his camp and hatchery, were all covered over by a reservoir of water destined to supply New York City.

CHAPTER SEVEN
Magalloway River, Maine

〰〰〰〰〰

Life is always flowing on like a river, sometimes with mur-
murs, sometimes without bending this way or that, we do
not exactly see why; now in beautiful picturesque places,
now through barren and uninteresting scenes, but always
flowing with a look of treachery about it; it is so swift, so
voiceless, yet so continuous.

—Faber

The beauty of rural Connecticut in the springtime has woven into
memory a tapestry of dark green spruce and hemlock standing tall in
groves of maples and elms, clothed in waxy green leaves—beautiful
islands of woods with fragrant wild laurel shrubs and chalky trunks of
white birch covered with silvery foliage that shimmered amid acres of
fields, pale green and contained by neat fieldstone fences.

It was my first visit to Connecticut and the year was 1931.
The contrast of the countryside to New York City made it all the
more beautiful, and I was surprised to find miles of rural land so
close to the busy metropolis. Jack and I were with Robert Fawcett,
a dear friend and talented artist who was taking us to his family's
home in Ridgefield. Having left the main highway, he was driving
us along a country road. Bob told us that Ridgefield was a small
New England village of large colonial homes and gardens bordering a wide main street lined on both sides with great elms (before

the Japanese beetles did them in). The village was surrounded by large estates originally inhabited by wealthy industrialists from New York City.

Jack and I enjoyed the visit and it didn't take long to convince him that we should move to that charming village. Six months later, we rented a furnished house in Ridgefield, bought a Ford Roadster for $750 and fourteen acres of wooded land three miles from the village center. The year after we had a house built which we could afford because the Depression of the 1930s and the US economy had dropped to an all-time low, along with the cost of building materials and labor, while Jack's income from commercial art had increased considerably.

We moved into our new house in the spring of 1932, shortly after our sweet daughter, Mary, was born. The house, a modest one of Connecticut salt-box architecture, sat in the woods overlooking a small, deserted marble quarry filled with some thirty feet of water. It became our swimming pool and was fed by underground springs with an underground outlet that emptied into a lake across the road. Our quarry bordered on the road so we had a high fence built on that side and many truckloads of sand brought in to create a beach. Rock ledges pushing out over the water served as natural diving boards, and across the back sheer marble reached some forty or fifty feet up to the edge of our front yard.

A deep pool in a natural setting resembled a stage set. Jack and I were sunning ourselves on the beach and two frogs were getting some sun on a rock ledge over the water. One was a large bullfrog and I assumed the smaller one was a lady frog. She seemed to be vying for his attention, but he ignored her. Lashing out a tongue and leaning into him with her body, she tried to nudge him off the ledge. He seemed to be dozing, and bit by bit she got him down to the end of the ledge. There, he refused to budge another inch. Did she stop pestering him then? No, indeed not. She kept right on shoving without success and, suddenly, she was gone!

It happened so fast I missed the moment, but I could see her kicking feet sticking out of the bullfrog's mouth and I could hear her croaking inside. When he jumped into the quarry and began swimming across the pool, he had to struggle to keep his bulging body from sinking. Finally, the miserable bullfrog disappeared under a ledge of marble at the other end of the pool. Astounded, I faced my chuckling husband and mumbled that Nature's creatures weren't supposed to eat their own kind.

"Nature's creatures, including humans, can stand just so much pushing and prodding and no more," Jack commented. Advising me to remember that the next time I started nagging him, he laughingly pulled me from the sand and we walked up the steep path to our house. Before going in, we stopped to admire the rock garden he had planted; and as we stood there, we became intrigued by a small silky white web, spun between the leaves on a trailing arbutus plant. A tiny spider had scrawled its signature at the bottom of the web in red silk. Just like a person's signature in red ink, I thought, awed by one of the natural world's mystical wonders.

Early the next morning outside I came upon a beautiful lunar moth, five inches from wing to wing, soft, jade green, and adorned with touches of ruby. It seemed in that moment to be one of Nature's greatest works of art in the world of insects. At last, we were living close and with the natural world, and we enjoyed working outdoors. Jack had planted the rock garden around a small pool at the back of the house. I had planted flower borders around the front lawn, and in the woods along the edge of the lawn, Nature had planted a beautiful bush of wild laurel and a clump of lady-slippers since it was impossible to transplant wild lady-slippers successfully.

Ours was a healthy way of life. We joined the Silver Spring Country Club in Ridgefield, raised our beautiful daughter, Mary, born April 17, 1932, played golf, and, during the coldest months, traveled to North Conway, New Hampshire, for skiing vacations. I joined the Ridgefield Hunt, a drag hunt, and Jack fished various trout rivers in Connecticut and New York.

Jack learned where to fish for trout from members of the Anglers Club, and from Pinky Gillum,[10] an ardent fly fisher and carpenter who had worked on our house and made wonderful rods. I'm not sure who discovered whom, but when those two perfectionists got together, I got out of the room. They could think of and talk about nothing but the making of split-bamboo fishing rods.

Their dialogue usually centered on the million and one details around building the perfect flyrod. Jack knew all about flyrods. He had made his own when he was only seventeen. Pinky had made several trout and salmon rods. Getting ready for the time when our country would get involved in World War II, he'd spent ten thousand dollars of his hard-earned cash to buy the best bamboo while it was still available. With it, he produced extra special flyrods, and each custom-made rod was designed to suit the individual owner, so there are relatively few, which makes them more valuable as collectors' items.

We could not get enough gasoline coupons[11] to make the drive to the Neversink, so Jack began fishing with men who lived in Connecticut and shared their coupons. Having not been invited to go along, I was delighted when one evening at a dinner party in Ridgefield, our host, Harris Colt, asked if I would go to Maine with him and his wife, Terry, the following September. Terry needed the support of another woman in a camp full of men.

---

10. Gillum lived and worked for most of his life in Ridgefield, Connecticut, although he spent a five-year period in Vermont helping Wes Jordan train rod craftsmen for the Orvis Company. Most authorities trace Pinky's introduction to making bamboo rods to Eustis Edwards who ran the Winchester rod shop in nearby New Haven about the time Pinky appeared on the scene. Gillum was a contemporary of Jim Payne and Everett Garrison and shared rod making information with both men. Harold S. Gillum has attained an exalted position among the top classic rodmakers, but it is a position some authorities feel exceeds what the quality of his rods actually deserves. For more information, please visit www.flyanglersonline.com/features/bamboo/part39.php.

11. Gasoline was rationed during the Depression and during World War I and World War II, as were other basic commodities such as sugar, and coupons also known as stamps were issued in limited amounts to allow people to purchase gas for their vehicles.

Jack encouraged me to go with the Colts. Harris said we would be at Parmachenee Lake the last two weeks in September and would fish for landlocked salmon. Fly fishing only was the rule, and everyone at the Parmachenee Club fished with streamers. So my dear husband tied some streamers for me, and some wet flies as well. One pattern, a Parmachenee Belle of red and white feathers, was stunning.

It was mid-September when I left with Jack's precious Leonard trout rod and the best fishing tackle to go with it, leaving John and our Mary with the housekeeper, and drove off to Maine with Harris and Terry Colt. An archaeologist, Harris had been working on his diggings in Palestine when the war drove his away. He went to the Isle of Malta where he met Terry, a daughter of the governor of Malta, and married her there.

On our way, as Harris drove north in the serene Connecticut River Valley, he related the story of the Parmachenee Club. After a small group of fanatic fly fishers in New York, including his father, discovered the spectacular trout fishing in Parmachenee Lake and the Magalloway River (flowing into the lake), they formed the club late in the nineteenth century. Harris explained that now—it was 1941—the trout fishing at Parmachenee was poor compared to what it had been. "My father always blamed the club for planting landlocked salmon there because the salmon feed on trout eggs."

Toward the end of the day Harris stopped the car at the White Mountain Inn in New Hampshire, where his father spent each summer. We were to be his guests that night and then go on to Parmachenee the next morning. Mr. Colt senior, a tall, good-looking grey-haired man, a retired lawyer from the days of the prosperous Industrial Age, sat waiting for us on a veranda. I liked him at once and was fascinated by the fabulous Inn, a huge, fashionable New England establishment with annexes sprawled over the landscape, all filled to capacity. Set on the side of a mountain, it overlooked the Presidential Range and offered a spectacular view.

That evening in the large formal dining room sparkling with crystal chandeliers, white linen tablecloths and polished silver, the

Colts and I were the only guests who had not dressed for dinner; but we were welcomed because we were seen as youngsters—I was thirty-five—and had been traveling. The guests' ages ranged from seventy to ninety; a few elderly gentlemen wore formal cutaways. Everyone knew everyone else because they had been summering at the White Mountain Inn for many years.

Mr. Colt noted that all of the Parmachenee Club members stopped overnight at the Inn when traveling to and from Parmachenee, and Harris commented that the Inn was popular because it catered to each guest's every need and provided all the comforts of a luxurious Victorian home. Having been given a glimpse into a past era and way of life I had no idea existed, I viewed it all with awe.

Before we left the next morning, Mr. Colt promised to join us at Parmachenee in a couple of days. During the drive, Harris explained that I would be his father's guest and then relayed the story of the Parmachenee Club. To get to Parmachenee Lake in the area of the Rangeley Lakes in Maine, the charter members traveled from New York City to Wilson Mills by train. From there, they and the guides paddled canoes fourteen miles up Richardson Lake. The guides carried the canoes over their heads to portage overland between lakes, and the club members carried heavy packs on their backs. The trip from Wilson Mills to Parmachenee took several days, but Harris said they were young and strong, and the fabulous fishing for Brook trout was worth the strenuous journey.

What luxury! Over the years, club members of the same vintage as those I'd met at the White Mountain Inn had added one luxury after another. Each log cabin had hot and cold running water and modern bathroom fixtures. I had a cabin and beautiful bathroom to myself. I slept on a sumptuous Simmons Beauty Rest mattress and every morning before I was up, the guide would come in and build a roaring fire in the fireplace. On exceptionally chilly mornings, he heated a blanket in the kitchen oven and wrapped it around me in the canoe.

The cabins ran in a line down an elevated boardwalk to the end of the island. Mr. Colt's cabin was at the very end of the line. Every evening after a day of fishing, we met in his cabin for cocktail hour. Mr. Colt enjoyed reminiscing about the good old days when trout were plentiful at Parmachenee, before salmon were planted in the lake and before the automobile and motor launch made getting there too easy.

By 1941 almost all the charter members were either gone or too old to travel that far. Mr. Colt was the only club member at Parmachenee that season. He, his family, and I were the only guests. He did not fish and, as Harris preferred wandering through the beautiful Maine woods in search of fossils, rather than fish, Terry and I had the fishing to ourselves.

Mr. Colt claimed he was too old to fish and arranged for his guide, Gerald, to take me each day. Terry, who had only learned how fascinating the sport of fly fishing could be when Harris took her to Parmachenee for the first time a couple of years earlier, was a wonderful angling companion, bubbling over with enthusiasm every time she hooked into a fish.

We fished the Magalloway from the shore. Soon, I learned how lucky I was to be with Gerald, one of the best guides in the Rangeley Lakes area. He taught me to cast out a fly using the old-fashioned method of holding a book under my arm. Later, Jack taught me to swing my arm and body a bit when casting, which worked better, but with Gerald's approach I learned to stop the rod on the backcast when it was only a bit past the perpendicular; and, when the line was straight out behind me, to cast forward with an extra hard drive of the rod at the end of the cast, which helped me shoot loops of line through the rod guides and drop the fly on the water with one cast.

Gerald advised me to fish the Magalloway, a small river, with no more than thirty feet of line. Standing behind me, he clasped my right hand, which was holding the rod, and then, with loops of line in his left hand, he told me to let him cast the rod for me. Finally, when I relaxed and let him cast without my interference, I felt the drive at the end of the forward cast shoot the line—as he released the loops of line with his left hand—and glide through the supple rod's guides. At the same time, I experienced the same exhilarating sensation and sense of accomplishment that had surged through me long ago in the Sierras when by chance I had cast out a fly with perfect timing, in harmony with my arm, body, mood, and the river's rhythms.

Gerald, having grown up around the Rangeley Lakes, had been well taught by member of the Parmachenee Club, some of the first fly fishers in America, and always took me to the best spots. He never stepped into the water and instead devoted the entire day to teaching me how and where to cast. Gradually, my technique improved.

Every morning Terry and I, in separate canoes with our guides and inspired by the beauty of the Maine woods in magnificent autumn colors and brisk invigorating air, started out anticipating an exciting day. At noon we would all meet at the Fireplace Pool for lunch. And each time, a lovely doe we called Molly joined us when she heard the guides chopping wood for the fireplace. The guides fed her pancakes, bacon, butter, and all of her other favorite foods, and they took along plenty each day so there would be enough for all of us, including Molly.

Unfortunately, the rich diet was probably the cause of the large lump that developed on Molly's neck. Everyone around the Magalloway felt concerned, and each evening when we returned everyone on the island asked for a report on Molly's health and we were happy to inform them that she was still in good health.

Terry and I caught no trout, but we had great fun catching land-locked salmon. The time to return home arrived too soon. The Colts had been wonderful to me. They had given me two marvelous weeks away from the frantic social life in Connecticut and, as there was no telephone or radio on the island, we had a rest from the grim news of the war abroad. On the way home, as Harris drove us down the Connecticut River Valley, I promised myself I would reorganize my life so I would have more time to go fishing with Jack.

The following year Jack drove me to Parmachenee, where we arranged to meet the Colts. Terry, Jack, and I were the only fishers. Harris was working on a book about his diggings in Palestine and he and his father remained in camp most of the time. The few surviving club members had given the buildings and fishing rights to the man who had run the camp for them for many years. He opened the camp to the public, but the change had not been advertised long, so only the Colts and the Athertons were there that fall.

There was no more trout fishing, but we had some excellent land-locked salmon fishing. Jack caught a record seven-pounder with a dry fly and a lightweight trout rod. His guide beamed with pride. It was the first time anyone had caught a salmon at Parmachenee with a dry fly, he said. And one day while I was watching Jack fish a wonderfully clear pool with a dry fly and a dropper fly on the leader, two salmon took a fly at the same time! Both fish jumped, one salmon breaking from the leader, but Jack managed to get the other one into the net. It was very exciting and I had been able to see it all through the crystal clear water.

That was the last time we had a chance to fish at Parmachenee. The next year we could not get enough gasoline coupons to make the drive. Meanwhile, we were very busy in Ridgefield. Jack had joined a group of artists at the Julien Levy gallery, a new gallery considered very avant garde in New York. He had been accepting only commercial assignments that were suitable to his talents so he could have more time to work on fine art rather than on what commercial art directors wanted; and Jack had begun to paint covers for the *Saturday Evening Post,* which paid well.

Jack also won a prize of $4,000 for a picture shown at the Artists for Victory exhibit at the Metropolitan Museum of Art (which still owns the painting) and that gave his morale, and his career, a great boost.

Unfortunately, in Connecticut we became associated with a group who seemed determined to have as much fun as possible before World War II killed far too many souls. Frequent, lavish parties were all the rage and we drank too much alcohol with little seeming reverence for the important things in life.

I had become involved in too many clubs and charity organizations, including one I found very worthwhile—the birth control clinic

Jack Atherton in his art studio. c. 1935.

in nearby Danbury. Nancy Rockefeller, a wonderful young woman from Greenwich, Katherine Hepburn's mother, and other dedicated women had helped establish birth control clinics in Connecticut. I believed then, as I do now, that the basis of so many of the world's problems stemmed at least in part from too many people pulling on the planet's natural resources. A volunteer worker and chair of the Danbury Clinic, before all the state's clinics were closed when an old blue law was enforced, had been carefully trained to assist the doctor and solicit and train other volunteer workers. It was depressing but important work, and while there never seemed to be enough time to do it all, I managed nonetheless.

One day when I was feeling particularly low with a hangover from a party the night before, I suggested to Jack that we move somewhere more restful. He refused to even consider moving. He was happy in his studio—where there was no telephone, no interference from the outside world—and he could shut the studio door on everything but his work and himself.

I had given up all hope of our family escaping from what seemed about to destroy me when a stroke a luck came to my rescue. It began one evening at a meeting of the Illustrators Club in New York, when Jack met two artists, Norman Rockwell and Mead Schaeffer. Jack was familiar with the covers they had painted for the *Saturday Evening Post*, and he was delighted to meet them. What interested him most of all, however, was that the Rockwells lived in Vermont near the Battenkill River. Our friend Lee Wulff owned a house on the bank of the Battenkill because, he told us, it was one of the best trout streams in the East.

Jack returned to me that night sparkling with excitement; and after hearing why, I thought the time was right to suggest a move to

Vermont, but I was wrong. Tossing my suggestion aside with a negative shake of his head, John went upstairs to bed.

The next morning while I was upstairs in the bathroom overlooking the rock garden and woods at the back of our house, I heard a foxhound in the distance howling at the top of his voice. The hysterical note in his wailing indicated he was on the scent of a fox, and I looked through the window just as a beautiful red fox ambled out of the woods. She stopped to drink from the small pool in the rock garden, licked her paws, washed her face, and rolled over on the lawn. Showing no sign of hurry, she trotted down our driveway and disappeared into the woods across the road.

In the meantime, the hound's eerie tones had become louder and I waited at the window until, ears and nose trailing the ground, he rushed out of the woods and over to the pool where the little fox had outsmarted him and somehow backtracked. Finally, the weary hound picked up her scent again and, still wailing mournfully, ran down our driveway after the fox long since gone. Every inch of me was pulling for the fox, despite a sense of empathy for the hound, but I wasn't

Max holding daughter Mary, Ridgefield, CT, c. 1932.

Max and John in their home in Ridgefield, CT, mid-1940s.

worried. I knew the hound would never catch up with the savvy fox because he had wasted too much time getting nowhere.

That night, after an exceptionally hectic day, I went to bed and had a strange dream in which I turned into a foxhound, running around in circles and getting nowhere all night long. At dawn, a mournful howl billowing out of my mouth woke me up. And it woke Jack, too. Jumping out of bed I faced my startled husband and vowed to move to Vermont even if I had to go alone.

The following fall we moved to Arlington, Vermont and became the proud owners of twelve acres of meadowland fronting on the Battenkill. Then began our new life and with it, great hopes for our future.

CHAPTER EIGHT

On the Battenkill (Vermont) & Miramichi (New Brunswick)

The river has taught me to listen; you will learn from it, too. The river knows everything; one can learn everything from it.

—Herman Hesse, *Siddhartha*

The Battenkill begins its journey to the Atlantic Ocean in Vermont. Winding down and around the Green Mountains, a part of the ancient Laurentians, the rivers weaves through dense woods, in some places resembling a chalk stream, and then wanders through meadowland and terrain dominated by marble and limestone. Just below the village of Arlington, the river runs down a narrow valley, protected on both sides by lofty mountains. Further on, where the river touches the Taconic range, it leaves Vermont, flowing into New York State to join the mighty Hudson River. Together, they enter the vast Atlantic.

Our house, set atop a slope facing the Battenkill and Green Mountains in the distance, was built in the middle of our twelve-acre plot of meadowland. The only sign of habitation visible from the front windows was a farm on the other side of the river. Dan Kiley had designed our house. An army officer in World War II, Dan was a well-known architect by then. The army had kept him in the service after the war to remodel the interior of the building to be used for the Nuremburg trials, and he had drawn the plans for our house while he was in Germany. With our suggestions, he created a contemporary house that featured a flat roof and many thermopane windows and walls.

Dan positioned the house so that the wide overhang on the roof shaded the front rooms during the summer months, and in the wintertime, when the sun was low, sunlight flooded the living room with warmth. The thermostat was in the living room and on a sunny day when the temperature dropped below zero outside, the thermostat seldom had to turn on the furnace until late afternoon, after the sun disappeared behind a mountain. Yes, we had passive solar heat as early as 1946.

We loved our modern home, made of natural cedar clapboards, glass and brick, and it fit perfectly in to the rustic landscape, we thought. The local Vermonters, however, expected us to build a large white colonial house like the Rockwell's and said it looked like a chicken house. It was Norman, who reveled in the Vermonters' droll sense of humor, who related that bit of gossip to us.

One day Norman came over to our place to tell us that Franky Hall, a retired vaudeville actor, had invited the Athertons, Schaeffers, and Rockwells to be his guests at the opening night of his new restaurant in Arlington. We all went, and it wasn't until we were all seated around a table that Norman, his eyes twinkling with mischief, announced that Franky had built the small stage at the end of the dining room for the purpose of displaying life-sized wax figures of Arlington's three *Post* artists.

An ominous silence—the calm before the storm—settled over our table as Jack glared at the stage and then at Norman. Knowing what was coming, I held my breath. Suddenly, shouting "over my dead body," Jack jumped up from the table and started for the door. It took the five of us to get him back to the table again, and Norman enjoyed every minute of the rumpus. Did Franky Hall really think the *Saturday Evening Post* cover artists would consent to such a crazy idea? I think he did, and in the end, when John's sense of the ridiculous came to the fore, the evening ended as a howling success.

Everyone adored Norman, loved him for his sense of humor and his sensibilities, especially his keen perception and understanding of the "little man," a quality in his paintings that made him famous. A few years ago at a lecture on art at Princeton University, the speaker discussed a slide of a Rockwell painting, a picture of a little man, a Casper Milquetoast character, wearing a sagging grey flannel suit and flat straw hat. Norman had painted the back of the man as he stood in a museum studying a large abstract painting by Jackson Pollock, and Norman's picture portrayed perfectly the intense confusion and bewilderment of the ordinary man trying to understand how this extremely abstract painting was considered a work of art worthy of a museum wall.

Norman's wife, Mary Rockwell was talented, too. I loved her charcoal drawings, which she produced when they lived in Stockbridge, and of some of her poetry, which she wrote when the Rockwells and Athertons were attending evening literature classes at Bennington College. Her poetry revealed a hint of brilliance. Unfortunately, she never had a chance to develop her talents. She devoted her life to the care of her husband and three sons, and I never heard her complain about her lot in life.

Jack and I were fond of the Schaeffers as well and pleased when the three Rockwell boys, the two Schaeffer girls. and our Mary became close friends. The Schaeffers had restored a farmhouse on the bank of the Green River, which flows into the Battenkill. They bought the house so Mead could fish for trout in the evenings when he was through working in his studio. Mead, an excellent and devout fly fisher and great fun to fish with, showed us all the best trout pools in the Battenkill. One of them bordered on our property and is now called the Atherton Pool. Lee Wulff's house was on the bank on the New York side of the river and sometimes we fished with him.

Yes, we were happy in Vermont. All through our married life we had been lucky, but our luck began to wane when Jack had a serious skiing accident in 1945. The excruciating pain, along with a concussion and having to endure being in traction, held down by a body

Schaeffer girls and Mary Atherton, c. 1948.

cast for over a month in the hospital and several weeks at home, was bound to be a claustrophobic ordeal for any sensitive being.

Jack suffered terribly, but he had made reservations to fish the Miramichi that year in New Brunswick, and the idea of having to cancel if he was not better by September provoked a superhuman effort to walk with a cane. As a result, we arrived at the Herman Campbell Camp on schedule in the middle of September. Herman greeted us with the news that he had arranged for Jack to fish from a canoe. No one fished Herman's pools from a canoe. Everyone waded. Herman made an exception for Jack, however. Jack hated the thought of sitting in a canoe and a couple of days, he began complaining. So Herman took us to the Cains River where Jack could fish from the shore.

Cursing his luck, Jack hooked his cane on his belt, stripped line from the reel, cast a wet fly into the river and hobbled along the shore, casting as he went. At the tail of the pool a salmon swirled but missed the fly. He waited a few moments, cast again, and dropped the fly a foot or two above the rise. That time the salmon nabbed the fly as it swung around in the current. Keeping a slight arch in the rod, Jack let the salmon run free. Suddenly, it turned downriver and when it showed no signs of stopping, Jack tossed the cane into the bushes and ran down the bank after the salmon. It stopped in the middle of the river when Jack got below it, and he managed to keep the salmon there, fighting the current. Twenty minutes later, when the fish tired, Herman netted it—a great salmon weighing over twenty pounds!

Smiling happily, Jack asked me to get his cane. My head shook an emphatic no, and when Herman started for the cane, I stopped him.

Dumbfounded, he glared at me and so did my astonished husband. Let me explain. I had come to the conclusion while watching him run after the salmon that he had been pampered long enough. Having been waited on by nurses in the hospital for over a month, and then by me at home, he was, I feared, on the verge of settling into a state of comfortable complacency from which he might never emerge.

Fortunately, my dear husband was not one to hold a grudge. Smiling sheepishly, he retrieved his cane from the bushes and from then on fished and waded in the Miramichi. He tied a wading staff to his belt but seldom used it, and of course the force of the current against his legs was good therapy.

I had never caught a salmon and the Cains was easier for me to wade, so one day Herman took us back there. I loved the Cains, a wilderness river wandering through woods and over a riverbed of dark stones, some jet black with orange spots. In the fall of that year, the flaming red and orange of the swamp maples, the yellow green of the poplar trees, and the forest green of spruce, all mirrored on the Cains' smooth dark surface, played tricks with my imagination. I had trouble keeping my mind on the serious business of trying to catch a salmon.

I was fishing in the middle of the Cains with an Oriole, a pretty wet fly Jack had tied with a black body and orange, yellow and green feathers, all the colors in the Cains; and I was wading in knee-deep water at the head of a run and daydreaming, imagining myself fishing in a stream of liquid jet, harboring wondrous mysteries such as silvery salmon as big as a whale, when the rod almost jerked out of my hand. I froze (hunters call it "buck fever") and then clutched the line tight to the rod.

I was with Charlie De Feo, another artist noted for the beautiful flies he tied, and he was standing on shore yelling at me, but I didn't hear a word. The tip of the rod was almost touching the butt, and the only reason the salmon remained on the end of the line was that Charley had tied the fly on a strong tippet in a double knot.

Perhaps the best way to describe what happened is to explain what Charlie meant when he told me to let the salmon "run." Wading out to me, he pried my hand away from the rood, took it from me, held it high in the air, and let the great fish run out line. Finally, when the salmon stopped and settled in the current, Charlie led me to shore, reeled in enough line to put a slight arch in the rod, and then handed it to me. I was lucky, he said, and advised me never to stop the run of a salmon.

The soothing technique he used to calm me worked. When the salmon began to run upriver again, I let it go, but when Charlie advised me to tighten the slack in the line, I had no idea what he meant. I had never played a heavy fish, knew nothing about playing one from the reel handle, and when I failed to react to Charlie's instructions, he reached over, held the line close to the reel and let it run slowly through his fingers until the salmon stopped in the middle of the current.

Everything seemed under control until Charley groaned and began yanking the line from the reel. He had discovered a backlash in the backing, and at that moment a great silvery streak leapt into the air, dropped back into the river and took the hook with it. The rod snapped back into place and I burst into tears.

Holding his arm around my shoulder, Charlie told me to cheer up because that salmon was a big female, carrying more than ten thousand eggs to the spawning beds, so someday I could fish for her offspring. Unfortunately, in my agitated state, I neglected to thank Charlie for his patience with me, and now it is too late. He is no longer with us. Not once did he blame me. That was his way, it was why those who knew Charlie De Feo loved him. I fished for two weeks without hooking another fish, but Jack had good fishing and that was important. He returned home looking well, with no need for a cane.

We fished the Miramichi each September and the Battenkill each spring and summer. Almost all of the fish in the Battenkill were Brown trout, and I soon learned that they were difficult to fool with artificial flies. The mayfly hatches in the river were spectacular then, before the farmers along the river began using DDT in their barns and then hosing it into sewers that emptied into the river. It was the summer of 1951 when we first noticed dead trout in the river and a decrease in the insect population.

The Battenkill favored the Hendrickson, one of the first mayfly species to appear in the spring. The hatch began in May about 1:30 p.m. if weather permitted, and it continued a little later each day after until the end of the Hendrickson period.

Various types of mayflies appeared over the Battenkill during the summer months. Usually we fished only during a hatch. The road from our house to the business district in Arlington followed the river, and if I happened to be driving to the village and notice a hatch over the river, I turned back to the house, rushed into the studios and notified Jack.

The most exasperating fishing I ever encountered in the Battenkill was during the summer when a large hatch of tiny dark duns emerged on the river. It seemed as if every trout in the river was moving in for the kill; but they were the most selective Browns I had ever come across and showed absolutely no interest whatsoever in my beautiful flies.

One day, having noted that particular hatch on the water, I rushed home, found Jack in his studio, and off we went to the river, where he demonstrated how I should fish for those ornery trout, rising for natural flies the entire length of the run. He tied a tiny artificial that matched the hatch to a fine leader and cast the fly to the last trout rising at the end of the line. If he hooked it, the commotion wouldn't scare the trout above it, he said. He seldom caught more than a couple during the hatch, sometimes he caught none, but I never caught even one; so when Jack commented that a hard-to-get trout was a challenge that made catching one all the more fun, I could not agree with him.

I had more success when I fished in the springtime, when trout were ravenous after a winter of fasting. I like looking back to the day

I gathered up rod and waders, drove the car down the road, crossed the old covered bridge, and parked the car at the Rockwell's house. From there, I walked a short distance down a path to a pool. I called it Rudi's Pool because Rudi de Wardener and his wife, Posie, had a summer home near there, across the road on the hillside above the pool. I had never had any luck there, but knew Rudi had. He seldom fished anywhere else in the Battenkill.

The river seemed to be asleep that still, warm day. I had not expected a hatch, so I was not disappointed. I knew the Battenkill was alive with trout, but the past few years had taught me to expect many fishless days. Simply content to rest near the river where I could escape from day to day domestic demands, I dropped down on the ground and leaned back against the trunk of an expansive maple.

I was almost asleep when the sound of a splashing fish brought me to my feet. Trout along the edge of the current were bombarding a great fleet of tiny mayflies! Hundreds of duns, their wings unfurled and upright like tiny sails, were traveling down the current. Never before had I seen so many mayflies on the water at one time. I found a dry fly that Jack had put in my box of flies and which matched the hatch, and I began fishing. The trout, however, were more interested in the real flies rather than my artificial.

Finally, I caught a couple of glutted trout and then, suddenly, the hatch was over and all activity stopped. But I was not ready to stop fishing. I decided to experiment and tied a White Wulff, a large dry fly I had used to lure grilse out of the Miramichi, to the leader. Standing on the bank, I cast it downstream at the side of the current, cast slack in the line so the dry fly would float on the surface without dragging, and the instant the fly slowed down, where the current fanned out at the tail of the pool, my fly disappeared in a quiet swirl and tore downriver.

Letting the line run out, I put enough pressure on the reel to keep the rod slightly arched, but before I had a chance to get in position below the fish, a great wake shot upriver and stopped close to the opposite bank. I managed to reel in enough slack line to arch the rod again, but sensed that the wily fish had looped my leader around a branch or log lying on the riverbed. Putting as much pressure on the line as I dared, I waded upstream a bit and jiggled the rod. There was no response, so I waded downstream and jiggled the rod. Still no response.

Finally, I gave up trying, tied my rod to a tree, ran up to and across the covered bridge, and down the road to the place where the fish line was coming out of the water. I slid down the bank, grabbed the line and gave it a yank. Up came the end of the line and a part of the leader. Yes, that smart old brownie had won his freedom and taken my fly with him!

He weighed at least seven pounds. I told everyone who would listen, but the smile on their faces said I was exaggerating. Everyone except Rudi de Wardener. He had encountered that great trout, too.

One of the millions who suffered in World War II, Rudi was living in Paris when the war started. Too old to enlist, he had volunteered to drive a Red Cross ambulance, had been captured by the Germans and imprisoned until the end of the war. That grueling experience and the ersatz food had ruined his health.

But his love for fishing, and for the Battenkill and Vermont, were helping him regain his health.

CHAPTER NINE

Rivers from Vermont to California, from Oregon, and New Brunswick

You could not step twice into the same river; for other waters are ever flowing on to you.

—Heraclitus of Ephesus (540 BC–480 BC),
On the Universe

A tiny mayfly perched on the outside of a windowpane drew me to the window as I passed through our living room. Quickly, I went for a magnifying glass. The mayfly, holding its double set of wings upright like an angel, resembled the Hendrickson duns Jack had tied. Its wings, a dark, smoky hue, and its body of burgundy colored segments formed a graceful arch from the head to the tip of the tail. The insect's bulging eyes intrigued me since I had read that our telescope was based on the same principles as the ephemeral mayfly's eyes. And my encyclopedia told me the mayfly was a most ancient species of insect and that fossils have been found in Devonian and Carboniferous formations during the Age of Fishes.

Suddenly, the fragile dun on the outside of the windowpane jumped out of its skin! As if by magic, the sub-imago of an Ephemerella subvaria, had discarded, like Cinderella, her dun-colored attire. Now biologically mature, her pale beige body, gracefully arched, was still holding up wings, now a rosy-beige delicately etched with a filigree of veins and flecks of pastel colors.

Surprised to see that the dun's empty shell was still intact, I examined it closely. With the exception of the split down the thorax, the entire empty shell—two sets of gauzy wings, the telescopic eyes, the gently curved legs and three filaments of tail as fine as a hair—were still intact. In fact, the entire empty shell of the fragile sub-imago remained standing beside the delicate imago on the outside of the windowpane. Another of Nature's impossible creations. I could hardly believe my eyes! Entranced, I stayed at the window until the tiny imago (called a spinner by poetic fishers) flew off to the Battenkill to find her prince at the mayfly ball.

During the nuptial period, the male spinners arrive over the river first. Later, the females begin to appear individually and the nuptial dance begins when each male chooses a mate. The strongest, healthiest male chooses the strongest, healthiest female, according to natural law, and hugs her close to him. He holds her from below, in a position that allows her wings to continue beating, so she can keep the two of them in midair, spinning up and down over the river. After mating, the female drops down close to the water and, dipping up and down above the surface, deposits the fertile eggs into the protection of the riverbed. The eggs resemble infinitesimal clusters of golden grapes. And each tiny female deposits some seven thousand eggs. Imagine that!

That evening I arrived at the Battenkill when mayflies, spinning up and down in the air over a gravel bar, moved like a maze of snowflakes in a whirlwind. I could scarcely see the sky and trout, who relish a diet of mayflies because they are rich in vitamins and minerals, were leaping out of the water to get the spinners before they deposited their eggs in the riverbed. Past experience and instinct down through the ages had taught the brownies that there would be no nourishment in the mayflies after they dropped their eggs into the water. And knowing from my own experience that it was useless to try, I dropped down on the ground, leaning against a tree, and watched. From my front row seat, I watched a magnificent performance of a mayfly ballet, choreographed by Nature. I stayed to the end, a sad one as a shroud of spent spinners covered the stilled pool.

The Battenkill abounded with fly life then and Jack and I felt pleased that the building of our house had not scared away all of the wildlife around us. Generations of deer had worn a path from the mountain behind us and across our meadow on their way to the river. Unfortunately, I discovered this only after having unwittingly planted a vegetable garden over the path they had followed for generations. The next year I planted twice as many seeds so there would be enough vegetables and berries for the deer—and for us.

Each spring herds of deer came down from the mountains to feast in the farmers' hay fields; and then herds of sentimental deer watchers, including yours truly, drove up and down country roads admiring all those lovely creatures with large soft eyes. Even so, as the deer population increased each year, the Vermont farmers complained when deer began destroying their hay fields. But they refused to approve a law that would allow hunters to shoot does as well as bucks.

In Vermont, the opening day of deer-hunting season seemed to be the most important day of the year. In Arlington, children stayed home from school and even men with no intention of shooting a deer stayed home from work. Herds of hunters trooped into Vermont from other states; and when slap-happy hunters began killing cows—by mistake, of course—Vermont residents including me, began barricading themselves inside their homes to remain safe during hunting season.

One day toward the end of the season that year, I glanced through a window in our living room and was surprised to see three lovely does within a few feet of the house—in broad daylight. Standing motionless, I stretched my neck to get a better look. They seemed extremely nervous and intent as they stood there staring at the slope across the river. I suspected that their buck had been killed and they had spotted another buck in the woods at the top of the hill across the river. Finally, they leapt over the fence in our yard and, with white flags waving, raced in graceful leaps and bounds down the hill and across the meadow to the river. Through the trees I watched as they crossed the river, ran up across the road, further up the long, cleared slope, and then disappeared behind trees into the woods.

Breathing a sigh of relief, I started to turn from the window and turned back as a car stopped on the dirt road on the other side of the river. Alarmed, I watched a hunter jump out of the car, creep across the cleared slope, crawl up behind a stone fence and sneak into the woods. As I heard a shot, I felt as though the bullet had hit me; and as I watched the hunter drag that noble creature with her large soft eyes out of the woods and down the hill through dirt, I hated him. I know I'm a hypocrite, given how often I have taken the life of a salmon or trout and enjoyed it as part of a fine meal.

The following spring I became engrossed in another episode of wildlife action outside of our house. It began when a robin built a nest in the fork of a small apple tree. The nest was only five feet from the ground and that worried me. Several days later, there were two robin-blue eggs in the nest. By the next morning, there were none. The broken shells were scattered on the ground and that mother robin was building another nest in the same place.

She was lucky and managed to hatch two chicks, but then early one morning after watching a skunk and her two babies waddle across the terrace, I rushed to the robin's next, found her babies gone and the nest strewn down the tree trunk. Distraught, I told Jack that he had to cut down the apple tree. He expressed sympathy but refused emphatically to take down the tree. The next day, Jack called me into his studio and there, just outside the door, on a rafter between the studio and shed, was a nest of tiny phoebe chicks—and huddled smugly on top of them was the robin! The poor phoebe mother, perched on a telephone wire close to the house, was peeping her heart out. Finally, her sad pleas drove me out of the house. I went fishing and when I returned she was gone.

The robin had pushed out and reshaped the nest to fit her size. She took good care of the babies she had kidnapped; and later, when the right time came around, she pushed them out of the nest, lined them up on the telephone wire, and taught them how to fly. After learning, they dove in the air for flies, which seemed strange to me because I had never seen the robin feed the phoebe babies anything but worms.

Soon I forgot about the robins. It was time to think about going to the Miramichi in New Brunswick. For us, the Miramichi River had become a haven from all the wars and violence in civilization. We were lucky to have Herman Campbell for a guide. We loved that jolly, good-natured man. He had grown up in Upper Blackville, New Brunswick, and he knew his river well. He knew when and where there would be salmon in his favorite pools. In September there were many more large salmon than grisles in the river, and not many sport-fishers. Herman took us to the best salmon pools in the river, and most were owned by his or Ada Campbell's relatives.

There was never a dull moment when Jack and Herman were together. Once, after fishing a week with Herman and catching some heavy salmon, Jack noticed a hole in Herman's net and advised him to mend it that evening. Herman agreed. He agreed every day for a week and then forgot about it. At the end of the week, I hooked a heavy salmon and when Herman scooped it up, it fell through the net. Jack exploded in fury. Jack's outbursts of temperament amused Herman. Chuckling, Herman advised Jack to calm down and said that now Mrs. Atherton had a chance to learn how to beach a salmon. It took a while, but eventually I managed, under detailed instructions from Herman—with the line going through the hole in the net to the salmon in the river—to maneuver the salmon up to the shore where it finally beached itself by means of a big flop.

Another day on the Miramichi, when the weather was hot, the river low, and the fishing poor, everyone in camp went to Mercury Island for a picnic. There were six fishers at Herman and Ada Campbell's camp, and as usual I was the only lady fisher there. We did not expect to catch fish but fished anyway. At noon, everyone quit. The guides broiled steaks over the campfire and one fisherman cooked fried potatoes. Ada Campbell had sent along coleslaw, homemade bread, and cake. One of the men had a case of beer and stored the cans in an icy spring. Needless to say, after that heavy meal, everyone fell asleep.

Everyone but me, that is. Feeling restless, I decided to explore the riverbed at the tail of the pool in a branch of the river flowing around Mercury Island. Standing in the river with feet far apart, I looked down just as a huge salmon passed between my legs! Suddenly, I was surrounded by a whole school!

Each year the largest salmon migrated up the Miramichi in September (as I recall, fishing season finished in the middle of the month and while I had been standing in the river, a pack of big salmon began entering the pool. My heart pounding wildly, I hoped to have a chance to fish with no interference from the men, so I started to sneak my way to shore. But before I got to my rod, Chip Stauffer, who had awakened and seen a fish roll near me, rushed into the river, hooked a large salmon and let out a loud whoop.

In no time at all every fisher was there beating the river with his line. They had appeared on shore and were catching salmon so fast there were not enough guides to net them. Furiously, I tried to get in the line, but that was dangerous. Those four crazed fishermen swishing barbed hooks around my head refused to budge. Dear Herman came to my rescue. He led me some fifty feet above the pool, positioned me on the shore where my fly could reach a large boulder lying on the riverbed beneath the surface, and told me where to drop the fly.

A heavy salmon took the fly on my very first cast! Bless its heart. The salmon started downriver and, holding the arched rod over my head, I let the salmon run out line and ran after it, making every fisherman below me pull in his line and stop fishing. Everyone but my darling husband. With a salmon on the end of his line, he held his rod high and I managed to pass under the line without getting my line tangled with his.

Herman netted my salmon and by then the fishing was over. The school of large salmon had moved out of the pool in a rush to get to the spawning beds, but every fisher had a salmon. Never again did I see such spectacular salmon fishing.

The next summer Jack decided to go out West. He was not feeling well and needed to get away for a while. His nephew, Don Harger, had asked us to visit. Don and his wife lived in Oregon, so in June of 1947, Jack, fifteen-year old Mary, and I started on the long drive across the continent. We had planned to stay a night or two at Lake Tahoe on the way, but the crowds, honky-tonks, noise, litter, and everything that belied how I remembered Lake Tahoe, saddened me. Instead of stopping in Tahoe, Jack drove right through the town to a motel in the woods far from town.

We drove to San Francisco, visited our families, and then to Carmel, which was full of arty gift shops and tourists. The change there was depressing as well. We left the next day, driving north to Oregon to Don Harger's. He wrote about fly fishing and trout rivers for magazines. Don and his lovely wife took us to the Matolius, Deschutes, and Crooked Rivers, all wonderful trout streams, still unspoiled. We found ourselves where there were no other fishers.

Our Mary returned to boarding school by train toward the end of August, on her own quiet adventure back. Mary Rockwell met the train in Albany and took her to their house. Jack and I went with Don and his wife to the Klamath River in northern California. We made ourselves a comfortable camp and had great fun fishing for steelhead, staying at the Klamath a month. We had delightful weather and

Max and Mary Atherton, Roaring Branch River, Vermont. c. 1948.

good fishing, but caught no large steelhead. (Jack wrote later about the Klamath and Oregon rivers in *The Fly and the Fish*.)

We were glad to get home to Vermont where life had been exceptionally kind to us.

A few short years later in September of 1952, Jack died unexpectedly, minutes after landing a twenty-five-pound salmon that had him screaming with excitement. The doctors declared the cause of death to be a major heart attack. John's sudden death came as a shattering blow.

Making it even harder, I realized that all of my life I had been a follower. As a small child I followed in my sister's footsteps, then in my father's, and after marrying Jack, I enjoyed following in his footsteps. But doing so robbed me of the confidence to stand alone. Suddenly, I was a widow, with no one by my side and no path to follow.

During that lonely journey home as I drove by myself, I asked fate why Jack had to die so young. He was only fifty-two. Thinking back to our walk in Muir Woods twenty-six years earlier, I recalled having asked Jack why, if trees could live a thousand years, people couldn't live longer. More interested in the dying steelhead, Jack shrugged and turned back to the stream. Still under the spell of those regal sequoias I had recalled a quotation from Edwin Way Teal's book, *The Lost Woods*, (written in 1945, the year of John's skiing accident) in which Teal wrote,

> *"In the presence of the redwood's eternity of hours we feel a sense of unavoidable awe, just as we feel a sense of pity a the quick rush of the mayfly's life-for-a-day. Somewhere between, but nearer to the mayfly, is man himself. His background of the redwood's cycle of life, ages long."*

Yes, but why? Why did Jack, with his unrelenting zest for life and artistic gifts beyond measure, have to be taken away, especially before he could reach his fullest artistic potential? Before his death, Jack had paintings in some of the nation's top museums of fine art. He had earned a good living painting for advertising agencies and creating covers for the *Saturday Evening Post*, but he had not had a chance to work on fine art for museums until after we moved to Connecticut.

Obviously, the museum curators who bought Jack's paintings recognized his genius, as Julien Levi had. Jack felt flattered to be a member of the Julien Levi Gallery, a modern gallery in New York City. Salvador Dali, also a member, was called a surrealist and a curator at the Museum of Modern Art described Jack's paintings as Magical Realism.

Later, Jack's style had changed dramatically to abstract works. The change came as a surprise to everyone, including me—and to Jack as well. I was surprised when some critics and curators liked his abstract pieces even better than the Magical Realism. Gradually I realized that Jack was painting not what he wanted, but what he was called to paint.

He seemed confused at times, and I was no help. Frightened by what I didn't understand, I avoided talking to him about what was happening, or discussing the change with anyone else. His behavior with changed, too. He was brusque in public and seemed to have a deep-seated need to ridicule or embarrass me, but never when we were alone at home. Then, he seemed sad and bewildered, and I was at a loss to explain the two different Jack Athertons.

When he asked my advice about a painting he couldn't seem to finish, I sensed that he had lost his confidence. Jack had no idea just how talented and admired he was, and I had a hard time accepting the unexpected transformation in Jack and in his art. Not until many years later did I allow myself to face the fact that the change in Jack might have been due to a stroke (or possibly several). Stroke sufferers can experience personality changes, and become irritable or even turn against the ones they love most; but Jack was never violent. His vituperative outbursts were harmless and typically ended in laughter. I have come to believe that Jack's skiing accident seven years earlier most likely had been caused by a mild stroke that led him to veer off course into a tree—or that the injury from the accident caused damage in his brain that led to later strokes. We will of course never know for certain.

Because he was by nature a gentle, kind man, I forgave Jack his unkind moments. At the time, I simply could not imagine what had caused the change in such a wonderful soul. Today, I reread the chapter, "Ladies and Guides" in Jack's book and realized for the first time that he had written about me very tenderly in that chapter—at a time when his behavior toward me was at its worst. In fact, the whole book was written after the skiing accident. So in spite of the strange outbursts, his core kindness remained within him.

Jack's abstract paintings revealed a different side of his creative abilities although he never had a chance to fully develop the new style as his own. If anyone thinks I overrate Jack's work, I suggest he or she make a trip to the Metropolitan Museum of Art in New York and ask to see its John Atherton collection. Or, go to the Museum of Modern Art or the Whitney.

Toward the end of Jack's life he suffered in pain most of the time. One might say his death came as a godsend. Although he still turned against me at times, I realized he could not help what he was doing; and so I pitied, loved, and stayed steadfastly with him to the end.

CHAPTER TEN

Chalk Streams, France

To put your hands in a river is to feel the chords that bind
the earth together.

—Barry Lopez, Author

After Jack's death, my Mary, a senior at nearby Bennington College,
came home on weekends to keep me company. She, too, was devas-
tated, having lost her adoring father. Jack had been Mary's musical
and intellectual inspiration and cheerleader as Mary pursued piano and
liberal arts studies. Not having any interest in her parents' obsession
with fly fishing, Mary's bond with her father revolved around a shared
passion for music, art, and literature.

Of course I shall be forever grateful to my friends for their kindness after Jack's death, and remember with deep affection Mary and
Norman Rockwell. They took me into their home until I could work
up enough courage to return to our house alone. I also received wonderful support from Posie and Rudi de Wardener. They lived in Paris,
although their summer home was in Vermont, and they invited me to
visit them in Paris the following spring.

Rudi offered to take me to fish in the chalk streams in Normandy.
Chalk streams in Normandy? Jack and I had talked about going to
England to fish chalk streams, but I was surprised to hear chalk streams
existed in France, too. Some fifty thousand years ago, France and the
British Isles were still joined together, and down through the ages

erosion and the Atlantic Ocean had cut through the chalk terrain and formed the English Channel. At first I was convinced I would never want to fish again, but Rudi's description of chalk streams in France stirred up a spark in the embers of my waning penchant for the sport, and its association with Jack. Finally, hoping that rivers in a foreign country might help me forget how much I missed my beloved husband, I decided to accept the de Wardeners' kind invitation.

Before going abroad I moved to New York for several months and while there I visited Mr. Hewitt. He thought my plan to go to Europe was a good idea and suggested I visit Spain after fishing in Normandy. He helped plan my itinerary. Late in April of 1953, well fortified with letters of introduction from Mr. Hewitt and Otto von Kienbusch,[12] another member of the Anglers' Club who had befriended me, I sailed for Europe on the luxury liner, the *Ile-de-France*. I went alone. Mary was busy finishing her last year of college, and I could find no woman foolhardy enough to go with me. They knew me too well as a fanatic fly fisher. When the ship's whistle blew for all visitors to go ashore, the idea that I was going abroad without Jack terrified me. However, the wise dining steward and his talent for putting the right guests together brought me out of that slump.

At dinner that night I was seated at a table for two with an Englishman, a widower who had been in America on a lecture tour. I asked him what his lectures were about, and his erudite answer went right over my head. My thoughts wandered a bit until he claimed to

---

12. Born in 1884, Carl Otto Kretzschmar von Kienbusch lived his entire ninety-one years at 12 East 74th Street in New York City. By the early 1970s, von Kienbusch devoted the entire second floor of his residence to house his collection of medieval arms and armor. Von Kienbusch graduated from Princeton University in 1906 and spent most of his life working in the tobacco industry. His family made their fortune in leaf tobacco. One of his earliest jobs, however, was working in 1912 working with the curator of armor for the Metropolitan Museum of Art. Prior to his death in 1976, von Kienbusch bequeathed his collection of rare books on angling, some paintings, manuscripts, and objects, as well as funding for men and women's athletics, the library, and art museum to Princeton University. Please see www.philamuseum.org/pma_archives/ead.php?c=ROO&p=hn for more information.

have communicated with his wife after her death. After that, I felt I was no longer with him in spirit (so to speak), but as I felt sorry for him and his loss, I somehow forgot to feel sorry about my own circumstances. I joined this Englishman in his nightly turns around the deck. We covered the acres of deck of the *Ile-de-France* in great strides while I scudded and weaved with the roll of the ship and trotted to keep up with him. Each evening I returned to the lounge breathless, shivering with hair stringy and tangled from the cold wind and salty spray, blinded by salty eyelashes and doubled up from grief and stomach pain after too much exercise immediately following the sumptuous meals I devoured in the ship's elegant dining deck.

My friend the Englishman left the ship when it reached England and I got out of bed to say goodbye. Quickly and nervously he shoved his card into my hand, kissed my hand, and asked me to call him if I came to London. Then he climbed down to the tender that had come out to the ship to pick up the few passengers going to the British Isles. I remained at the railing and watched as the tender moved out toward England and my lonely friend, the only person standing in the boat, gazed out to a foggy horizon.

I wrote about all this in a notebook years ago. Now I realize that I was the lonely one gazing out to a foggy horizon. But everything seemed brighter when Posie de Wardener came to meet me at the Paris railroad station. She explained that Rudi was salmon fishing in England and would return to Paris later that afternoon. They were living in the Hotel St. James & Albany and had reserved a room next to their suite for me. When Rudi returned, he outlined the plans for our fishing in Normandy.

We would go as guests of his friends, Geoff and André, who shared a lease of several boats in the Charentonne. They were business men, too busy to leave Paris until the weekend, and we couldn't fish unless accompanied by one of them, so we would go there only on weekends, Rudi explained.

Dear Posie cared little about fishing, but she was patient while Rudi acquainted me with some of the history and fishing of chalk streams. He explained that there was very little public fishing in France and that the chalk streams were owned by the gentry, or farmers who generally leased their waters to Frenchmen living in Paris. The method of fishing a chalk stream was the same as in England, allowing for the French temperament, Rudi said.

We had a few free days before traveling to Normandy, so the de Warderners took me to Versailles, to the elaborate gardens and palace built for Louis XIV. I thought the gardens were impressive, but there were too many trees and shrubs pruned into unnatural shapes to suit me. In the palace, Rudi showed me the long table on which the Versailles Treaty of 1919 had been signed, the treaty that brought an end to World War I, but failed to prevent World War II.

On our return to Paris in the train, Posie and I sat together, and Rudi sat at the other end of the car since there were no empty seats near us. It was then that Posie told me what had happened to Rudi during World War II, before they were married. He had been living in Paris and, too old to enlist as a soldier, had driven a Red Cross ambulance. During the attack on Paris, Rudi was captured and imprisoned in Germany by the Nazis. Tears ran down Posie's cheeks as she described the way many millions of innocent Jews were herded like animals to the slaughter by the Nazis, into gruesome concentration camps; and then murdered in gas chambers. That night I had no appetite for dinner.

The next day I found happier distractions as Rudi took me to the Louvre. Having been an art student in Paris, he was an excellent guide and I enjoyed seeing the originals of the old masters, although I wondered why Leonardo da Vinci's *Mona Lisa* had become such a famous work of art. Rudi thought it was overrated, too. The pictures in the annex, where the contemporary art was hung, were more exciting—especially the Van Gogh and primitive Rousseau paintings. The Impressionist and Post-Impressionist paintings reminded me of the exhibition long ago at the California School of Fine Arts, the show that Jack had enjoyed and helped me to appreciate.

From the Louvre we walked across a bridge over the Seine and stopped in the middle to watch boats and barges chugging up and down the river. At the end of the bridge, we climbed down an ancient flight of stone steps worn by billions of footsteps to the river. Stopping near the water, we watched old fishermen as they fished with long bamboo poles and bait and to Rudi's question, "Any luck?" they answered with a benign smile and negative shake of the head. Occasionally one of them caught an eel, but not often, since too many sewers emptied into the Seine and not many fish could survive the pollution. But that didn't stop the fishermen. They came back again and again. I asked Rudi if Atlantic salmon migrated up the Seine. He shook his head. "They used to, as far back as the time of Caesar, in 53 BC, when the island of Paris was nothing more than a little fishing hamlet that eventually became the center of medieval commerce and Scholasticism."

What was Scholasticism, I wanted to know. "Essentially it was the philosophy and theology of Western Christendom. During that period Paris suffered severely from what we call the Hundred Years War." Everything seemed gloomy again, but then Rudi changed the subject and reminded me that we would be leaving for Normandy the next morning.

Friday morning Geoff, a dapper Australian living in Paris, came for us in his little Renault, and that brilliant clear day we drove, intermittently touching the Seine, past miles of fragrant orchards. Each fruit tree stood like a giant bouquet of pink and white blossoms, glistening after a spray of April showers. When we came to the orchards of blooming espaliers, each manipulated into a ridged shape like a candelabra, I was less euphoric.

A couple of hours later, we turned off the parkway along a country road that wound through pastoral Normandy—past scenes I had thought existed only on postcards, by meadows rich with new grass, by picturesque villages of stucco, thatched-roof cottages tinted white or pastel colors. In the sunlight, everything seemed immaculate. The landscape, blue sky, and puffs of brilliant, white cumulus clouds appeared to have been scrubbed and waxed. Rudi had been talking to Geoff, who asked about the trout fishing in Vermont. Taking advantage of the lull in their conversation, I asked for more details about the chalk streams in France.

"They are much like those in England," Rudi answered. "They flow through the same kind of terrain and through what the English call water-meadows, meadows flooded by means of dams and sluices." That was why they produced such large crops of hay. And due to the riverbeds of chalk (or limestone) and the careful control of the water-weeds, the nature of the chalk streams, particularly the water level, remained about the same—except when the sluices were opened to flood the meadows.

Geoff added that the chalk streams were leased and well guarded throughout their entire length, and that all the chalk streams were under the jurisdiction of French law. That was important, for if an owner neglected cutting the weeds in his beats, the neglect had an ill effect on the entire river.

In other words, unlike the French salmon rivers, they had been well managed and, as a result, there were almost no poachers. The water-weeds produced a protective cover for trout and excellent vegetation for nymphs and larvae, thereby producing a tremendous amount of insect life, especially mayflies. When the river keepers cut the weeds, they were careful to cut downstream, to give the nymphs or larvae a chance to fall off in their part of the river, instead of being carried down to other fisher's water. They cut a patch of weeds, left a patch, and so on to the end of their beats; and since the weeds grew thick and fast, they were cut twice a year.

The good fishing started around the first week in May. The big hatches of mayflies began later, and the last two weeks in May produced the best fishing. Trout rose constantly in May. Geoff suggested that I stay in France until the end of the month. I thanked him and explained that I had plans to go on to Spain that could not be changed.

Upon arriving at our destination, Beaumont-le-Roger, Geoff decided that since we still had a few hours before dark, we should drive on to the Charentonne River, to La Dame Blanche, an ancient, deserted farmhouse with a mellowed ambiance of the ancient past.

Geoff used it as a sort of a lodge, a simple one, and we changed quickly into our fishing clothes. "One does not wade in chalk streams. One fishes from the bank," Rudi explained. He advised me to tiptoe along the banks because the trout in the Charentonne were very wary and the least vibration put them down. Geoff took me to a pool near La Dame Blanche and asked that I release any trout I caught as there was no refrigeration available, and then Rudi went upriver and Geoff when downriver.

I had been warned that there might not be any mayflies yet, but that balmy evening a few were spinning up and over the Charentonne. While tying a dry fly on the leader, I caught a glimpse of a trout rising for a natural. It was feeding about twenty feet above me, on the same side of the river and a bit below a small belly of bank protruding into the water. For me to catch that trout would require a difficult cast. I would have to send about thirty feet of line directly above my stance, and cast enough slack in the line to float a fly down the current, around the belly in the bank, and down to the lie of the trout before my fly started dragging in the current. The only possible way to do that was to cast to so that the leader would fall on the water in a left-hand curve.

Jack had tried without success to teach me the curve cast (he describes how in *The Fly and the Fish*). Knowing it was the only way to interest the trout in my fly, I tried over and over again until, by sheer perseverance, I succeeded. The bouncy dry fly bobbed down on the current and around the protruding bank and suddenly disappeared in a large swirl! I let it run out line and then, holding the arched rod high, I got the trout into the net as soon as possible.

Before releasing the trout, I had a chance to examine the large fat German Brown. Its olive-green back and sides were studded with red dot as brilliant as rubies, and with white dots the size of seed pearls. The ivory-colored belly was brushed with strokes of pink around the anal fins, and its entire body was covered in a golden sheen. Surely, the name "Brown trout" is a misnomer. I stopped fishing and stood on the bank awhile, mesmerized by the nocturnal beauty of the river, as my imagination took me into the mystical realm of Ceres, where the quiet Charentonne turned into a stream of liquid silver, flowing quietly through meadows of black jet in dusk's fading glow.

We stayed the night in Beaumont-le-Roger, at a simple little hostel dating back to the seventeenth century, and that chilly night I slept under a comforter stuffed with down, but only five feet long, so I spent most of the night trying to decide whether I wanted my feet or shoulders sticking out in the cold.

The next morning, we returned to the Charentonne and Geoff took me to a lovely spot where the river, flowing through meadows, turned and ran through a profusion of flowering apple trees. The ground around the river was dotted with daisies, buttercups and swamp primroses. I had no trouble catching six- to eight-inch trout, one after another, with a dry fly. Releasing each one carefully, as Geoff and Rudi stood on the bank smiling and nodding, I was fairly certain that someone had planted those trout there especially for me to catch.

I caught no more trout that day. There were no flies in the air, so we stopped and returned to La Dame Blanche. Sitting around the warmth of the huge fireplace, originally used for both cooking and heating, we sipped a delicious Burgundy wine that Rudi had brought along. As we reminisced about the wonders of trout fishing in chalk streams, we spoke the universal language known only to the most devout fly fishers.

Jack's name had not been mentioned since my arrival in France, but that evening when I went to the other end of the room to get my coat and stopped beside a table littered with fly-tying material and feathers, I noticed *The Fly and the Fish* lying open at the center of the table. My eyes were too blurred with tears to read the script, but Geoff and Rudi cured that condition as they stood beside me praising Jack's book.

We were invited that evening to a dinner party in Quetteville, to the country home of Rudi's friend, the president of Morgan's Bank in Paris, and his wife, an American Southern belle. Geoff drove us to the Chateau de Quetteville, a massive structure of Norman Gothic architecture regally enthroned on top of a hill overlooking a wide valley of apple orchards in the county of Calvados, famous for its delicious apple brandy. We approached the most impressive and important chateau in the area by way of a long driveway and made our way straight up the hill to the front door.

Our hostess and Posie, a houseguest that weekend, led me upstairs to a bedroom. I complimented my hostess on the chateau's interior and learned that they had redecorated the whole place, a challenging experience since the war had made it almost impossible to find workmen and servants.

Downstairs, Posie introduced me to our host, a handsome Frenchman, and to two other house guests, an elderly aristocrat and his young wife. Everyone but the fishers had "dressed" for dinner, but we were wearing our very best tweeds. In the dining room, two small children and their governess joined us. Dinner was served by a butler—dressed in Quetteville livery—and a waitress. The service was impeccable, a different wine served with each course, and special champagne accompanied dessert.

In the living room after dinner, sipping a fabulous Calvados brandy, I complimented the host on the brandy and wines he had served. "Well, we have our butler to thank for being able to serve you France's finest wines and brandy. He's worked here through several changes of ownership, and had the brilliant idea of burying every bottle in the ground beneath the cellar before German officers took over the chateau as their regional headquarters during the Occupation."

Later that night, in the hostel at Beaumont-le-Roger, I dreamed about the Chateau de Quetteville and everyone in it. The dream turned them into tortured ghosts, suffering from all the ghastly killings and ravages of World War II. In the light of day at least, fishing the peaceful chalk streams of Normandy, I could forget what that horrible war had done to Europe and the world.

CHAPTER ELEVEN

Charentonne and Risle Rivers, Normandy

Rivers are the primal highways of life. From the crack of time, they had borne men's dreams, and in their lovely rush to elsewhere, fed our wanderlust, mimicked our arteries, and charmed our imaginations in a way the static pond or vast and savage ocean never could.

—Tom Robbins, *Fierce Invalids from Hot Climates*

Rudi had been an art student and member of the Ernest Hemingway Group in Paris—a group of idealists who following World War I succumbed to disillusionment. He knew all of Paris's best inexpensive restaurants and took Posie and me to a different restaurant on the Left Bank every evening.

Meanwhile, Rudi was planning another trip to Normandy and told me that André, a Parisian who shared the lease of the long stretch of the Charentonne with Geoff, the Australian businessman based in Paris, would be our host. Lowering his voice, Rudi added, "Max, you should know that some consider André a traitor since he stayed to manage his factory after the Germans confiscated it during the Occupation. He got his factory back in one piece when the Germans were driven out of Paris, but he still bears the stigma of a traitor. On top of that, André's wife, an American, was killed not too long ago in an automobile accident."

André drove us to Normandy and I sensed a barrier between us from the beginning. So, I turned my attention to the landscape while he talked to Rudi. As we drove through the Normandy countryside, we passed a farmhouse, partially demolished by a bomb, and a story I had written years earlier in high school flashed across my mind. It was my first attempt at creative writing and now I remember vividly the frustration I experienced drafting it. I wrote a couple of pages quickly and then a lack of ability to express all my ideas flooded my head, stopped the pen and my story came to a dead end. I had wanted, oh so very much, to go on and give the story a happy ending but simply could not write another word; so when the class bell rang, feeling terribly frustrated and discouraged, I handed the unfinished story to the teacher. I thought I had failed and was surprised when my story appeared in the high school yearbook. It was the only story in it that year, and I was proud of myself but could not imagine why the judges had chosen to publish an unfinished piece. The story, about a young French soldier who had survived World War I and returned home after the war, began with him standing before the ruins of the family farm. Alone, he faced for the first time the end of all he had held dear in his childhood. Somehow, I had expressed, in my description of the scene and the soldier, his agony—and that of thousands of other soldiers like him.

Of course, if I had given it a happy ending the story wouldn't have been published. There were no truly happy endings in war. What puzzles me now is how, at the age of seventeen, I was able to write about something that happened in Normandy. Outside of the fact that one of my early Breese ancestors came from France, I had known nothing about that part of the world, or the life of a soldier.

André interrupted my thoughts when he stopped the car at the hostel in Beaumont-le-Roger. Early the next morning he drove us to the Charentonne. André suggested I start fishing near La Dame Blanche and work my way downstream, and then he and Rudi went off in different directions. There were no mayflies in the air that chilly morning. I fished a while, had no luck, and started downstream when

I came upon André. So I sat down on a bench at the side of the river and watched him fish.

"Would you like to fish, Max?" he asked. "No, thanks," I said. "I prefer to watch while you fish for now." André stayed a while longer and then came over to the bench and sat down with me. Motioning to a large hole in the ground beside the river, he said, "Believe it or not, there was a small textile mill here once, but a bomb destroyed the place."

Surprised, I responded, "Why on earth would anyone would want to bomb a poor little textile mill?" André replied, "The story goes that an American plane dropped a bomb there during the Occupation when young American pilots with limited training and experience dropped bombs at random to get rid of them after a raid before returning to their base in England." Bowing my head, I groaned. No wonder I had sensed resentment against Americans almost everywhere I went in France. For the first time in my life, I felt ashamed of being an American.

Fortunately, André changed the subject. "There is a farm in Normandy I think you would enjoy visiting," he said. So he made arrangements for us to have lunch in the farmhouse of a farmer who owned the land on which we were fishing. At noon, André, Rudi, and I drove to the farm. On the way, Andre explained that the farmer and his wife had two sons, but both had been killed in the war. So now the poor man did all the work by himself. When we arrived, the farmer, a quiet little man, showed us around his farm, small but rich in produce. Not once did he look at or speak to me and I couldn't help but think that he resented me as an American.

I had no such thoughts when I met his wife. The rapport between us delighted me. A plump, motherly lady in a long, full, grey wool skirt with a white shirtwaist trimmed with crocheted lace, she proudly showed me around her immaculate domain. The white lace curtains, the pictures of the Virgin Mary and Christ in gilt frames on the wall, the tinted family photographs, everything about the house reminded me of the farmhouses I had visited in French Québec.

Our energetic hostess's sparkling eyes embraced me when I praised her home and admired the tablecloth she had crocheted. She served us a delicious lunch: a mushroom omelet, local cheeses, fresh warm crusty bread, a salad of garden lettuce, fresh strawberries, and dry white wine. All but the wine had been produced on the farm.

We returned to the Charentonne that afternoon and fished until a squall developed that scattered our artificial flies everywhere but over the river. Ah, wind. Woe to fly fishers and dreaded by fishers at sea, it battles the best of human-made contrivances. That evening we dined at the hostel in Beaumont-le-Roger, and the barrier I had once felt between André and me seemed to have softened. After dinner, Rudi phoned the Duke of Magenta. He wanted to fish the Duke's water in the Risle, and I was surprised when I overhead Rudi introduce himself as Baron de Wardener. I had heard that his family was driven out of Austria during the war, but I had no idea he had a title—and using the title as a means of getting permission for us to fish the Risle amused me. As it happened, the Duke was in England, but the duchess answered the phone and invited us to visit her that evening.

André went with us and the Duchess of Magenta, elegant in a chic black silk dress, greeted us and apologized for her living quarters. "We live in Paris most of the year and when we come to Normandy, we stay in the superintendent's cottage since the Chateau Magenta was attacked by bombs during the war." A charming hostess, the Duchess served us scotch (with soda) and American cigarettes, both of which were difficult to get in France.

She explained, "My husband is in England visiting our son, who is in boarding school there, but you have my permission to fish the Risle at will." Rudi smiled. "Thank you, Duchess." He added, "Max is a sportswoman from America who has come to Normandy to fish the famous chalk streams." Turning towards me, the Duchess asked, "Do you like to hunt, too?" I nodded and she said, "You should see our kennel of stag hounds—the only one still in existence!" When I noted, "I mostly participated in drag hunts in Connecticut," the perplexed look on her face indicated that she had never heard of a drag hunt, so I explained. "Instead of a hunting fox, the hounds follow a scent from a dead fox that had been dragged across country to the end, where there is a pile of meat and bones instead of a fox." Suddenly, I felt that she was miles away, And no wonder—the contrast between a drag hunt and a stag hunt, a royal sport, a serious ritual dating back to the time when hunting was the only means of acquiring meat for food, is enough to distract anyone. However, I preferred not to watch the hounds tear a little fox into pieces; but I had sense enough to keep my mouth shut with the Duchess.

The next morning André drove off to fish the Charentonne and as the Risle was only a short distance from the hostel, Rudi and I walked there. Beaumont-le-Roger had built up around the Chateau Magenta, now a bare spot in the landscape, and the path to the river took us past tree-lined lanes spreading out in all directions, past paths worn by generations of farmers walking back and forth from their farms to the hostel for a friendly glass of wine. When we arrived at the assigned place, the river keeper was there waiting where the Risle wound its gentle course through vast acres of peaceful meadows and gorgeous orchards in bloom. The river keeper, also the superintendent since the chateau was destroyed, waited near a small trout hatchery. A kind, shy man from a long line of Magenta river keepers, he wore the Magenta livery, proudly, and the look in his eyes expressed a tender love for his river as he placed me on the bank and then took Rudi downriver.

There was nothing behind me to interfere with my backcast, and there were no flies over the water, so it was an ideal place and time to fish with a nymph. Using the greased line technique Mr. Hewitt had taught me, I felt no need to hurry. I had as far as I could see to myself. Greasing the silk line, I tied a nymph on the leader and, standing well back from the river, cast the nymph to the opposite bank. There was no activity, a peaceful quiet had settled over the river and environs, and as I fished my way downriver I felt confident with every cast that sooner or later a great trout, snoozing beneath the overhang of the opposite bank, would wake up and see my luscious nymph.

Fishing in this leisurely way, I covered every inch of the opposite bank until finally, when I least expected it, the rod jerked into a deep arch. At first I thought it might be the most important trout I had ever caught, an aristocrat in the royal world of trout, but it was too fat, almost deformed. Nevertheless, I netted it for my breakfast the next morning and then fished down to where Rudi was casting. At once, I knew by the smile on his face, that he had caught "the big one." Never before had I seen Rudi display such excitement. A dry fly purist, he had caught a huge trout, an old-timer who lived in a deep hole beneath a sluice gate, with a dry fly.

We had to go back to Paris the following day, a Sunday, but we fished the Charentonne that morning and then André suggested we drive to Serquiny for lunch. Serguiny was only a few miles from Beaumont-le-Roger and near the Atlantic coast. André took us to an inn that reminded me of the country inns in Maine at the beginning of the fishing season. I was the only woman in a dining room buzzing with fishermen who had waited impatiently all winter for the beginning of trout season. No one seemed to notice me, and I liked that. It gave me the easy feeling of being one of them.

André suggested I order coq au vermouth, the favorite on the menu. It was delicious. I said as much when the waiter asked if I like it, and I inquired about whether it would be possible to have the recipe. Nodding, he disappeared into the kitchen and returned with the chef. Delighted that someone in the dining room of crazy fly fishers appreciated one of his masterpieces, he quoted the recipe in one word a paragraph long, or so it seemed, but Rudi translated it so I could write it down on a paper serviette.

It is a very simple recipe. Split a broiler in half, place on a broiling pan, season with salt and pepper, cover the top of the chicken with butter, and broil over an open fire until a golden brown, cooked through and juicy. Put the pan and chicken on the stove, pour a cup of Noilly Prat vermouth over the chicken, simmer and baste a while. Remove the chicken from the pan, turn up the heat, stir the drippings and wine, simmering until there is about half a cup of sauce. Pour the sauce over the bird and serve. The vermouth gives the chicken a gamey flavor.

After lunch, André and Rudi took me to where the Charentonne and Risle meet, left me there, and drove to a garage for gasoline. I felt no desire to fish. I simply wanted to say goodbye to the two sister rivers that given me so much pleasure. They joined at Serquiny, flowed on to Pont Audemer, arrived at the Seine and, together, flowed into the great Atlantic's vast eternity.

As I recall, the only completely peaceful moments I had in France were while fishing along the banks of its chalk streams. In that era, seven years after World War II, France seemed fraught with sorrow. Everyone I met had been hurt in one way or another by that futile war. Nearly every story had an unhappy ending, and two years after our visit to the Duchess of Magenta, I learned from Rudi that the Duke had been killed in an accident while stag hunting. The unfortunate Duchess lost both her husband and her home in Normandy.

In researching the Magenta duchy recently, I learned that in 1859 the Comte Patrice de MacMahon, a descendant of the Irish family who went into exile with James II, "was in command of French and Sardinian forces in Italy when he distinguished himself by defeating the Austrians, thereby enabling the French to secure victory." Apparently he won the Battle of Magenta in Italy partly by good luck and partly through his boldness and sagacity; and by pushing forward without orders at a critical moment in the Battle of Magenta, the Comte defeated the Austrians. The cost in lives lost was terrible but the Comte enabled the French to secure victory, and for that he received his marshal's baton and was named Duke of Magenta.

But why oh why must great heroes be created by such a terrible cost in lives?

CHAPTER TWELVE
Saja River, Spain

A river does not just happen; it has a beginning and an end. Its story is written in rich earth, in ice, and in water-carved stone, and its story as the lifeblood of the land is filled with colour, music, and thunder.

—Andy Russell, *The Life of a River*

I will never forget the kindness of Rudi and Posie, and when I left France they took me by taxi to the railway station. From Paris I traveled to Spain by train in a compartment by myself. Rudi had arranged for me to contact a Señor Enrique Camino in Santander and beyond that, I had no idea of what lay ahead. I wanted to fish for trout and salmon and recalled Mr. Hewitt saying that during Spain's Civil War starving Spaniards had depleted their rivers of fish. But in 1949, when he travelled there, Atlantic salmon were returning to the rivers after General Franco had outlawed all commercial netting and restocked the rivers.

In the train I had a copy of *The Anglers' Club Bulletin* (1946) in which there was an article by Mr. Hewitt who wrote:

All the conditions which make for the best reproduction and protection of salmon are controlled by one central agency. This is not the case with any other salmon river with which I am acquainted. Unless all conditions can be maintained favorable to the salmon, it will never be possible to secure the maximum number of salmon returning to the river. The natural hostility of the local population to the preservation of the rivers for sport had been entirely overcome by a wise and original system. These rivers have been divided into beats, and as many beats are allotted to the local population for their fishing as are rented to sportsmen. Local fishermen are now killing far more salmon than they ever did by unrestricted fishing and poaching in former years and are cooperating fully in the preservation of the rivers. Poachers get ninety days in the chain gangs. . . . As to the future of these rivers, their rapid improvement in the six years during which they have been under management of the Turismo leads one to expect still greater improvement in the next few years. In the Deva-Cares, for instance, only sixty spawning fish were counted six years ago. The next year the number was three hundred.

I knew much more about Spain's salmon fishing after reading Mr. Hewitt's article, but at the moment was more concerned about Spain's astonishing trains. Pulled by a coal-burning engine over rough tracks, the train jerked and jiggled me unmercifully all night long. The suffocating heat in the compartment forced me to open the window and by morning my beige silk suit, hanging on the wall, was covered in soot. I gave it a good shaking, washed the soot from my hands and face, and donned the suit, now charcoal-grey.

Once we crossed the border into Spain I left the train at Irun, a picturesque hamlet surrounded by the majestic Pyrenees. I boarded a bus heading to Santander and like the train, it proved to be somewhat of a shock. No one had prepared me for the condition of public transportation in Spain because everyone I knew had better sense than to travel by train or bus in Spain. Nearly all vehicles dated back twenty or so years to the time of Spain's Civil War, which had left the country beyond repair.

On a road that ran along the Cantabrian Mountain Range, a continuation of the Pyrenees, the bus rattled around hairpin curves at frightening speed. Once, to get around the sharp curve, the ancient bus had to stop, back up, maneuver back and forth, and stop just in time to avoid backing off a cliff and falling thousands of feet to the Bay of Biscay. To make matters worse, the bus was full to capacity. Each time it stopped at a station a din of voices rose to a high pitch of excitement and stopped abruptly when the bus started again. I must admit that the deep silence as the bus bumped along alarmed me. It seemed that everyone was holding their breath in expectation of approaching disaster.

In fact, it turned out that I was the only once concerned about our safety. A lady sitting next to me seemed particularly calm. She asked me a question, but knowing only a few words of Spanish, I failed to understand what she was saying. Realizing my predicament, she patted my arm and smiled. She had been sitting in the back of the bus with other ladies, but when I entered the bus and sat down, she moved up to occupy the empty seat beside me.

Before leaving New York my friends had all expressed concern about my going to Spain alone. Women did not travel in alone in Spain, they told me. As it happened, I was given special care everywhere I went in Spain because I was an American women traveling by myself.

The señora at my side had deliberately placed herself by me to prevent a man from sitting with me. At noon, when the bus stopped in San Sebastian, she stood up and motioned for me to follow her. Her three companions joined us outside and those kind ladies escorted me to a nearby restaurant where a waiter seated us at a large round table. I knew enough Spanish words to ask them to order for me and from then on we had great fun conversing in pantomime and giggles.

The señoras left the bus before it reached Santander, and after an enthusiastic and lengthy adios, all talking at once, they gave the bus driver instructions that I failed to understand until he helped me off the bus at Santander. He took my bags and guided me to a taxi, delivered a series of orders to the driver, and then explained to me in English that the señoras on the bus had instructed him to escort me to a taxi and tell the driver to take me to the Bahia Hotel and not charge me a cent more than anyone else.

The Bahia Hotel catered to foreigners. Members of the hotel staff were familiar with several languages including English and that made things easier. The next morning, I asked a clerk at the reception desk how to get to Enrique Camino's house; and with his instructions, I left on foot. A charming little seaport town of stucco houses with red tile roofs, clustered around the Bay of Biscay, Santander spread a short distance up a mountain slope. Señor Camino's house was located on the slope in a residential district overlooking the picturesque Bay.

Enrique Camino was a retired lawyer and lived alone. His housekeeper answered the doorbell and led me inside. Señor Camino greeted me in the hallway and we sat in his trophy room. As I introduced myself, I handed him the letter of introduction from Rudi. Glancing through it, he seemed surprised and at the same time amused that *una mujer* was traveling alone and wanted to fish in Spain. After reading the letters, he showed me around his trophy room. Mounted heads of wild animals hung on the walls, but what he really wanted me to see was a table covered with equipment and feathers for tying flies, and boxes of trout and salmon flies that he had tied—all after British patterns. Then he took me to the Turismo in a taxi, explaining that all fishing and hunting in Spain fell under the supervision of the Turismo, which operated under the jurisdiction of Max Borrell, Franco's right-hand man, according to Mr. Hewitt. Señor Camino remembered meeting Mr. Hewitt and said he admired him for what he had done to improve Spain's rivers.

At the Turismo I sat beside Señor Camino's desk while he helped some French sportfishers with reservations—he dealt only with foreigners. When he finished with them, he turned to me. "Señora, you should have made reservations many months in advance, but I will see what I can do." After many phone calls, he was able to arrange for me to fish the Saja, a trout river, and the Nansa, a salmon river.

In the meantime, I had a few days to spare before I could start fishing and was fortunate to meet an American couple at the hotel who invited me to join them for a visit to the Caverns of Altamira. The couple, touring Spain in a rented car, said the caves were not far from Santander and that evening loaned me a book about the caves.

The book was fascinating. It described how cave men had evolved during the Paleolithic Era, how these ancient hunters discovered the use of fire during the Magdalenian phase and that stone lamps, found in the caves, indicated they used burning fat to light the dark caves. The book also talked about Neanderthal men who were cave dwellers of the Mousterian Era and lived during Paleolithic Era, and that the study of the river-drift-men's skulls at that time had revealed that these cavemen were among the most brutal of all known humans. When I read that I pictured them beating women, dragging them around by their hair, and relegating them to an inferior position in the hierarchy of Homo sapiens. I was feeling a bit annoyed because not once did the book mention the word "woman." After all, there wouldn't have been any cavemen without some cavewomen, would there?

I returned the book to the American couple the next morning and we left for Altamira. An old Spaniard donning baggy cotton trousers and a tunic of hand woven fabric belted with a rope, greeted us at the entrance to the cave, which proved to be nothing more than a large hole in the side of the mountain. The guide with his flashlight led us through a dark tunnel and into a small cave. There on a low rock ceiling, a great artist had created a mural some twenty thousand years ago. Beneath it was a boulder, high enough for the artist to lie on his back and work on the mural.

Now, I am looking at a reproduction of that remarkable mural in my encyclopedia. The composition and drawings of the bison, wild pigs, deer, all animals that the ancient, carnivorous hunter knew well, had been drawn in line and engraved in the stone by a gifted artist. The lines had been filled with some kind of dark coloring and the drawings were simple, but surprisingly accurate, abstracted down to the pure essence of each. The colors—earthy browns, reds, ochre, and black—were, I'm guessing, added to the mural at a later date; and I suspect the shading had been added by someone else years later. It added a sophisticated perspective which I doubt cave dwellers living twenty thousand were capable of creating on stone. But what talent! It surprised me and my companions as well. On our way back to Santander, I thanked the couple and told them that seeing the caves had been a marvelous experience that I would have missed if they had not taken me with them to Altamira.

The next day, Señor Camino came to the hotel to give me my permit to fish for trout and salmon in Spain, and I was pleased to have a chance to learn more about that charming gentleman, an elderly aristocrat and sportsman who had fished and hunted with King Alfonso. He spoke of the king affectionately, so I was stunned when he also said that he admired Franco and enjoyed fishing and hunting with him. He praised Franco for having built schools for the poor and orphanages to care for the army of homeless children living on the streets after the civil war. Franco was a fine sportsman, he said, and a dedicated conservationist who was doing wonders to restore Spain's rivers.

Señor Camino had made a reservation for me at the Saja, a trout stream running through and around Puerto del Sol, and I traveled there in a cranky old train that huffed and puffed up the mountain at a snail's pace. Two guides met me when I finally arrived and escorted me to an inn just a short walk away. Puerto del Sol was a hamlet of farms spreading out in all directions high up in a fertile mountain valley, lush and green and protected from rough weather by a range of snow-capped peaks rising above the horizon and sparkling in the sunlight.

Yet to be discovered by tourists or much of anybody, Puerto del Sol seemed little changed from what it must have been been hundreds of years ago. Señor Camino sent me there because the inn was owned and managed by two sisters. They greeted me with smiles at the door. The guides left me in their care but returned an hour later. Noting that I had changed into fishing waders, they explained in Spanish that the Saja was *turbulento*. That was the only word I understood in the flood of Spanish words pouring from their mouths, but it was enough for me to know what to expect. They were young, polite and charming. In unison, they told me, "Pesca es imposible" and then they took me fishing anyway. Yes, whenever I planned on doing something in Spain, someone said it was impossible and then made it possible.

With the help of an English-Spanish dictionary and a great deal of pantomime, I learned from the guides that the previous night a gush of heavy rain had melted snow in the mountains and muddied the river.

Otherwise, it was an ideal trout stream winding through a serene valley with a dramatic backdrop of snow-capped mountains.

The day was sunny and warm, and as there were no automobiles in Puerto del Sol, we walked a mile or so to the river. One morning we rode in the one and only bus, with farmers carrying their produce to market, including a bunch of live chickens tied together at the feet and slung over the back of a seat, and a bleating lamb on the floor with its four feet tied together. After that ride I suggested we walk to the river, no matter how far!

I caught no fish that weekend but gained a great deal by associating with the friendly locals. Each day as I left or returned to the inn, a group of curious Spaniards awaited my arrival outside of the front door. When the sisters sent me out the back door, the crowd moved to the back door and the guides had to push them aside to get me through the doorway. The townspeople wanted to talk to me about America. I felt sorry that I could not converse more with them and also the two sisters, who had turned the large family house into an inn. I often wondered about their men. Had the civil war taken husbands or brothers from them?

I realize now more than I did then that despite the cruelty of their civil war, the people in that lovely valley were generally happy, living in a world untouched and unspoiled by civilization at that time—the Machine Age. Señor Camino seemed pleased when I returned to Santander and told him that although I had caught no trout, my visit to Puerto del Sol had been delightful.

CHAPTER THIRTEEN

Nansa River, Spain

The rivers are our brothers. They quench our thirst. The rivers carry our canoes, and feed our children. If we sell you our land, you must remember, and teach your children, that the rivers are our brothers and yours, and you must henceforth give the rivers the kindness you would give any brother.

—Suquamish Chief Sealth, 1854

I was on my way to the Nansa River, riding in a compartment on the same ancient train that had taken me to the Saja. This time two Americans were seated across from me and I soon learned that one was a mining engineer and that the other was in Spain on some kind of business. The mining engineer asked me where I was heading and I told him I was going to the Nansa, a salmon river that began in the Cantabrian Mountains and emptied into the Bay of Biscay. He said he had fished the Nansa one weekend and stayed in Arrudo overnight. When he asked where I was planning to stay, I said I didn't know but expected to be met at the train by someone who would know and take me there.

The poor old creaking train was climbing up a mountain at a speed one could follow on foot. The slow pace game me a chance to enjoy the landscape, however, and I was surprised to see, on the side of another mountain and across a ravine, a long-legged man astride a little donkey riding along a trail as his wife, carrying a huge bundle of sticks on her head, trotted behind him on foot. I was surprised because I thought by the year 1953 things like this happened only in the movies.

A little further on, I was surprised to see buckets of ore, spaced four or five feet apart on a cable, being pulled up the side of the mountain. The mining engineer explained that they still brought all the ore up to the mine that way. The mining industry was not yet modernized and that was why Franco had asked him to come to Spain and help improve their mining operations. He was on his way to that mine and left us at the next station.

A couple of stations later, I left the train and was met by a young man who greeted me affably. I could not understand a word he said and tried to get him to speak more slowly, but he simply did not know how to slow down his speech, so I began answering his questions with a shrug. Finally, he showed me a telegram which I was unable to translate and when he asked me a questions again, I smiled and nodded my head.

Bowing politely, he picked up my suitcase and leaving the huge duffel bag at my feet, strode happily down the road. He did not wait for me and I could hardly believe my eyes, but then I recalled the man on the donkey and his woman carrying a load on her head. That must be the custom in Spain, I told myself, and picked up the duffel bag. In a state of dismay and bowed down by the heavy bag, I stumbled after him. Custom or no custom, I could not go another step. I dumped the duffel bag on the ground, dropped down on it, and let out a howl.

The young man rushed back to me. He seemed terribly concerned and tried to lift me from the ground. I refused to be lifted. With my feeble knowledge of Spanish, I asked him how far it was to the Nansa. The words *doce kilometros* brought me to my feet immediately. No, no, no, no, I said, and when he mumbled something about a taxi, I shouted *Sí, sí, sí* . . . . Quickly, he placed the suitcase at my feet, told me to wait, and ran down the road toward the railroad station.

I was alone on top of a strange mountain in the loneliest of spots where there were no buildings, no telephone wires, no person in sight. Nothing but sky and a vast wilderness. I waited and waited. Finally, wondering if I would ever see that young man or anyone else again and just when the intensity and power of fear and isolation was transforming itself into full-scale panic, an ancient car rattled down the road.

The young man had found a taxi! He jumped out, helped me up to the front seat beside the driver, and put my luggage on the back seat. Wishing me a pleasant journey, he beat a fast retreat. The driver wanted his fee (a very modest amount) right there and then. After I paid him, he glanced at me and muttered, *¿Dónde?* The realization that he had not been told where to take me almost scared me out of my wits again. But then I remembered the mining engineer saying he had gone to Arrudo, so I told the driver to go there, and off we went. As we drove down the dirt road all fears vanished behind the spectacular view of the river valley far below, lovely and modeled by distance into an exquisite miniature.

Eventually, we came to a man who was leading a burro along the road. I understood not one word of the conversation between the man and the driver, and when the driver started down the road again, the look on his face indicated that he was becoming more and more discouraged. However, a few miles further down the isolated road we came upon another man who, pointing a finger toward the valley, muttered something about *una mujer americana.* The driver smiled, thanked him and we were on our way again.

We had gone about ten kilometers down into the valley when we came to a lone tavern. The driver stopped the car and went inside. A few minutes later, he emerged with the tavern owner. Bowing his head politely, he spoke to me in English. What a relief!

I explained that I had a permit to fish the Nansa River and was looking for a place to stay. He asked me to wait a minute, went inside, returned with his wife and introduced me. A forlorn looking woman, she acknowledged me with a frown and turned toward her husband. They spoke quietly in Spanish and I gathered from his gentle persuasive tone that he was urging her to let me stay with them. Her head kept shaking no, but he persisted, and finally she turned, faced me and said that I could stay but wouldn't like it there. She spoke English which surprised me, but I quickly assured her that I would not be fussy. She pondered awhile, shrugged, and invited me inside. Quickly, the driver dumped my bags on the ground at my feet and drove away before I could change my mind.

Gradually during the week I lodged with this couple, I learned why the Señora had not wanted me to stay with them. At first she avoided me whenever possible and pretended she could not understand English well. But I persisted in talking to her and finally, she relented and explained that she had grown up in America and thought she had forgotten how to speak English. "It's been more than twenty years since I've spoken English with anyone," she confessed.

The Señora's parents had moved from Puerto Rico to California when she was a child, and she had inherited the family grocery store in Los Angeles after both parents were killed in an automobile accident. Señor was born in Arrudo. An enterprising man, he managed to escape the debilitating poverty of that area and somehow worked his way to America. He met and married the Señora while visiting relatives in Los Angeles, and together they had turned the grocery store into a profitable business, saving enough to visit his family in Arrudo.

Unfortunately, the civil war broke out and prevented them from getting back to America. For twenty frustrating years, the Señora had tried but failed to get "back home." She and her husband had left relatives in charge of their store, but now the relatives claimed that after two decades of paying taxes and maintenance, the store belonged to them. Señora and her husband had cashed their return tickets and the high exchange for American currency made it possible for them to buy the tavern. They tried to save enough cash to get back to Los Angeles, but the cost of getting there and the struggle to survive in Arrudo during and after the war had made the journey impossible. When I came into her sad life, she had given up all hope of getting home to the United States.

They had two lovely daughters, ages eleven and fourteen, and she had sent them to school in a convent. Señora was very proud of her daughters, and extremely bitter, understandably, because their son had died from lack of medical care. The nearest doctor and clinic were in Santander, and getting her sick baby there had been impossible during the civil war. Señora blamed Spain for all of her troubles and Señor, a gentle, kind man, blamed himself for bringing her to Spain.

With no one else around who could understand English, the Señora began to confide in me. I was an American woman, a mother, who could understand the reason for and depth of her grief; and whenever we were alone together, all of the agony and frustration simmering within her poured out.

In the meantime, Señor found a young guide for me and arranged for the one and only car in the vicinity to transport us to the river. The driver arrived in his ancient car each morning and returned me to the tavern at sundown. I liked my guide, Alfonso, but sensed that he resented having to guide me. He was a commercial fisherman, no longer allowed to net salmon in the Bay of Biscay, and could fish the river with a rod but he seemed to prefer fishing for himself, even though I paid him well, and made no effort to extend himself beyond the minimum required.

The Nansa, a dramatic mountain river that tore down a narrow valley, was banked with ferns and dainty alpine plants. All around it spring had burst into bloom. Sitting on the ground by the river, high in the spectacular beauty of the snowcapped Cantabrian Mountains, I had no trouble communing with Nature and marveling over a miniature iris growing out of the ground at my side. Beautifully formed, the plant was no more than an inch high.

Again, I caught no fish. Catching fish in that paradise seemed almost irrelevant. The car came to pick us up late in the afternoon and when the driver stopped in Arrudo to let Alfonso out, a crowd gathered around us. At once, the car windows were plastered with noses that changed into smiling faces when I saw myself through the eyes of the crowd and burst into laughter.

Back at the tavern, Señora served me dinner in a cold, dark dining room. The only heat in the tavern was in the kitchen and barroom. Both rooms were heated by coal-burning stoves. After dinner, I went into the kitchen and asked Señora if I could eat future meals with her and Señor in the kitchen. She said I wouldn't like eating with them since they ate only beans. I like beans, I said. No, she said firmly. So I ate alone in the gloomy dining room and the next evening she fed me canned squid, cold and slimy. Squid was very expensive, she told me. I simply could not convince her that I preferred beans, even if they were cheap.

One evening when I went into the kitchen, Señora asked me to sit down beside her at the table. She wanted to show some of her favorite possessions, two old issues of the *Ladies' Home Journal* and *Women's Home Companion*, both of which she had thumbed through so often the pages had become worn and torn, especial those with ads picturing electrical appliances such as electric stoves, washing machines and refrigerators. She had planned, twenty years earlier, to have those things when she got home, she told me.

Poor Señora. In Arrudo they were too poor to buy electrical appliances, and they had electricity for just a few hours each evening. Señor explained that the government had built the dam in the upper Nansa. The only running water, supplied by means of a hand pump, was in the kitchen and bar—and there was no bathroom. There was a privy and I bathed in my room using a washbowl, dressed quickly and ran downstairs to the kitchen stove.

I was beginning to understand why Señora had not wanted me to stay there. She was ashamed of the way they lived and she was ashamed because she had to do the weekly wash in the river. Señora blushed when I told her I had seen her, but when I said I had washed clothes in many rivers, a weak smile passed across her face. Yes, she was ashamed, but only when she was with me. In Arrudo, she and her husband were considered to be a prosperous couple who owned a tavern.

One morning Alfonso took me to a long, deep pool. Standing on the bank ten feet above the river, we could see a half dozen large salmon, fanning fins and tails at the head of the pool. Magnified by sunlight in the clear water, they seemed huge. It was what I call a holding pool, the kind in which salmon usually stop overnight during their migration upriver and are in no mood to go after flies. Generally, the only times I had caught salmon in such a pool was when fishing the fast water at the tail of a pool.

Unfortunately, no one in Arrudo knew anything about fly fishing, so I had been taken to pools ideal for spinning lures, but not for casting flies. Now I suspected the salmon in that clear pool could see me and would never take a fly in such deep water. But I had no choice, so I tied a dry fly, a large White Wulff, on the leader and cast it over each salmon. It didn't scare them. They seemed oblivious of its existence. However, as I persisted, they gradually backed down to the end of the long pool. Alfonso paced the bank restlessly. He had brought his bait-casting rod and spinning lures, but I knew that if he cast a metal lure into the pool, I might as well quit fishing for the rest of the day. Slow, gradually, the salmon moved from the end back to the head of the pool. I tried several different dry flies while following the fish back and forth with no success. Finally, in a fit of exasperation, I asked Alfonso to take me to another pool. *No es posible*, he said.

While I was trying to convince him that it was possible, a look of fear spread over his face. He was staring at three men who were walking across the bridge, a stunning stone bridge over the river, gracefully arched; and from the immaculate uniforms and black patent leather tricorn hats and boots, I recognized the men as members of the Guardia Civil and wondered why Alfonso seemed so terribly frightened.

The men greeted me in a friendly manner and then two of them moved back to Alfonso, while the other one, a tall robust Spaniard, began talking to me. He understood a few English words and I understood a few Spanish words; and I motioned to the bands on his sleeve and asked what they meant. He explained that his rank was the same as that of an American lieutenant and that the Guardia Civil was the equivalent of the American Military Police.

A large salmon interrupted our conversation when it leapt into the air at the head of the pool. The lieutenant looked straight through me and rushed over to the bank. I followed and he asked why I wasn't fishing. I tried to explain that the salmon in the deep, too-clear pool would not take a fly, but he was too excited to listen, so I called to Alfonso and asked him to bring his bait-casting rod to me. He pretended not to understand, so I walked over to him, helped myself to his rod, and took it to the lieutenant. He glanced at me helplessly, so I went back to Alfonso, led him over to the lieutenant and told him to show the man how to cast the rod.

What followed and the change in the lieutenant was a joy to behold. After a short lesson, he discarded his mask of military formality and laughed and shouted joyfully every time he plopped the metal lure into the pool. He drove the salmon back and forth from the head to the end of the pool, but that failed to spoil the fun. Even Alfonso smiled. Suddenly, though, the lieutenant stopped fishing, handed the rod to Alfonso, buttoned his collar, put on his hat, clicked his heels together and faced me.

Why, I asked, had he stopped fishing. He said he shouldn't have fished and added that members of the Guardia Civil were not allowed to fish.

Come what may, sometimes I cannot stop saying what I am thinking and so thinking how lucky I was to have been born in America, I said that in America our military police were allowed to fish. And then, to make matters worse, I said I'd heard that Spain's notorious dictator, General Francisco Franco, was fishing nearby at the Carves-Deva and asked if he was fishing the Nansa. The sudden change in the lieutenant signaled that I had blundered. He glanced at me suspiciously, bowed formally and left me without answering my question. The two guards joined him, walked down the road and across the bridge, and then I turned toward Alfonso. I could see terror in his face but was too naive to fully understand why.

Late in the afternoon when I returned to the tavern, Señora surprised me when she met me at the door and led me hurriedly through the barroom, which was full of Franco's guards. She took me into the kitchen and shut the door. Franco and some two hundred guards came to Arrudo every year, she whispered. Sometimes whole families were moved into one room to make space for them. Seeing that she was extremely nervous, I decided not to tell her about my experience with the guards at the river.

The next morning Alfonso took me to the same place, to the clear deep pool. I protested but realized it was hopeless. I suspected he had been ordered to take me there and only there. All salmon had moved out of the pool, so I fished the fast water running beneath the bridge. I had no luck there, either, and when the three guards came down to the river, I quit fishing.

The lieutenant stationed the two guards on a ledge jutting out from the slope above the river and then asked why I wasn't fishing. Instead of answering, I handed him my rod. He accepted it and began fishing. I assumed he was given permission to fish and while there were no fish in the pool he became intrigued with casting a fly, so I left him and joined Alfonso in the background. While we were watching the lieutenant, a little boy walked across the bridge and down to the river. Quiet and holding a piece of paper in his trembling hand, the boy stopped beside Alfonso. Sensing it was a message, I gestured for him to take it to the lieutenant, but he seemed frozen. His dark frightened eyes stared right through me and I had difficulty getting the message out of his clenched hand. Finally, he let me take it and I walked over to the lieutenant. He looked at me quizzically and I explained that the little boy had delivered it and was afraid to bother him. He read the message, handed the rod to me, stood at attention and blew a shrill police whistle. The two guards on the ledge stood up.

Turning, the lieutenant blew the whistle twice. Behind the top of a high hill bordering the river, a line of Franco's guards popped up along the horizon. Turning to face the hill on the other side of the river, the lieutenant blew the whistle three times. A line of guards behind the hill popped up as if by magic.

Flabbergasted, I muttered, "Muchos guardias". He replied, "Sí, viente y ocho" and quickly added, "Mucho protección por la Señora." Twenty-eight of General Franco's guards had been watching me all morning! Doubting that they were there to guard me, I waited for an explanation but received none. In the meantime, the guards were talking and laughing and marched down the road, passed over the bridge to the guards on the other side of the river and disappeared around a bend in the road. Bowing politely, the lieutenant wished me a good day and hurried after his men. Alfonso breathed a deep sigh of relief and went for the lunch basket. After we'd eaten, Alfonso took me a short distance upriver. The instant I saw the pool I forgot all about Franco's guards. It was ideal for fly fishing. Time and the strong current had created a pool after the river split around a small island, and the force of the two currents coming together at the tail of the pool had dug out an excellent place in the riverbed for salmon to lie while the splashing current churned up energizing oxygen. As a resting pool where salmon were likely to take lies, it was ideal for fishing with wet flies.

I fished down the run with no luck, changed the fly, and had started down the run again when a large salmon rolled at the end of the run. Suddenly, Alfonso, who had been sitting on the bank below me, jumped up, grabbed his rod, cast a metal lure over the salmon and hooked it. Seething inside, I reeled in my line, stomped past him and strode down to the bridge.

I was furious! However, I now realize that Alfonso simply could not resist the urge to step in front of me to catch that salmon. I had been fishing several days with flies and had caught no fish. To him a salmon was a very valuable fish. He could get the equivalent of a dollar a pound for a fresh salmon in Madrid at that time. The salmon he caught weighed over twenty pounds—a fortune to him. At the tavern Señora told me that Spain's economy had dropped to an all-time low. People were starving and when Alfonso was not fishing, he was working on the roads for twenty-five cents a day. After gaffing the salmon, he sat on the bank, sulking. I could see him but he did not see me. Suddenly, he jumped up and started fishing again. Almost at once he caught another large salmon. That one he hid in the bushes and then brought the first salmon up to the bridge and waited behind me. We both sat on the ground sulking until the taxi came for us.

The driver helped me get settled on the back seat and Alfonso put the salmon and our fishing tackle on the floor at my feet. When he started to climb into the car, I stopped him and told him to get the other salmon. He pretended not to understand what I said and sullenly refused to move. I kept insisting until the driver interrupted and began questioning him. Interrupting the driver, I tried to explain what had happened. Confused and concerned, the driver turned back to Alfonso and asked for the truth. Alfonso kept denying having caught a second salmon. I kept insisting he go get it. Finally, Alfonso turned away from me, went back to the river and returned with the salmon.

He placed it at my feet beside the other one and sat on the front seat beside the driver. No one spoke. An embarrassing silence settled around us and I yearned to vanish from the whole ordeal which had become a much more unpleasant problem than I had intended. I had wanted no part of the salmon, only to prove to Alfonso that he would gain nothing by lying. When the taxi stopped in Arrudo, Alfonso jumped from the front seat and turned away from me. I called him back, motioned to the salmon, and told him to take them. Surprised, he stood there staring at me as though he couldn't believe his ears, but I kept insisting until he picked up a salmon and shut the car door. Again, I called him back. Motioning to the other salmon, I told him to take it, too. He froze, but I continued to insist. Finally, he snatched up the salmon and promptly disappeared behind the crowd that had gathered around the car.

If my behavior has confused the reader, I must admit now that it confused me as well, and no doubt confused Alfonso more than any-one. Later, when I told Señor and Señora what had happened, their reaction surprised and frightened me. Señora said I shouldn't have given the salmon to Alfonso (she expected any salmon to go to her). Señor said Alfonso shouldn't have fished, that any salmon he caught belonged to me, and then explained that the fishing laws were strictly enforced. I felt deeply concerned. I had no desire to get him or anyone else in trouble with the law.

I decided I should tell them about my experience with General Franco's guards. Their reaction alarmed me again. Señora seemed scared out of her wits and Señor shook his head and said it was important that there be good relations between Spain and America since the United States had recently built an airbase outside of Madrid. I knew that he was counting on the US to help build up Spain's poverty-stricken economy and the thought of stirring up trouble between the two countries almost scared me, but I simply could not believe it possible for one little American fisherwoman to cause a serious international dispute. With that I went to bed and had a good sleep.

In the morning Señora asked me if I would return from the river early that day and go for a walk with her. I promised that I would and at the same time wondered what had happened to relieve her of yesterday's worries. She seemed unusually cheerful and avoided mention of yesterday's problems.

I noticed a change in Alfonso and the driver, too. They greeted me as though nothing unusual had happened and took me fishing, to a branch of the river where water poured over a dam of boulders and rocks. At the bottom of the low waterfall, salmon were rolling and cavorting all over the pool and as there was no current, the only possible way I could fish for those salmon was with a dry fly. I chose a large White Wulff, cast it to the foot of the dam and started stripping in line.

Suddenly, Alfonso grabbed my arm and pulled me away from the pool and up the steep bank to the road. By the time we reached the top, the water in the pool had raised a foot and was still rising. Form Alfonso's explanation, I gathered that water had been released out of the large dam above us. The pool had been allotted to us for the day so, realizing it was the end of our fishing, I asked the driver to take us back to the tavern.

It was my last day at the Nansa, and when the driver stopped the car to let Alfonso out in Arrudo, a Franco guard—the top guard—opened the back door, smiled and wished me a good journey back to Santander. Surprised, I wondered how that friendly guard knew I was leaving the next day but kept my thoughts and questions to myself this time.

At the tavern, when I told Señor about the morning, he said that was unfortunate, but that the Franco government had built the dam to give the people in the valley electricity, and that only recently had a fishladder, the first ever in Spain, been built beside it.

I lunched at the tavern that day and when I started upstairs, Señora asked if I would put on a skirt and go with her to visit Señor's mother. The only skirt I had with me was the one with the tweed suit I had worn when traveling, so I put on the suit and accompanied Señora to her mother-in-law's house.

Sitting in a line of poor, meager homes with thatched roofs, crowded together along the side of a dirt road, the house was little more than a hut. Señora led me into a room lit by one small window and introduced me to Señor's mother. Wearing a long black dress with black lace mantilla over her white hair, she greeted me with a sweet smile. She sat in the center of the room in a straight-backed chair. It was the only piece of furniture in the room, with the exception of a bench built into the wall at one end of the room—a room in which solidly packed dirt was partially covered with a large carpet. And yet, in that gloomy room, as Señora and I stood facing Señor's mother, her pride and dignity created a regal atmosphere. It was a special occasion and I felt sorry for not having brought an appropriate dress to Arrudo.

We left after a brief visit and out in the bright sunlight I simply could not associate that venerable lady with the poverty surrounding her. Nor could I imagine how Señor had grown into a tall, handsome, intelligent man despite such crushing poverty. I had often said that poverty made people mean, but not in Spain. There, pride seemed to have made the poorest Spaniards immune to its worst effects.

Señora was ashamed of her poverty, but she was an American; and it suddenly dawned on me that probably after spreading misinformation around Arrudo that all Americans were rich, she had hoped to impress her mother-in-law by introducing her to me, a friend from America, the country she proudly called home.

Concluding that both Señora and I had grown up in America on a foundation of false values, I turned to her and asked where we were going. She was taking me to a new power dam, she said. We walked a mile or so up the road to the dam and I was very impressed by its size and construction. The man in charge seemed to have been expecting me. He led across the board walk on the top of the dam and exuded pride as he showed me the fishladder at the side. I suspected that Edward Hewitt had in some way been responsible for that fishladder. Señor Camino told me that Franco was doing everything possible to industrialize Spain and had invited Mr. Hewitt to visit, fish some of its rivers and suggest ways of increasing the salmon population. At the same time, I suspected the reason everyone had become more cheerful that day was because somehow Señor Camino had finally contacted Señora, assured her I was not a spy, and asked her to take me to the dam. Now I guessed that since I had not gone where I had expected, Max Burell[13], the fishing pundit of the Ministry of Tourism in Madrid and longtime fishing companion to General Franco, and probably Franco himself, learned about my presence in Arrudo from the lieutenant.

It was my last day with Señora and her husband and on the way back to the tavern, she invited me to eat with them in the kitchen that evening. She cooked a special recipe: beans with onions, herbs, red wine, and bits of meat. With it, she served delicious homemade bread. After dinner, Señor served a rare old brandy. He had been saving it over many years for a special occasion, he told me.

Señora drank a toast to America. Señor drank a toast to me. And I drank a toast to them both and to Spain, and our very special occasion ended in happy hugs.

---

13. In *The Best of Ed Zern—Fifty Years of Fishing* And *Hunting From One of America's Best-Loved Outdoor Humorists*, Zern writes: "After the Civil War, Franco indulged to the full his passion for hunting and, in the later 40s, discovered the delights of deep-sea fishing. He fished for salmon in the Atlantic, particularly in the company of his friend, Max Burell. His [Franco's] main objective seemed to be to kill as much as possible, suggesting that hunting [and fishing], like soldiering before it, was the outlet for the sublimated aggression of the outwardly timid Franco. . . . He once commented while at work in his office, " . . . if it weren't for hunting or fishing which give one back a bit of nature, I couldn't put up with all this." His trips "became notorious as the occasions for the distribution of favours and government contracts. Important sums changed hands as aspirants to Franco's favour sponsored hunts in order to gain access to the fount of patronage."

CHAPTER FOURTEEN

Tormes River, Madrid and Salamanca

There is no music like a little river's . . . It takes the mind out-of-doors . . . and . . . it quiets a man down like saying his prayers.

—Robert Louis Stevenson

Before leaving Santander, I relayed my experience with the General's guards to Señor Camino. He grinned, but before I had a chance to question him he quickly changed the subject. I guessed that the trouble had started when I failed to go where I had been expected. No one, including the staff at the Turismo, knew where I was until Franco's lieutenant phoned to check on my credentials. To this day, I have no idea what really took place behind the scenes, except that Spain's longtime dictator General Francisco Franco was fishing nearby and I could have gotten myself into serious trouble if he had considered me an ideological threat and not just an eccentric and stubborn American woman encroaching on his fishing river.

At home in the United States the consensus seemed to be that Franco and his Guardes Civil were as evil as Hitler with his Gestapo; but after my contact with Señor Camino and Franco's guards, I realized that when it came to river conservation and salmon, Franco had a more forward-thinking side. If during World War II I had expressed my own view of Franco, I would no doubt have found myself branded as a traitor by impassioned patriots, as was the case with some of my more intellectual friends.

I told Señor Camino that I wanted to go to Madrid, spend a week, and go on to the Tormes River. He arranged the trip and made a reservation for me at a hotel in Madrid. I traveled by train and found myself in a small hotel in the middle of Madrid where I will never forget the bathroom off my room. I could find no way to flush the toilet and had to ring for help. The Spanish bellhop arrived, all smiles. I asked how one flushed the toilet and when he finally understood what I wanted, he pranced to the other end of the bathroom, a long narrow room, and proudly pressed a button on the wall which promptly caused the toilet to flush in a great roar.

There were several astonishing experiences in Madrid. I recall walking along a crowded sidewalk when someone bumped into me and pushed me straight into the man just ahead of me. It happened in a flash, and I only realized what had happened when I could not find my wallet in my purse. There was nothing I could do about it, the hotel proprietor told me. Luckily, there had been only a couple hundred pesetas in my wallet and my American money and passport were enclosed in a zippered pocket. Nonetheless, it seemed incredible that I had been completely unaware of someone opening my purse and removing the wallet as I strolled down a city sidewalk in the middle of the day.

In the meantime, I had arranged to meet friends, Mary and George Dunbaugh, who were in Madrid that week. Mary and I had been close friends in art school and I enjoyed visiting the Prado with her. I found its famous collection of primitive paintings wonderful, but Goya's *The Third of May 1808*, painted during the Napoleonic invasion of Spain, more exciting than any other picture in the Prado. I had seen several reproductions before, but standing in front of the original was especially exciting since its undefinable brilliance did not come through in the reproductions. The next day, George took us to Toledo, to what had been El Greco's house. It had been transformed into a small museum filled with fantastic paintings. From there we walked outside the town to the spot from which El Greco had painted a view of the ancient Roman aqueduct with Toledo in the background—the original is now in New York's Museum of Modern Art—and I was surprised that the landscape seemed unchanged.

The following day George took us to El Escorial, a monastery, palace and church, all in one, outside of Madrid. We were in the foothills of Spain's Sierra Nevada mountains, and I felt right at home as I came across a shrub like the wild shrubs that grew in the Sierra Nevada foothills around Nevada City. There we called it broom, a plant of sweeping evergreen spears covered with small yellow blossoms like sweet peas.

El Escorial, built by order of Philip II, a gloomy, religious king who used it as a retreat from all of his problems in Madrid, had a famous art collection. I was fascinated by an El Greco painting, a large picture composed of heads, portraits of important men in King Philip's court. It had been painted freely and brilliantly as only El Greco could paint, with the exception of one head at the center that was meticulously painted, more like a photograph. It ruined the painting, I thought. I conjectured that either El Greco had been forced to repaint it or someone else had painted over his work, and Mary Dunbaugh agreed with me.

The next day, George took us to watch a bullfight. We hated the experience. Mary, who walked out of the stadium before the kill, was booed by zealous Spaniards passionate about their cultural tradition, and I yearned to go with her but felt obligated to remain at the side of my host.

Each evening, George escorted us to a different outdoor cocktail lounge. We sipped, moderately, until dinnertime. As was the custom, we never dined before ten, and each night we went to a different restaurant and George always chose one of the best.

At the end of the week after the Dunbaughs had flown off to Paris, I visited one of Madrid's large cathedrals. A guide, a young intellectual and obviously a victim of Spain's dire poverty, offered to show me through the cathedral. He spoke English fluently and startled me by mumbling "dirty pig" as we passed a priest draped in the elaborate finery of priesthood and holding out a cup for change. Surprised, I stopped and stared at the guide. With a sweet of an arm covering the cathedral's valued treasures, he said that the cost of it all would feed thousands of starving children. But, he whispered, the priests had bled the people dry. I was shocked. Back in the States I had heard that General Franco was a fervent Catholic and no one in Spain dared speak against the Church. I began to sense the powerful, fear-filled spell Franco cast and the dire consequences on the average citizen.

I left for the Tormes River the next day and took the train to Avila, south of Madrid. I had been given special instructions to visit Avila's church, which was said to be exceptionally beautiful; but having read that the Inquisition had killed thousands of Jews in a bloody massacre at Avila, I had little desire to visit anything there. Instead, I got into a taxi and went directly to the Parador Nacional de Gredos, one of the government inns. The view was spectacular! I stood for a long time on the Parador veranda, looking out at the Tormes River valley. At the horizon the beauty of the Picos Gredos, in the Sierra de Gredos with its dramatic mountains capped in shining white snow, rose above the backdrop of breathtaking blue skies. And it all felt intensified by the sun's sparkling light in the clear, rarefied air.

Inside, when I explained to the manager that I wanted to fish the Tormes, he announced, "That, Señora, is impossible because you do not have a reservation." But he was a gentleman, a tall, handsome man, another aristocrat working with the Franco government; and the next morning, he made the impossible wonderfully possible.

First, he arranged for the Parador truck to take me with a guide to the Tormes and return for us at the end of the day. The following day, he introduced me to Lord and Lady Brookback. They had arrived the previous night in their chauffeur-driven car. The Brookbacks were a friendly, attractive couple, probably in their early forties—and they promptly invited me to fish with them that day.

The Parador's manager, who I assumed had encouraged Lord Brookback to take me with them, instructed their chauffeur to take us to a certain beat in the upper Tormes where we could fish from the bank. There were no flies in the air over the river, but Lord Brookback fished with dry flies, and I fished well above him with dry flies while Lady Brookback sat on the bank and surveyed the scene.

As we fished from the bank of this beautiful trout stream during a glorious day in an idyllic setting and caught not even one fish, a man fishing below us caught one trout after another in quick succession. Shouting loudly every time he hooked into a trout, he lifted his rod and tossed the fish up to the bank. Quickly, the guide released the fish from the hook, tossed the line back into the river, and dumped the trout into a basket, again and again.

The fisherman was American. He used a metal spinning lure rather than a dry fly, as I recall. I felt sorry about that and would have felt better if Lord Brookback had protested. Instead he was every bit the gentleman and kept quiet. Suspecting that trout had been planted in the river for us, I moved down to the American's water, stopped fishing and sat on the bank with Lady Brookback. Later I enjoyed a picnic lunch by the water with the Brookbacks and since we had caught no trout and could not fish another beat, we decided to return to the Parador.

The following day the inn manager introduced me to the American who had been fishing below, a Texan, and he invited me to fish with him. We drove in his great Mercedes to a little stream winding its gentle course through acres of meadows. It resembled a chalk stream, but I knew I had no hope of catching trout there as my restless companion fished ahead of me caught nothing. After his exciting experience the day before, he soon became bored and discouraged. So we sat on the bank and, feeling gloomy but talkative, the American shared his life story with me. He had been a Texas Ranger during World War II. Only he and one other man had survived. All of the other Rangers, his buddies, had been killed. Indeed, he had every right to be gloomy.

After the truck came to take my guide and me to the Tormes, I enjoyed fishing that beautiful river alone, even though the trout were still not cooperating. At lunchtime, while the guide and I were sitting on a large boulder by the water, three little boys (in clothes that were little more than rags) came to the river and sat nearby. I greeted them but they did not respond. Eating our picnic lunch I soon lost my appetite as they sat watching us. Their wan faces seemed to be all eyes—sad, hungry eyes. Deeply touched, I offered the boys some of our food and again they did not respond. The guide, speaking to me in English, suggested I leave the food on the boulder and then go over to the river and fish with my back toward the children.

The next day we returned to the same place and I groaned when I saw what was in our lunch box. The cook had given us two large cold potato omelets, blood sausage, large slices of buttered bread, cake, and fruit. I started to complain to the guide but he stopped me by motioning to a boulder in the background. Four little boys were perched on the rock, quiet. Waving to them, I picked up an apple and went fishing. The guide lost his appetite, too, and took a slice of bread, told the children the rest was for them, and joined me at the river. The boys and the lunch were gone when the truck came for us.

This was my first encounter with true hunger. The realization that those starving children were too proud to accept the food we offered them had come as a shock at first. But, yes, pride seemed to be a strong trait among the Spanish I had encountered. When I left the river, I sent silent wishes for an angelic force to watch over those boys and help them find nourishment and the opportunity to make a decent life for themselves.

Back at the Parador, the manager seemed concerned that I had caught no fish and suggested I go to the upper reaches of the Tormes. I said I could walk there and explained exactly how and where to go. That morning I caught all the trout I wanted in one pool. They were small trout, eight to nine inches, so I returned them to the river; but I had fun catching them with a dry fly. When I returned to the Parador, the manager seemed very pleased to hear about my "good luck." I was fairly certain, however, that he had arranged for the little pool to be stocked especially for me. This was becoming a familiar pattern.

I would have liked fishing the Tormes when Hemingway fished it, before Spain's Civil War, when it was alive with wild trout. Nevertheless, my visit was enjoyable. And on my last day, Max Borrell appeared at the Parador and I met him for the first time. He was traveling with an American couple who had been hunting wild cabra for the Museum of Natural History in New York. I wished I could have more time to get to know the couple and Burell, but the next day I made the return trip to Madrid.

From Madrid, I traveled to Gibraltar, to the famous rock; and also to The Rock, a modest but famous hotel built on a cliff with a view of North Africa in the far distance and the Mediterranean to the east and the Atlantic to the west. Over the years, the hotel and Rock of Gibraltar had become romantic legendary sites, but not for me. That balmy night, alone in one of the most romantic spots on the planet, I missed Jack painfully. Finally, it was time to return to New York. I left on an Italian luxury liner—the Biancomano—but was in no mood to enjoy the luxury or social whirl.

In the end, I caught no salmon in Spain. But I saw many salmon in its rivers. There was no doubt that Franco's plan to outlaw commercial fishing and rehabilitate the salmon rivers under the supervision of Max Borrell was successful. If I had wanted to fish with metal lures, I would have had good fishing.

Thirty-eight years later in 1991, I read in the Atlantic Salmon Journal a charming account by J. L. Jenkins about his recent fishing excursion at the Cares-Deva, where the Cares meets the Deva, in the same area I had fished on the Nansa. Sadly, Jenkins mentioned there were diseased fish among the returning salmon and that in four days of fishing he caught no salmon. I am almost certain the disease he saw was furunculosis. We can only hope that Spain today has voices as powerful as Franco's when he outlawed commercial netting in the Bay of Biscay and ordered Spain's Atlantic salmon rivers restored. And I hope Spain's Ministry of Tourism is as strong as Canada's Atlantic Salmon

Federation, with David Clark at the helm and American members like Lou Rossi. Lou introduced me to David and helped ensure publication of my writing about the threat of furunculosis to the Atlantic salmon population and the need for commercial fisheries to stop netting and selling these salmon.

CHAPTER FIFTEEN

The Anglers' Club & My Hewitt Reel, New York

To the lost man, to the pioneer penetrating a new country, to the naturalist who wishes to see the wild land at its wildest, the advice is always the same—follow a river. The river is the original forest highway. It is nature's own Wilderness Road.

—Edwin Way Teale

Members of the Anglers' Club of New York were wonderful to me after Jack died. Edward Hewitt and Otto von Kienbusch, both well known at the Spanish Ministry of Tourism, had made traveling easier in Spain by paving my way with letters of introduction. Now, looking at an issue of *The Anglers' Club Bulletin* published the month after Jack's death, I am feeling sentimentally fond of that men-only club. There is a photo of Jack on the cover, with an obituary inside written by the editor, Alfred Miller whose pen name was "Sparse Grey Hackle," known to many as "Sparse".

One of the first major clubs for fly fishers in the United States, the Anglers' Club was formed in 1906 and patterned after London's Fly Fishers' Club. Like the Parmachenee Club, it was founded by a group of devoted fly fishermen in New York City. As I write this, copies of *The Anglers' Club* bulletins particularly the early issues, grant me a marvelous source of authentic information about the origins, development and traditions of fly fishing in America.

Fundamentally, the Club is a place for members and their guests to meet and chat about their fishing exploits; and it has also been an eating establishment. The charter members included industrialists with offices near the Stock Exchange on Wall Street, so they chose a location for the Club headquarters in the rooms over Fraunces Tavern at 101 Broad Street. I knew three of the most prominent and active early members—George La Branche, Edward Hewitt, and Otto von Kienbusch, and I think their names should be recorded in the annals of fly fishing history since, having had the opportunity to fish extensively in England and Scotland, they left Americans a wealth of information about what they had learned abroad and practiced in the US. La Branche and Hewitt wrote some of the most informative books ever produced on fishing, and Kienbusch left a valuable collection of fishing literature and manuscripts dating back to the fifteenth century up through the nineteenth century, along with some charming old prints and original paintings. The collection is small in quantity, but great in quality, and housed at Princeton University.

George La Branche, Edward Hewitt, and Otto von Kienbusch were close friends. George was the oldest of the three, and Otto the youngest. I found Mr. Hewitt the most relaxed and congenial of the trio. Otto claimed George was the finest technician with a fly rod he had ever known. I would say Jack Atherton holds that title. Mr. Hewitt saw George as the leader in developing dry fly fishing for Atlantic salmon and the first fisher to use flies in salt water, at Islamorada in Florida. Mr. Hewitt cast a somewhat sloppy line, but he knew more about how and where to drop a fly, on or in a river, than anyone I knew. Yes, even more than Jack. About George LaBranche, Lock Scott wrote the following toward the end of his book, *Greased Line Fishing*:

The reader will notice that Mr. La Branche became enamored of the greased line, thereby following in the footsteps of Mr. Grosfield and many other fishermen . . . . I find it hard to express in cold print the strange fascination which the greased line method exerts over its devotees.

In fact, La Branche's book, *The Dry Fly and Fast Water,* is still the best book I ever read on the subject of casting methods, for both wet and dry fly fishing, particularly greased-line fishing with nymphs; and I found his instructions easy to follow. I knew George La Branche as a bright, peppery man and Mr. Hewitt liked to say George was a rich man who had become richer because during the stock market crash of 1929 he had been salmon fishing in Canada, somewhere at a camp where the fishing was great and there were no telephones or roads. His stockbroker desperately wanted to sell George's stocks before they hit bottom, but couldn't reach him. By the time George returned to New York, he was millions of dollars richer since his stocks had recovered and later soared beyond all expectation!

Jack and I were living in Connecticut when George La Branche invited us to visit him in upstate New York one weekend. I knew nothing about him then and was impressed by his country home, which resembled an English manor house. Inside the guest wing, the long hall featured bedrooms and bathrooms on each side and seemed to go on forever. We had arrived early in the afternoon and were the only guests. The other guests along with George's wife would arrive late that afternoon, the housekeeper told us. George offered to take us hunting, so we changed into hunting clothes.

The stately manor sat in the middle of a series of fields in which pheasants had been planted. Behind the house they kept a kennel of German short-haired pointers, recently imported from Germany. Jack, who had been acting as official gun at springer and cocker spaniel field trials, was an excellent shot—he never missed a bird. I wondered if George had invited us there that weekend because he wanted the best "gun" he could get to prove that German short-haired pointers were the best hunting dogs on earth.

The hunt was reminiscent of a traditional drive held at manors in England. The kennel man "ran" the dogs, George and Jack followed behind with their guns, and I followed behind as the only spectator. The dogs performed beautifully and I was particularly impressed by the fact that the only two hunters had all of those pheasants to themselves.

The other guests turned out to be one of the La Branche sons and his wife, and George's wife. She was too young to be the son's natural mother and that strange weekend in an American mansion amid vast, cleared fields holding doomed pheasant, we dressed for dinner. Mrs. La Branche asked if I had a dinner dress (a semiformal dress with long skirt and sleeves), which I did. The gentlemen wore their best tweeds. Sunday supper consisted of turkey hash, leftover from Sunday dinner, served to all but George. He was served a whole wild duck, rare, as it should be, and cooked in a marinade of red wine and spices. Since I was seated next to our host, he let me taste a sliver of the meat and it was delicious.

The last time I saw George La Branche was years later at a reception given for Mr. Hewitt by his publisher shortly before he died. Both men were in wheelchairs. Unlike La Branche and Kienbusch, Hewitt had never succeeded as a business man and he had no desire or need to since he had inherited a fortune; but he was a hard worker, a true conservationist, and very productive. With his books he left us important information and wisdom about fly fishing, and about salmon and trout rivers. He was my favorite, and he was always very fond of Jack.

Mr. Hewitt's father, Abram Hewitt, had made his money as an industrialist and one of the pioneers of the US iron industry, associated at times with J. P. Morgan and Andrew Carnegie (and son-in-law of Peter Cooper, the industrialist and inventor who founded Cooper Union). Hewitt, Jr. began fishing for trout on his father's estate in New Jersey as a small boy. When he was a young man, Abram Hewitt took his son to the Carnegie family castle in Scotland. While Carnegie and his father talked business, the Carnegie gillies[14] took him salmon fishing at a river on the estate. Later in 1866, Abram Hewitt was elected mayor of New York City and became known for the construction of Cooper Union and innovative financing—and years later, for the construction of New York's subway system.[15]

Mr. Hewitt's maternal grandfather, Peter Cooper, was responsible for finally getting the telegraph cable laid across the Atlantic, and for building the first locomotive in the United States. Mr. Hewitt was proud of his grandfather. Indeed, he had a right to boast about Peter Cooper, the philanthropist who gave New York City Cooper Union and the New School of Social Research, the first free night school for working people in America. While comparing his grandfather to Rockefeller, du Pont, and other industrial tycoons from that time, Mr. Hewitt noted that all of Cooper's male descendants had become hardworking scientists rather than prodigal dependents.

Peter Cooper's parents came to American as poor immigrants. From this humble beginning, Cooper had amassed and founded—through honest hard work and talent—not only a great fortune, but also a dynasty of truly altruistic Americans who felt no need to emulate the customs and way of life of the British aristocracy.

---

14. A ghillie or gillie is a Scots term that refers to a man or a boy who acts as an attendant on a fishing, fly fishing, hunting, or deer stalking expedition, primarily in the Highlands or on a river such as the River Spey. In origin it referred especially to someone who attended on his employer or guests. A ghillie may also serve as a gamekeeper employed by a landowner to prevent poaching on his lands, control unwelcome natural predators such as fox or otter and monitor the health of the wildlife. The origin of this word dates from the late 16th century, from the Scottish Gaelic gille, "lad, servant," cognate with the Irish giolla.

15. Abram Stevens Hewitt (July 31, 1822—January 18, 1903) was a teacher, lawyer, an iron manufacturer, chairman of the Democratic National Committee from 1876 to 1877, US congressman, and a mayor of New York. He was the son-in-law of Peter Cooper (1791–1883), an industrialist, inventor, and philanthropist. He is best known for his work with the Cooper Union, which he aided Peter Cooper in founding in 1859, and for planning the financing and construction of the New York City subway system, for which he is considered the "Father of the New York City Subway System".

Cooper sent Edward Hewitt, after he graduated from Princeton and became a pharmacist, to a university in Germany noted for its unique science program. While Hewitt was there he met and fell in love with Mary Ashley, who was traveling abroad with her mother. This was a period in which wealthy American women took their daughters to Europe, hoping to find titled sons-in-law. Many were successful since impoverished but legitimate aristocrats were plentiful.

Jack and I learned that Mary's father, James Ashley[16], had been the governor of Montana until 1870 and an abolitionist during the Civil War, using his political talents to help free the slaves in Washington, DC. And so Mary and Edward Hewitt were married in the governor's mansion in Montana and settled in New York. One of their daughters, Eleanor, later became Princess Viggo of Denmark[17] and another became a doctor. As I recall, she was a popular psychoanalyst.

Mary Hewitt was an invalid when she and I first met, and Mr. Hewitt was doing everything possible to keep her alive. Never had I witnessed a more devoted husband. He was seventy and I imagine she

---

16. James Mitchell Ashley (November 14, 1824 – September 16, 1896) was a US congressman, territorial governor of Montana and railroad president. James Ashley was an active abolitionist who traveled with John Brown's widow on the date of Brown's execution and reported the event in the still-extant local newspaper, the Toledo Blade. In 1858, he was elected to US House of Representatives of the 36th United States Congress as a Republican. During his three terms in Congress he served as the chairman to the Committee on Territories. He took an active role in supporting the recruitment of troops for the Union Army during the American Civil War. During his term, he wrote a bill to abolish slavery in the District of Columbia, introduced the first bill for a constitutional amendment abolishing slavery, and initiated impeachment proceedings against President Andrew Johnson (1867). He was defeated for re-election in 1868. During the Civil War, he authored the Arizona Organic Act. Following his defeat, Ashley was appointed the Territorial Governor of Montana and served until 1870. He then returned to Toledo. Ashley was the builder and president of the Ann Arbor Railroad.

17. Edward and Mary's daughter, Eleanor Margaret Green (1895–1966) married Christian Adolph Georg, HRH Prince Viggo of Denmark (1893–1970) in 1924. She acquired the title Eleanor Margaret, HRH Princess Viggo of Denmark.

was in her late sixties. I visited him in their New York house after she died and he showed me two lovely urns, one on each side of the fireplace mantel in the living room. Her ashes were in one, and the other was for his ashes when the time came. His wish was for both urns to be sprinkled into the Neversink River after his death.

Hewitt died in 1957 at the age of ninety-one and I was with him at the hospital the night before the surgery that took his life. After commenting that he would be glad when it was over, Mr. Hewitt sat up in bed as though he had no intention of dying and asked me to visit and fish with him the following spring at the upper Neversink, and then questioned me about my trip to Labrador. When I told him about the Inuit and their plight with tuberculosis, he began telling me how to cure them. Having graduated from Princeton as a pharmacist, he had an intense interest in health and the vitamins, minerals and natural elements needed to keep the human body well. He survived the operation the next morning, but a couple of days later his old heart stopped beating.

I remember Otto von Kienbusch (he dropped the von later) as more of a collector than a devotee of fly fishing. Other than that, I knew nothing about him. He asked me to visit him and I had no idea why, but I went to his brownstone off Fifth Avenue. When I rang the doorbell, a strange man opened the door and ushered me into a large hall. He told me to go upstairs and open the door at the top. The stairs went up the side of the hall wall and seemed to go on forever. Finally, at the top, I opened the door and stepped into a dark room, nearly running into the long spear of a man mounted on a horse—both in armor!

It was somewhat of a shock because I had never heard of Otto's armor collection. Later, Mr. Hewitt had a twinkle in his eye when he told me that Otto collected armor for the Metropolitan Museum of Art until he infuriated them by bidding on the best pieces for his own collection!

I was about to run out of the room and back downstairs when a blaze of light flashed over the room and Otto, with his slight build and grey hair, walked through the doorway at the other side of the enormous room. A most dramatic entrance, indeed, and greeting me graciously, he led me around the massive collection of every kind of armor imaginable and led me to a smaller room. There, I toured a massive collection of antique rare books, manuscripts, paintings and prints, all related to fly fishing. Then we went back to the armor room and he offered to help me plan my trip to Spain. Ed Hewitt, it seems, had told him I was going there.

A week or so later Otto phoned and asked me to visit again. He had prepared some letters of introduction for me to use in Spain and while we were sitting on the sofa in the armor room, a voice spoke from up above the spectacularly high ceiling, "I'm ready."

I craned my neck and saw, high at the top of a narrow iron stairway on a side wall, a very large lady draped from head to toe in black silk—somewhat like a nun's habit—standing on the landing by a door. Otto told her to go ahead with their chauffeur and we would go later by taxi. Silent, she came down the stairs, walked across the spacious room to the door in back, and vanished. I assumed she was Mrs. Von Kienbusch, but why hadn't she stopped to greet me? And why hadn't Otto introduced us? It all seemed very strange, like the movie Dr. Jekyll and Mr. Hyde; while Dr. Jekyll, or Mr. Hyde (I wasn't sure which) went on talking as though nothing unusual had occurred.

Otto had not informed me that he planned to take me somewhere and I did not know where he was taking me in the taxi until we go there. We went to a tea at The Guild of Rare Books, of which he was president, and the minute we arrived I walked straight over to Mrs. Von Kienbusch, who sat at the head of a table pouring tea. I introduced myself and a man sitting next to her offered his chair. I sat down and stayed by her to the end. We talked about art rather than rare books and I was delighted to learn that Mildred von Kienbusch was familiar with (and admired) Jack's museum paintings.

Later, after I returned from Spain, Otto invited me one weekend to go with him to the Wyandanch, an exclusive club for trout fishermen on Long Island. I have been told it is now a state park with fishing open to the public. I would have loved to fish there but was afraid of becoming a collector's item and so declined the invitation. Otto was ninety-one when he died, and although he became blind, he never stopped fishing. Some years later I met his daughter and was surprised to learn that Otto had been a talented artist who never had (or seized) the opportunity to develop his gift. Mr. Hewitt told me that Otto's father had made a fortune in the tobacco business, which Otto had inherited and was obliged to manage. What a pity!

Other members of the Anglers' Club of New York helped me as well. To show that fly fishers are no ordinary creatures, I will relate a true tale about the adventures of my precious Hewitt trout reel[18] Mr. Hewitt had made it by hand and Jack bought the reel and gave it to me on my birthday. Mr. Hewitt had made several reels, carved out of solid aluminum, and sold them to special friends who were members of the Anglers' Club. My reel was not as polished and finished as the others, but it was special because it was the first, the original, and Mr. Hewitt had become a very special man in the world of fly fishing. I was at the Parador Tormes in Spain when I unpacked my duffel bag and discovered it was gone. Luckily, I had another trout reel with me, but I phoned Señor Camino immediately and told him I had lost the reel, probably at the Saja, and asked him to try and find it for me. One week later I received a letter from Señor Camino saying the reel had not turned up, but he would keep looking.

I was forced to return to New York without the reel. The following December of 1953 I sent a Christmas card to Señor Camino and a week later received a note from him informing me that he had

---

18. Photo of Hewitt Reel and reference to Maxine Atherton's Edward R. Hewitt Reel, c. 1945, aluminum frame, nickel-silver fittings. Hewitt made about 20 reels, all when he was in his eighties and all for fishing friends. The Atherton reel is believed to be among the first. Please visit http://content.yudu.com/ Library/A18crl/FishFlyVol12/resources/54.htm for more information.

the reel and would have written sooner if he had known my address. Mr. Hewitt had engraved his signature and my name on the reel, and Señor Camino, a devoted, fly fisher, appreciated the importance and sentimental value of the reel. He said he preferred not to send the reel through the customs office in Spain where things got "lost" and advised me to send him the name of a reliable gentleman who was going to Santander and could get the reel there and deliver it to me in New York.

Delighted to learn that the reel had been located, I telephoned Sparse and read Señor Camino's letter to him. He agreed to do what he could, which consisted of putting a notice in the Bulletin, and one on the bulletin board at the Anglers' Club, asking any member going to Spain in the near future to get in touch with him. A few days later, Sparse phoned to say that Acheson Harden, a member of the Anglers' Club who had ships going back and forth from New York to Santander, had answered the notice and promised to have a captain of one of his ships pick up the reel. Acheson did business with the president of the bank in Santander and would ask the ship's captain to ensure the safe retrieval of the reel.

I knew Acheson Harden because we had met during a field trial at Hot Springs in Virginia years earlier. I had been seated next to him a dinner in the ballroom one evening after a day in the field with Springer Spaniels, and it wasn't long until I found I was sitting next to a fly fisher and most attractive man. During our conversation I told him I had fished at Parmachenee in September, without my husband but with his precious Leonard trout rod. I described every detail of catching landlocked salmon with flies, described the beauty of the Maine woods, about the sunsets, and how the guide taught me to cast with a book under my arm (to keep the rod from going too far backward). I loved Jack's Leonard rod, I said, and I didn't want to give it back to him.

My dinner partner said little (I know, he didn't have much chance), but he seemed amused and interested, and I simply could not stop talking about fishing. The ballroom was almost empty when Jack came for me. He saw I had been talking to Acheson Harden. Then, a friend who had been watching us wanted to know what I had said to hold the attention of the most sought-after bachelor in the East. I told her I had been talking about fishing and she seemed astounded; but, not surprisingly, she knew nothing about the powerful, magnetic lure that never fails to fascinate a true fly fisher.

I never saw Acheson Harden again, and I never attended another field trial because over time they were taken over by professional dog handlers and owners and faded into a nonentity of commercial competition. Several months later, however, I received a mysterious package in the mail. A fly rod—my first, very own rod! It was a Powell rod, and inside the package a note from Mr. Powell explained that Mr. Harden had asked him to make the rod and send it to me. I loved it! Powell fly rods, made in California, were the most popular custom-made rods in the West at the time and I sat down at once and wrote Acheson an effusive thank-you note.

I heard nothing until Sparse told me Acheson Harden was going to get my Hewitt reel back to me. Sparse advised me to write to Senior Camino, tell him about Acheson, and ask that he take the reel to the president of the bank in Santander. I wrote to Señor Camino and a few weeks later the bank president personally handed my Hewitt reel to the captain of one of Acheson's ships. The captain stowed the reel in the ship's safe and sailed it across the Atlantic Ocean to New York. There, he personally delivered the reel to Acheson Harden who phoned me to let me know he had the reel in hand and would be sending a courier to deliver the reel and asked that I let him know when I had it in hand. After the messenger completed his mission and my beloved Hewitt reel was safely back home with me, I called Acheson, thanked him profusely, and never heard from him again.

Indeed, if that trout reel had been the crown jewels, it couldn't have been better cared for.

CHAPTER SIXTEEN

Adlatock River, Labrador

Who hears the rippling of rivers will not utterly despair of anything.

—Henry David Thoreau

On the fourth of July 1956, I flew out of sizzling hot New York to Montreal and from there to St. John's, Newfoundland. I made my way north on the SS *Kyle*, an icebreaker used as a small passenger ship that traveled back and forth from St. John's to the US Army base in Labrador's Goose Bay. Why Labrador? I had always thought the crisis of the North resembled that of a beautiful woman—cool, magnetic, mystical. But I soon discovered that the North could be just as cruel, and that time and plans meant nothing. Weather dictated my every move, and stop.

Now, traveling along the Newfoundland coast through and around a massive archipelago, past lonely lighthouses and isolated settlements, the Kyle took me to Goose Bay. I had been booked to change to the Trepassey, the only passenger ship going north along Labrador's coast. The Trepassey was not, however, at Goose Bay when the Kyle docked there, and after waiting there several hours, the Trepassey started back to St. John's!

Rushing around the deck, I tried to find someone who could tell me what was going to happen to me, but everyone who might know was too busy trying to get the Kyle safely through Hamilton Inlet, a difficult passage around islands and shoals of solid rock. Finally, a deckhand explained that a storm was brewing and the captain wanted to get his ship back to St. John's as soon as possible. A half-hour later the Kyle stopped abruptly. It had run aground, so we would all have to spend the night aboard. Alarmed, I asked if he was going back to St. John's. No, I would be boarding the Trepassey the next day—at sea.

The following morning, once the high tide lifted the Kyle off the sand bar, we sailed out to the Trepassey, which was anchored outside of Hamilton Inlet in the North Atlantic. Standing on deck, I became more and more alarmed as I watched the crew tether the two ships together at the hand railings. When the mate said, "You're going to have to jump—we'll help you," I was too stunned to argue. I let him lead me over to the railing where he and a crew member boosted me up on top and instructed me to leap. Glancing down at the treacherous North Atlantic's icy water and recalling having heard that it would take a person four minutes to die in that water, I could not bring myself to jump. That is, until the squeaking, groaning railings of the two ships rubbing together convinced me they were about to pull apart. My eyes shut tight, I finally took a deep breath and jumped, falling into a cushion of arms, and was set safely on my feet.

The railings were quickly untied and the Kyle started south, while the Trepassey moved north. Late that night the brewing storm rose up full force. In a cabin with four bunks and three roommates, I had chosen an upper bunk since claustrophobia always threatened to smother me in the lower bunks. I had more privacy in the upper bunk, too, and after an exhausting day of stress and strain, I actually managed to sleep through the storm. No one was in the cabin the following morning when I climbed down out of my bunk. In the dining room, only the captain was seated. He had been up all night and was surprised to see me in such good condition. I was surprised when he said no one else had slept through the storm and that a woman in my cabin had been terribly seasick. He explained that he and his brother were the sole owners of the Trepassey, and that the storm last night was the worst it had ever weathered. It was a beautiful old schooner, but realizing the dangerous ramifications of the storm, I longed for the comfort and safety of a clumsy old icebreaker like the Kyle.

The captain, due to relieve his brother at the wheel, invited me to visit the wheelhouse. He introduced me to his brother and showed me an instrument that resembled a television screen. It was a new invention, he said, and it made this a historic voyage for the Trepassey. Pointing a finger at the dark specks on the screen, he showed me the icebergs dotting the area around the ship. I groaned and he quickly added that he would never have left Goose Bay during the storm if he hadn't had it and the ship-to-shore phone, also a new invention just on the market. The phone made it possible for the schooner to travel as far north as Nain, but only during summer months. This was the ship's first trip north this year.

Standing beside him at the wheel and staring out at the icebergs in the distance, I shuddered recalling the fate of the Titanic; but he assured me that he was careful to keep the icebergs in the distance and to travel close to the coastline. Still, his words were less than comforting because I knew that the Labrador coastline—a part of the ancient Laurentian plateau, sometimes called the Canadian Shield and still rising, consisted of a massive archipelago of islands, land, shoals, and underwater mountaintops, all requiring extremely expert navigation.

A day or so later, the wonderful devices of electronic science had us safely into Hopedale Bay. About twenty Inuit, who has been at St. John's all winter, were on board the Trepassey, returning to Hopedale or Nain. Almost all of them had been at a hospital for months and were especially anxious to get home. The arrival of the Trepassey had become the most important event of the year for the isolated Inuit; and when it dropped anchor in Hopedale Harbor, excitement ran high as Inuit in all kinds of boats rushed out to meet the ship and poured over its railing to greet their friends and family members and take them to the settlement.

This was my first experience getting to know the Inuit and that cold, gloomy day as I stood on deck shivering and waiting, their focus was not on me. Suddenly I realized I was the only person left on board! If the captain or any crew members were still aboard, they were not visible. At that moment, a man appeared, leaping over the railing and running past me. Chasing after him, I shouted that I wanted to go ashore. He was not Inuit and said he had come to get the mail and would take me to shore with him. Reverend Grubb, a tall, handsome gray-haired Englishman in his early sixties, greeted me on the dock and said I would be staying with him and his wife in the mission. The main mission building, the church, and the Hudson Bay store on the other side of the mission formed a line along the Bay shore. The wide dock led up to the mission and from there branched into boardwalks built high over muddy ground, around the Inuit homes. Reverend Grubb explained that he and some of the Inuit men had built a school building behind the mission.

We waited for the baggage to be unloaded and once it was on the dock, I could not find my tent and the large duffel bag that I had packed with sweaters, wool clothes, rain coat, fleece-lined jacket and more. Where were they? No one knew, and no one seemed especially concerned, either. But I couldn't fish without my cold-weather gear, I said. It was probably still on the Trepassey and I could get it when the ship returned, Reverend Grubb told me. "When will that be?" I moaned. "In a couple of weeks," he replied. The Trepassey sailed on to Nain and later we learned that heavy ice had prevented the ship from reaching Nain. I had yet to accept that weather would dictate our every move.

Now resigned to my fate, I followed Reverend Grubb up the dock to the mission. In that part of Labrador, there were no streets, no roads, very little plant life, and at that moment there was no joy in my heart. But the Grubbs were kind to me. They took me into their home and treated me as a member of the family. However, I was expecting to head someplace near the Adlatock River, where there would be guides to take me fishing and I was shocked to learn that I was nowhere near the river and there were no guides in or around Hopedale.

Reverend Grubb seemed more like an adventurer than a minister. In England, he had been one of the famed Coldstream Guards. After being ordained in the Moravian Church and getting nine months of medical training in England, he was the only doctor and dentist for the Inuit in Hopedale. "It has been a historic year for Hopedale and Nain since the Grenfell Mission at Goose Bay has started sending a bush plane to take patients back and forth to its hospital," he told me.

I was surprised to learn that two hundred fifty Inuit in Hopedale had TB, or had had it, or were carriers. There was nothing I could do but wash my hands frequently with soap and water and then try to forget about it. I had been opposed to missions and missionaries whose purpose was to convert so-called heathens into Christians. Especially the Inuit, who my father always claimed were the sanest people on earth. Nevertheless, in Hopedale I soon realized that if it had not been for the Moravian Mission and Reverend Grubb, there would be no Inuit left there, since commercial fishermen had brought in tuberculosis, influenza, colds, and other diseases, and they had almost depleted the whale population.

There was a Moravian mission in Nain as well. These missions were responsible for gathering all Inuit who were left in Labrador, settling them in Nain and Hopedale, and supplying them with food and medical care. Before the whites and "civilization" discovered the "Eskimos" in Labrador, they were a healthier, established race. The name Eskimo is a misnomer of an Indian word meaning eaters of raw meat. Québec's government has officially changed the name Eskimo to Inuit, which is as it should be.

Whale abounded in the North Atlantic around Hopedale at one time, Reverend Grubb told me. He spoke of Hopedale Bay nostalgically, as it was in the days of whaling ships and all the excitement that surrounded their presence. But, Grubb admitted, hunters had almost depleted the North Atlantic of its precious whales and the Labrador tundra of its caribou.

Waiting for my bags to arrive gave me time to learn more about the Inuit, a culture that struck me as optimistic and wise as they always seemed to turn their disappointments into a joke. Every summer Québec's lieutenant governor came to Hopedale on the Trepassey. It was one of the big events of the year, and while I was there great preparations for his arrival kept everybody busy and in a state of excited anticipation. The Girl Scout troop, consisting of five teenagers, made new uniforms and practiced the song "Oh Canada" for days, which they were planning to sing as their honored guest made his way down the dock to the mission.

A reception was planned in the Grubbs' quarters and I helped Mrs. Grubb polish and shine everything in the living room, and then went looking for something to put into a floral arrangement of some sort. Not an easy task in a tundra! There were no flowers but, having won prizes for my arrangements in flower shows, I found a dwarf pine tree and using pine boughs, mistletoe, and some other interesting plant life, I created what I thought was a fascinating arrangement and placed it proudly on a table in the living room. Rev. Grubb took one look at it and muttered, "Parasite," but he knew nothing about modern garden club flower arrangements, so I paid little attention to his lack of appreciation.

The day of the lieutenant governor's arrival came around, but cruel weather and wind with driving rain battered the North Atlantic. Undaunted, the Girl Scouts and all of the other Inuit in the settlement gathered on the dock in the pouring rain and waited until a messenger from the telegraph station ran down to us with a message from the lieutenant governor. The storm had prevented him from boarding the ship to Hopedale. Standing on the sidelines and watching as the Inuit turned back to the settlement, I was surprised to see them laughing and joking about what I expected they would see as a devastating disappointment. The lieutenant governor never made it to Hopedale that year, but the Girl Scouts loved their new matching uniforms, wearing them every day, and the whole community enjoyed the cakes and punch that had been prepared for the occasion.

From the Inuit I befriended, I learned a very important lesson: It felt so much better to make lemonade out of life's lemons and turn disappointments into jokes and occasions for shared laughter, rather than allowing complaints and regrets to ruin one's peace of mind. And, as the Grubbs showed no signs of being disappointed, I concluded that the Inuit had taught them something far more valuable than anything the Moravians could teach the Inuit.

The Trepassey came again, this time with my bags. I was elated until I realized they weren't all there. I forgot all about laughing and was on the verge of tears when Rev. Grubb suggested I go up to the telegraph office, get in touch with the woman at the St. John's travel agency and ask her to locate the missing bag. There were no telephones in Hopedale, only the one-way phone at the telegraph office, a recent and well-appreciated addition to the mission.

I had shipped my baggage from New York by boat freight, with my tent and fishing clothes wrapped together in a tarpaulin, and the travel agent found the bundle in the baggage room. It had not been picked up when the other bags were put on the Kyle. She promised to send it to me on the Trepassey's next trip to Hopedale. When I complained to Mrs. Grubb, she said it was the usual plight of travelers to Labrador and should be expected. So, instead of complaining I decided to laugh and felt more cheerful. The Trepassey would not be back for another two weeks, but I had slacks and an old sweater in my suitcase, so when the weather warmed a bit, Rev. Grubb arranged for an Inuit couple, Dan and Bertha Kimusigak, to take me to the Adlatock River. I suppose he chose Bertha because she was one of the few adults who spoke English and was more educated than most of the Inuit there. As a baby, Bertha had been raised at the Grenfell Mission after being left to die on the ice, a custom Inuit considered kinder than slow starvation.

While we traveled by motorboat down the coast to Adlatock Bay, Bertha spoke of Sir Grenfell proudly and lovingly as her father, and during our voyage she recounted the tale of Sedna, who according to Inuit religion ruled the sea. Like sand, the sins of the Inuit got into Sedna's hair and when they got too thick she got angry and roused some stormy weather, so people were careful not to do anything that might offend Sedna. Bertha claimed to be a good Christian and was not supposed to believe in Sedna, but there was no doubt in my mind that she did. Dan, who was busy steering the boat, remained silent during the entire voyage. Bertha explained that he didn't speak a word of English.

Late that afternoon we arrived at Adlatock Bay. I climbed out of the boat and followed Bertha down the dock and past a most astonishing house. Quite large, it looked old and deserted and sad. There were three large dormers across the front and it seemed palatial in that lonely wilderness. More like a fortress than a home, the house, and a couple of small buildings were fenced in by a highboard fence. Who in the world would want to build such a house in that godforsaken part of the world? I wanted to go inside and explore, but Bertha was waiting impatiently for me to follow her.

I walked with her into the entry room of a three-room cabin and began gagging. It was where they cleaned seals and was the most important room in the house, she told me. Smiling, she drew in deep breaths of stale seal oil effluvium as though it were the sweetest smell on Earth. Quickly, I followed her into the kitchen and closed the door on the worst odor I had ever smelled.

The only furniture in the kitchen consisted of an old iron stove for cooking, a table, one chair, and a large wooden box. Bertha announced that she and Dan would sleep in the box. Protesting, I suggested it looked more like a coffin. Giggling, she said that it was and that she loved to sleep in it with Dan.

I simply could not imagine how two adults could get inside that coffin, let alone get a good night's sleep, but I kept quiet out of fear that she might change her mind and tell me to sleep there. We put our bundles on the table and she took me into the only other room in the cabin. There was a wire bed spring minus a mattress. That was where I would sleep. Thankful I wouldn't have to sleep in a coffin, I smiled and put my eiderdown sleeping bag on the bed spring, my duffel bag on the floor and joined Bertha in the kitchen.

There was no running water in the house, of course. I washed my face and hands in the ice cold Bay, and Dan brought in buckets of salt-free water, probably from a nearby spring. Dan never spoke. Bertha did all the talking and made all the decisions. There was no doubt that Bertha was the boss. Dan and I dared not defy her.

Whenever I attempted to ask Dan a question, he answered only with a sweet smile or a blank expression. It had become obvious to me that neither he nor Bertha was one bit envious or impressed by me, a white woman from the great United States of America. Well, at least I thought my country was great.

I had brought my own food and we ate independently. The Inuit had no specific meal hours. They ate when they were hungry. Packaged dehydrated foods had only recently come on the market and I had a good supply. That evening, I cooked a package of vegetable soup, a package of rice and chicken and I mixed up a bowl of instant chocolate pudding. I let the bowl of pudding stand overnight to thicken and the next day I offered some to Bertha and Dan. She said she would like some, but Dan wouldn't eat it. He thought it looked like shit. Shocked, I grabbed the bowl of pudding and marched it into my room.

The next day Dan took me to the Adlatock River. We traveled in the motor boat a mile or so, down along the bay shore and then walked over a trail to the river. Following behind Dan, I congratulated myself for having worn a head net and covered all exposed skin with fly-dope. The back of Dan's light colored parka was now black with black flies and mosquitoes. He was carrying my duffel bag and a .22 riffle (held together with tape) and I was carrying my fishing rod and flies. Suddenly Dan stopped and circled around something on the trail.

A large pile of dung, still steaming, had stopped Dan. Motioning to the dung, I looked at him questioningly. "Bear shit," he said. Frowning, I glared at him. Calmly and deliberately, still smiling, he placed my bag on the ground beside me and then, with both hands on his gun, walked forward on the trail.

Somewhat subdued, I followed close behind. Dan's calm and tolerant manner made me ashamed of myself. He was not vulgar—the few English words he knew he had learned from rough British, American, and Canadian commercial fishermen. Of course, there is nothing bad about the word "shit." It means excrement, but I had been brought up in a Victorian social system that condemned the use of words related to bodily functions such as sex and the elimination of bodily wastes. With a big smile on my face, I told Dan that if all the sins the Victorians had caught in Sedna's hair, her fury would whip up a worldwide tidal wave.

I was not afraid of the bear, wherever it was. I was afraid that if we came upon the bear and Dan took a shot at it with the .22 rifle held together with adhesive tape, we would be in serious trouble; but we arrived, finally, at the Adlatock without mishap. The trail came to an abrupt end on an expansive flat boulder at the edge of the river. Dan put my bag back at my feet, gave me a sweet smile, turned and went back down the trail.

Frantic, I called and asked when he would be back. He turned, answering with only his smile, and then continued down the trail. Of course, he had not understood my question. I considered running after him, but just then a salmon jumped in the middle of the Adlatock. With a pounding heart I picked up my rod and surveyed the river. Banked with great rocks, it ran clear and cold. Another salmon splashed near me in the strong current. What a wonderful salmon pool! I wondered how to approach it. Between the river and the boulder on which I was standing, the space was too deep to allow me to cross, so I decided to head downriver.

Following the river, I kept close to the bank and cast a wet fly at random into water unlikely to hold a salmon. Finally, I came to the end of the river—a most dramatic finale! The entire river ran head-on into a granite wall, turned abruptly, and roared into Adlatock Bay at the side. Down through the ages, the great force of water and ice had pounded a hollow in the rock wall, and while I stood trying to decide how and where to fish, two large salmon began fighting, splashing, lashing tails, and jumping on top of each other in the bay at the mouth of the river. No doubt there were hookbill salmon fighting for the privilege of escorting a beautiful silvery female up to the spawning beds.

Certain that a big run of salmon was entering the river, I yearned to be in a canoe on the bay where I could cast a dry fly, a big White Wullf, into the mouth of the river. I tried to reach it from the other direction with a wet fly but failed. Fishing there was hopeless, so I returned to the spot where Dan had left me. While sitting on the boulder eating a sandwich, I noticed a place where I could fish that salmon pool from the bank. It was about a hundred feet above me and to get there, I worked my way back and around some large rocks and thick brush and then started circling back to the river. Suddenly I realized I had lost the sound of the river. I glanced at my watch. I had been out a half-hour. Realizing that I had been going away from the river rather than toward it, I panicked.

My heart beating wildly, I felt faint and dropped down on a large rock. I was on the border of the timber line, in an area along the coast where the growth of brush and dwarf pines was approximately the same height. There were no tall trees, nothing to mark direction, and the sun was in the middle of the sky. No one travels alone here, not even the Inuit. Dan would never look for me alone—he would go back to Hopedale for help and that might take days. I recalled my father saying that whenever I was lost, I should work my way downriver, where there would most likely be some kind of habitation. But how could I find the river if I couldn't hear it? Finally, as I sat there pondering the possibility of never being found, terror pried me off the rock and instinct took over.

At long last, the wonderful sound of the river's roaring waters in my ears stopped me. I had been lost for over an hour and was now standing at the top of a hill, looking far down to the Adlatock, which was shooting white spray and foam into the air as it flowed at lightning speed through a narrow granite chasm. Above, from the hazy silhouette of mountains upon the distant horizon, the river flowed in a straight line through miles of flat tundra. The lush carpet of lichen on the tundra grew a foot high. What a wonderful place for caribou! Alas, Rev. Grubb had said there were no caribou left in the area.

I wanted to fish the river where it flowed through the tundra. I could fish from the bank, but the thought that Dan might be waiting for me sent me hurrying downriver. Careful this time to stay within the sound of the river, I had no trouble and worked my way down to where Dan had left me; but he was not there. Somewhat alarmed, I waited with one thought in mind: Had he come and gone without me? He appeared thirty minutes later and while I followed behind him on the trail, I decided not to mention to Dan or Bertha that I had been lost.

The following day Bertha explained that Dan had left me at the river and returned to get his bear trap, and that he couldn't take me fishing now because he had gone to get the bear. He came back that afternoon with a large bear's toe. Smiling from ear to ear, he stepped out from the boat and held up the toe for us to see. Bertha began to giggle. Why were they laughing, I asked? Ignoring me, Bertha ran over to Dan.

I knew they needed meat and fur. But I could not understand why they were laughing and it was clear that Bertha was very happy to see Dan and nothing else mattered at the moment. This, too, was difficult to fathom. Dan was the smallest and least attractive Inuit man in Hopedale, and Bertha was the most attractive woman. At least, I thought she was. I was beginning to realize that my idea of an attractive person differed from that of the Inuit. I told myself that beauty was only skin deep and admitted that something much deeper than beauty attracted these two to each other. The idea of them probably thinking I was funny-looking started me laughing.

I had no desire to return to the Adlatock unless Dan would take me down the bay shore to the mouth of the river, and stay with me while I fished from the boat. Or, take me to the river where it flowed across the tundra, and then stay nearby. Bertha said no before asking Dan and intimated to me that he had better sense than to go where no one else dared to go, so I asked them to take me back to Hopedale.

Back in Hopedale, when I recounted my day to Reverend Grubb, including my adventures getting lost, he said no one ever went there and he was quite sure no one other than a few Inuit had ever been to that part of Adlatock.

CHAPTER SEVENTEEN

Little River between Lakes, Labrador

~~~~~~~~

It is pleasant to have been to a place the way a river went.

—Henry David Thoreau

Finally, the Trepassey brought my belongings to Hopedale, and then Reverend Grubb started making plans for my trip to Little River. Two Inuit boys, ages fourteen and fifteen, were going with me. Jona and Joel were the only two members of the Boy Scouts in Hopedale, and since its agenda required that all members participate in some kind of excursion each summer, Rev. Grubb had arranged for them to go with me to Little River. To this day, I have no idea of its exact location. No detailed map of that area had been published in 1955. In fact, I had the latest map of Labrador, on which the whole area above Hopedale was nearly blank, and Nain was the only settlement north of Hopedale.[19]

A Mountie, a member of the Canadian Mounted Police, on a boat rather than a horse, took us to Little River. Riding with him in his wonderful motorboat with a small cabin was the most exciting adventure the boys had ever experienced. We had been out a couple of hours when we passed through channels between islands and shoals, and entered an unusually calm bay in the North Atlantic. There, the

---

19. Hopedale in 2014 boasted a population of 520.

vanishing sun, tinting the sky, horizon and glass water a soft hazy pink, reminded me of the rosy fairyland in my childhood conch shell.

I came out of my dreamy haze when the Mountie stopped the boat at a tiny dock. Motioning to a rowboat and deserted cabin on the shore, he explained that Joseph, an older Inuit who had accompanied us from Hopedale, periodically came here to net salmon. Joseph and I did not speak the same language, but he was a gentle, kind man who never stopped smiling and he talked to me with his eyes. The boys had learned some English at the Hopedale school, so we had no trouble communicating.

The Mountie, a nice looking young Canadian, left us on shore at the mouth of Little River and went fishing. He anchored his boat in the bay and fished around the mouth of the river with spinning lures. Joseph and the boys loaded our bags and supplies in the rowboat. I still had no idea what to expect. No doubt Joseph and the two boys were getting ready to take the rowboat upriver, but at the last minute, Joel refused to go with us. Concerned, I tried to understand what they were saying. If he didn't go, I would have to return to Hopedale.

I now realize I should have given Joel credit for having more sense than I did, knowing that we were heading into truly desolate wilderness far far away from Hopedale and the rest of the world. But after a great deal of compassionate persuasion by Joseph, Joel agreed to go and we all breathed a deep sigh of relief.

Joseph helped me get into the boat and then started poling it upriver while the boys, wading in the shallow water at the stern, helped maneuver the boat over the rocky riverbed. They took it a short distance up to the foot of a dam at a small lake and there we unloaded our supplies. Joseph helped the boys pull the boat overland to the lake and then walked back to the mouth of the river, where the Mountie was waiting to take him back to Hopedale. Alone with the boys, I suddenly realized the seriousness of my responsibilities. Our camp was very basic. The boys at least had a fairly large tent. I had a small tent and a two-burner Primus stove and all the food we would need.

The next morning, when salmon began coming into the river with a rising tide, I decided to fish a pool at the foot of a natural dam of rocks and boulders. I could see no way to reach the pool from the rock-piled banks, so I advised the boys to fish from the boat in the lake and cast a fly down to the pool at the foot of the dam. Joel had a long bamboo pole with about ten feet of line tied to the tip, on which I tied a heavy leader, one used for tarpon in saltwater. I tied a wet fly onto it, the largest salmon fly I could find in my tackle box. The boat was on the shore of the lake and Jona rowed it out to the top of the dam, which was six or seven feet high, and anchored it where Joel could stand in the boat while fishing.

In the meantime, I had managed to crawl over boulders along the bank of the river and was fishing the tail of the pool when I heard shouts from the boys. Joel had hooked a huge salmon at the bottom of the dam. Tide water had raised the water level several feet and half of his fishing pole had been pulled beneath the surface!

It was his first experience with fly fishing, his first salmon; but his chances of landing this salmon were slim. There was no reel on his pole. I began yelling instructions. "Don't pull, try to hold onto it without pulling," I shouted. Clutching the pole, he began heaving it up and down. Again, I yelled at him, "Stop pulling, that won't help!" But when he stopped, the heavy salmon dragged the rest of the pole beneath the surface. Joel started heaving again, and again I yelled, "Stop pulling—let the salmon fight the current until it gets tired." Joel, beyond hearing a word I said, shoved the pole into Jona's hands, grabbed the line and with it tried to lift the heavy fish up to the top of the dam. Soon realizing this was impossible, he grabbed the rod, jumped into the boat and told Jona to row like hell. Finally, when the water was only a few feet from the top of the dam, after much pulling and rowing, they managed to get the salmon up to the top, but then a sharp rock cut the leader and the salmon fell back into the river.

A deadly sorrow-laden silence followed. After a moment, Joel began beating the lake with his pole and sobbing. Again and again, he sobbed that he had caught a great one and lost it. His reaction surprised me. I had never seen such an outburst of emotion from an Inuit.

He forgot about the salmon when I hooked into a grilse in the pool below the dam. He and Jona rushed down to net it. They had never netted a fish and were extremely excited. Joel held the net in the water as I instructed and when the grilse tired, I guided it up to the net, but when Joel scooped up the net the grilse teetered on the rim and flopped back into the water. Quickly, I guided it back to him, and when the grilse eluded the net Joel grabbed the line and, in a lunge that almost swept him off his feet, he scooped up the grilse, stumbled to shore, pulled it out of the net, embraced it tightly, carried it over to our camp stove and dumped it on the ground. Indeed, it was extremely important we get that grilse for our dinner—we were very hungry for fresh protein.

Joel didn't hook a salmon again, but he never stopped fishing; and he fished with the patience of a seasoned angler. He had no interest in anything else. Jona, on the other hand, with the finesse of a diplomat, persuaded Joel to help with camp chores such as carrying buckets of water from the lake to our camp. Joel seemed to feel no resentment toward Jona for being the leader and they did not quarrel once on our trip.

One day, while I was sitting on the folding canvas chair beside a fallen log a ptarmigan—a kind of grouse—was walking with two tiny chicks along the log and passed within inches of me as though I was nothing more than a big rock. Joel came running in from the other side of our damp, holding his gun. I jumped up, yelling at him not to shoot. Stunned, he dropped the gun. Looking unimaginably sad, he did not protest or complain, he simply stood them, staring at the ground. The Inuit never yelled at or scolded their children. If they did something wrong, they showed them the right way to do it. Joel's reaction upset me. I knew he had experienced pangs of hunger many times. "If you shoot the bird," I explained, "her chicks won't be able to survive."

Later, while I was on the river fishing, I heard a gunshot, smiled, and forgot about the chicks. I caught all the trout we could eat. Rev.

Grubb had sent us to Little River because Joseph had told him that a good run of salmon was migrating upriver at that time, but fishing for them was challenging. It could have been fabulous had I been with a guide who knew where to take me so I could wade in the river or fish from a boat. I never caught a really large salmon, such as the one Joel hooked, but I had wonderful fishing for Brook trout in that river between the lakes, both within walking distance. We called the upper lake (in which the salmon spawned) Big Lake, and the lower one Little Lake.

The boys drank gallons of chocolate milk—made with powdered milk—and lemonade made with dehydrated lemon juice. Rev. Grubb claimed it was good for them because they needed more calcium in their diet and as the water in Hopedale came primarily from melted snow, it lacked minerals. I cooked the fish and lots of dehydrated vegetables on the Coleman gas stove, and my boys consumed everything I cooked, plus a half-gallon can of marmalade during our first week in camp.

One morning I went fishing and returned to camp late in the day. Jona was there waiting for me alone and I sensed something was wrong. Joel was in their tent because he didn't have any pants. Having been down at the bay fishing at the bay of the river, Joel had taken off his pants, left them on shore, and was wading out to where he could reach salmon as they entered the river. The tide came up and carried his one and only pair of pants out to sea. I was furious, but more frightened than angry. The boys could not swim. The water in the north was too cold for them to learn and if the tide had been strong enough to knock Joel off his feel, that would have been the end of him. "He has only those pants," Jona told me. Well, I wasn't going to give him mine. "He'll have to make do with his long underwear," I countered. Jona looked worried. "No long underwear." I groaned.

Finally, Jona worked up enough courage to tell me that their precious bottle of fly-dope was in Joel's pants pocket. This created a very serious problem. The black flies and mosquitoes in the Labrador woods have been known to drive a person crazy. I reminded Jona that

I had instructed them not to remove the fly-dope from their tent, that we were running low. "I know." Frowning, I insisted that I wasn't going to give them anymore. "I know . . . I'm sorry." How could I stay angry? His honesty and humility completely disarmed me. I relented and gave them my extra bottle of fly repellent and Joel my extra slacks.

Another day, Jona brought Joel to me and told him to show me his finger. The whole finger was black and purple. He had a wound with a sack of pus the size of a dime. A fish hook had gotten caught and torn his finger. I knew at once that I had to lance the finger. It would be almost a week before I could get him to Rev. Grubb. Terrified, I went for my Red Cross kit. After reading the directions for lancing, I sterilized the razor blade, explained each move to Joel and lanced the finger. But the first time I lacked the courage to cut deep enough so I had to do it again, and that time pus spurted in all directions. Joel winced when I cut the second time, but he held his hand still during the entire fumbling operation on what must have been a painfully sore finger. He was the most stoic, brave boy I'd ever known, I told him, and bandaged the finger.

Yes, those boys were careless. They were adolescent boys. Many times, I found Joel's bamboo pole, the only one they had, lying on the riverbank; and once I rescued it from the lake. More than once I found his only sweater on the trail near the river. They had no idea of the value of possessions, little concern for comfort, and rarely if ever planned ahead. And yet, they appeared to be two of the most contented and kind teenagers I had ever known.

Finally, I found it easier to adapt to their way of life than to try and make them adapt to mine. Settling down into a natural, peaceful routine, I ate when hungry, slept soundly, fished when I was in the mood, and stopped scolding. I forgot all the past woes and lived for the moment—very pleasant moments. Generally, the boys found what they lost, or managed without it. Why, I asked myself, had it taken such a long time to learn what Father had tried so long ago to teach me, the meaning of true contentment and how to live with gratitude for the small moments of life.

Jona and Joel.

One evening I returned late to camp. The fish had ignored my flies and I was in no mood to cook or live for the moment. The boys had gone to bed and our supplies were low. The only food I could find that required no preparation was a can of beets. So I sat on the canvas chair and ate cold beets from the can. At that moment, I was definitely not content. Why, oh why did I insist on such crazy adventures!? For that I blamed my pioneering ancestors, from whom I had inherited the spirit of adventure.

The next morning the sun was shining and so were my spirits. Glancing at my watch, I noticed that I had neglected to wind it. I had no way of knowing the right time and could not even remember if it was Monday or Wednesday. What a relief not to have to worry about time! Later that morning in a contemplative mood, I was fishing Little River when my thoughts wandered back to fishing with my father in the Sierras.

I glanced over at my trout net, which was lying on a boulder by the riverbank. It had belonged to Jack, and for a moment a trace of sadness filled my thoughts, but I found it difficult to concentrate on him. Even his profile seemed dim. In a moment of remorse, I tried visualizing each feature. But why, I asked myself, should I?

I shall never forget him, but I can and must live without needing him. At last, I was beginning to realize that the rosy shell in which I had escaped after John's death was no longer rosy, but rather dull and lonely. Would I ever learn? Probably not. When there is nothing more to learn, there is nothing to live for, I told myself cheerfully, recalling the passage I had read somewhere that learning is wisdom, and in the search for wisdom lies the spirit of adventure and a vital interest in living.

CHAPTER EIGHTEEN

Rivers and Lakes, the Laurentian Club, Canada

Rivers flow not past,but through us; tingling, vibrating, exciting every cell and fiber in our bodies, making them sing and glide.

—John Muir

One evening during the summer of 1956 Watson Wyckoff, a friend from our days in Connecticut, came to my apartment in New York and told me in one breath that he was on his way to Canada to go trout fishing, that he would be staying at the Laurentian Club, and that he had to leave at once because he had a date to meet a guide at ten o'clock the next morning. And in the next breath, Watson asked if I would go with him.

The Laurentian Club was not far from Three Rivers, a small town in Québec. Chuckling over the idea that he was even crazier than I was, I declined the invitation. But after an hour of listening to his pleading and the description of the trout fishing there, I was sitting in Watson's car and we were on our way to Canada.

During that exhausting all-night drive, Watson relayed the early history of the Laurentian Club. It was formed around 1900, when American fly fishers were discovering wonderful trout fishing in their own country and in Canada. A group of fly fishers from New York negotiated a lease with the Québec government for access to a vast territory of lakes and streams in the Laurentian wilderness between Montréal and Québec City in the vicinity of the St. Maurice River.

The territory of the Laurentian Club was much larger than that of the Parmachenee Club, and the Laurentian Club had built lodges at a few of the best lakes and employed a staff in the lodges which had all the comforts of home. It also employed caretakers, river guardians, and guides. They were Indian—Native American, rather—guides from the Algonquin tribe that had been driven out of the United States by white settlers, and traveled up the Connecticut River by canoe to Canada and across to the Laurentians where they settled near the St. Maurice River.

These Native Americans were fantastic guides—the best—and the fishing was superb in both the lakes and streams that connected the lakes. Now, very few of the Laurentian Club's charter members were alive and there were about twenty new members, but the fishing wasn't what it used to be and the average member came no more than once a year. Watson warned me not to expect too much since the upkeep was exorbitant and the club had cut expenses quite dramatically. There were only a couple of caretakers now and no cooks. We would have to do our own cooking and housework.

Watson's father had been a member of the original Laurentian Club and Watson became a member at his father's death. Watson dreaded the possibility of the Québec Government terminating the lease. That did happen seven years later, as it should have. It did not make sense for only twenty individuals to retain all that fishing for themselves. In the meantime, Watson and I enjoyed some marvelous fishing there, as well as each other's company.

In 1960 Watson and I were married. Although in the end, a decade later, I was not right for Watson and he was not right for me and we eventually drifted apart, everything was more than right for us when we were together at Lake Hauteur, at the highest altitude in the Laurentian Club territory. We lived in Montréal in those days and drove to Hauteur every weekend and holiday we could. Almost no one else fished Lake Hauteur or even the streams and lakes nearby. Getting there was too difficult for poachers, and for club members, too. There were almost no roads throughout the Laurentian territory and no motorboats, so everyone traveled by canoe—or not at all. Peace and quiet reigned and traveling to Lake Hauteur at any time of year rewarded us with a complete escape from civilization's increasing pace of life with its stresses and strains.

The trail up to Lake Hauteur was tough and we had to carry in all of our supplies, so we flew there in a bush plane on pontoons that could land on water or ice. Once there, we reveled in the quiet beauty of the wintertime, when everything was covered in layers of sparkling, untouched snow. We loved our trips over the trees in the bush plane.

Once, while we were in the air after a rain, the plane flew into the arch of a rainbow, with another rainbow below us, and the rainbows seemed to stay with us. It was a magical experience of Nature's beauty and rather than spoil the mystical feeling, I shut out the pilot's voice when he explained the science behind that amazing phenomenon. The rainbow vanished when a cloud blocked the sun and the plane dropped down on the waters of Lake Hauteur. But the fantastical illusion of the rainbows guiding and protecting us enhanced the beauty of the lake and pines, and stayed with me forever.

There was no lodge at Lake Hauteur, but there was an old loggers' cabin that Watson restored. He installed a large picture window that overlooked the lake and surrounding landscape. We loved it there, completely isolated from the outside world and deeply connected to the land and its history. The area was part of Canada's Laurentian Plateau, known today as the Canadian Shield. It is more than two billion years old and contains the Earth's greatest area of exposed Archean rock. During the Pleistocene era, sheets of continental ice dug into the land's surface and scooped out thousands of lake basins, carrying away a great amount of the region's soil.[20]

---

20. The Canadian Shield, also called the Laurentian Plateau, or Bouclier Canadien (French), is a vast geological shield covered by a thin layer of soil that forms the nucleus of the North American or Laurentia craton. It is an area mostly composed of igneous rock which relates to its long volcanic history. It has a deep, common, joined bedrock region in eastern and central Canada and stretches north from the Great Lakes to the Arctic Ocean, covering over half of Canada. It also extends South into the northern reaches of the United States. Human population is sparse, and industrial development is minimal, while mining is very prevalent.

Our camp was built on a huge flat boulder at the edge of the lake, beside a dam at the outlet. During our first weekend, Watson cleaned out the clutter of debris around the old dam, only to have it all back in place a week later when we returned to camp. The beavers had replaced the debris, which to them, of course, did not seem like debris at all. These were very important sticks and logs they had instinctively masoned together with mud in an ingenious job of engineering and construction. Each evening a beaver sentinel came down the dam to inspect it and be sure the silly creatures staying in the cabin had not ruined the dam again.

Once the dam was repaired by the beavers, the water in the lake rose by a foot. I learned this from a wise Native American guide and friend, Ralph, who was also a professional piano tuner. He spoke of the beavers with a note of tenderness as he paddled us up to the foot of another beaver dam at the opposite end of the lake. In order to keep the lake at a level suitable to their needs, the beavers raised or lowered the water level by opening or closing a trapdoor they made under the dam. If the lake was too high, it would flood their houses, and if it was too low, if would leave them high and dry with the entrance exposed.

Lake Hauteur was long and narrow, large enough to accommodate three beaver houses, and each beaver house included its own nursery and toilet room. Having watched a fascinating documentary that took the viewer inside a beaver home with a nursery, a raised platform in the main room, and a separate entrance to the toilet room at the back, I asked Ralph how a photographer could get a camera view in a beaver house. But our conversation was interrupted by a large beaver that was circling our canoe and slapping the water furiously with his flat tail. I had planned to fish there, but Ralph said there was no use fishing there now that the beaver had notified any trout in the vicinity of our presence.

The stream flowing over the dam was coming from Parkman Lake, another spot Watson and I liked for the fishing. We anchored our canoe about twenty feet back from the dam. It seemed as if every large trout in the lake came down to the dam in the evening to feed on drifting insects, worms, larvae, minnows and anything edible. In June and July, the supply seemed endless. Parkman was another lake the poachers found too difficult to get to and almost nobody from the Club fished there, so we had that entire lake to ourselves as well.

One clear morning, Watson took me to a lake filled with thousands of Brook trout averaging no more than eight-to-nine inches in length. The lake didn't produce enough underwater vegetation or larvae to feed that many trout, Watson thought. We caught a small trout on almost every cast and released them all. Of course, it would have been better for the trout population in that lake if we had saved them for the frying pan, but we never killed more trout than we could eat. What had happened in the lake was a good example of what can happen when trout populations become too prolific. And human populations, too.

All the trout in the area were Brook trout—gorgeous, plump, and colorful, adorned with olive green backs and golden sides studded in ruby-red dots, with creamy bellies and touches of pink and red around the anal fins. In the autumn, near the spawning period, the males were even more colorful.

Another day, each of us with a guide and canoe, Watson and I decided to go down to Wessoneau, the main lake and lodge of the Laurentian Club. When we portaged between lakes, the guides carried the canoes on their heads and shoulders, the Native American way. It was not an easy trip for them, although they never complained. Brush and fallen logs covered the old trail, so late that afternoon when we came to a lake where there was a comfortable camp with a caretaker, Watson suggested we stop there for the night.

The guardian was delighted. It had been days if not weeks since he had seen another human being. At sundown, he took us fishing, without the guides. He placed Watson on the bank at the top of a man-made dam and me on the other side. We would have good fishing there, he told us, because each evening the trout came down to the dam to feed on all the drifting insects and worms before the current carried them over the dam.

We could see dozens of trout in the clear water behind the dam. Generally, the club members fished with streamer flies, and Watson began fishing with one; but the trout ignored it, so I decided to fish with a dry fly, a Spider. Every time I skated it across the water, splashing trout exploded over the surface. It was the first time the guardian had seen what a dry fly could do to his trout. He stood beside me, speechless and wide-eyed.

Almost at once, I hooked a trout and the camp guardian netted it. Examining the fly, he advised Watson to change to a dry fly and then took me by the arm down a steep slope to the foot of the dam. There, the fish coming up from the lake to feed on whatever was being washed over the dam were large brook trout. But they spurned my dry fly. They wanted something more meaty, like a minnow, so I changed my fly to a Streamer and caught large trout until I was ashamed of myself and quit fishing, despite the groans of the hungry guardian who said he needed fish to salt down for winter.

The next evening, he paddled down to where a brook flowed into the lake. Anchoring the canoe a bit out of the mouth of the brook, he told me to cast my dry fly as far upstream as possible and let it float down to the lake. All the big trout in the lake would be there. They came every evening to feed on the minnows that were there to feast on the insects and larvae being washed into the lake by the brook.

I followed his instructions, casting a large Spider a good distance upstream, with slack at the end of the line to avoid drag on the fly. While I was watching it bounce down the current, a big sleek round head popped up and, with its nose almost touching the fluffy fly, followed the Spider downstream. I froze. What on earth was that head? The guardian laughed and said, "It's only an otter." Luckily, it didn't touch the fly. If it had, I would have lost both the fly and fishing line, and the otter would have had a very sore mouth. We caught no fish that evening because the trout had sense enough to stay far away from the otter. However, since the camp guardian had not invited Watson to fish with us, he had gone back to our fishing spot from the previous evening. As a result, Watson arrived back at camp with enough trout for supper—for the five of us.

The following morning, we started down to Wessoneau Lake and arrived at the lodge late in the day. The place was empty. We found all that luxurious space without inhabitants depressing and the next morning we decided to return to Hauteur.

The wildlife in the Laurentian Club territory was as exciting as the fishing. There was a day on Lake Hauteur when Watson and I were in our canoe paddling, and passed a baby moose, standing alone and staring curiously from the shore of a small island. Watson stopped a few feet away and I tried to photograph the adorable creature. There is something about the long, funny face of a moose that is very appealing; but before I could get the camera in focus, the mother rushed out of the bushes and with her nose pushed the calf back into the brush and out of harm's way.

We waited in the canoe and watched as they reappeared on the shore a short distance above us. The mother moose was trying, with come-hither grunts, to persuade her precious baby to follow her into the lake; but the young one refused to budge and stood at the shore whimpering. It had probably just been born and was afraid of the water. Finally, the mother gave up, hid her calf once again in the brush, and then waded into the lake and began swimming toward the opposite shore. She kept looking back at us and Watson remarked that she was trying to get us to follow her and forget about her calf. I imagined how worried she must be so we paddled in the opposite direction to leave the mother and her calf in peace. The minute we turned away, she started her swim back home to her little island.

Another day, when Watson and I were paddling back to camp, we neared the shore by our cabin and were surprised to see a beautiful— and large—black bear. He, or she, was sitting on the shore between our cabin and the dam. The bear waited for us to get out of our canoe and then ambled off down the trail in the direction of Bode Lake.

Watson also kept a canoe at Bode Lake, just down the hill from Hauteur. One evening when we were there in the canoe, we came upon a large cow and bull moose. Watson said the bull had the largest rack of antlers he had ever seen. Standing in shallow water on a piece of ground jutting into the lake, the cow moose was busy nibbling water lily pads. Nudging her tenderly, her mate tried to get her to stop eating and pay attention. Never have I heard such affection grunts from any animal, including man, as that great moose used to get his ladylove's attention.

We were only a few feet away from the moose pair and they seemed to have no interest in us, nor did they show any signs of fear. We sat quietly in our canoe, observing, until the cow moose stopped eating, lifted her head and followed him as he lowered his antlers and pushed aside a large swath of brush and small trees as easily as if they were blades of grass. Sauntering slowly, they disappeared into the thick brush. I tried to take a photograph of them, but the excitement made my hands shake and since I am not a good photographer, the effort failed.

Each morning at Lake Hauteur, the repetitive call of a loon's liquid trills in treble pitch, sounding like hysterical laughter, woke me up smiling. And outside the cabin a friendly chipmunk talked to me in a throaty clucking voice, or scolded me with a rapid raspy chirping. There was an osprey, too. It had built a nest at the crest of a tall dead pine and my spirits soared with the osprey as I watched that rare bird in graceful flight—soaring and gliding high in the cloudless sky.

One day, Watson had to go back to Montréal and I stayed at Hauteur alone with a young Native American guide. That night, I was sound asleep when the door flew open and in one leap through the doorway, the guide landed in the middle of the cabin. A bear had tried to get into his cabin, he explained, trembling from head to foot.

I laughed and accused him of having a wild imagination. He spent the rest of the night sleeping on the floor in my cabin and the next morning I found him outside sitting on the front steps with Watson's rifle in his lap. When he saw me, he stood up and gestured for me to follow him. We walked to his cabin where he pointed to the front door. It was covered with deep grooves, newly made by bear claws. I apologized for having laughed at him and he stayed close to me, gun in hand, until Watson's return a week later.

There was a wolf at Lake Hauteur, too, but she was too smart to let me see her. I knew she was there because I'd seen her tracks in the snow. There was also a playful otter. One warm summer's day he came to the big boulder in the water outside of our cabin, not to fish but to play. I watched him from the cabin window. Using the smooth slant in the boulder as a slide, the happy creature had a wonderful time sliding down the boulder into the water, again and again and again. Watson, however, was not aware of the otter. He had been fishing and returned with four trout for our dinner. He put them on the wharf, came into the cabin for a knife, and when he returned a minute later, the trout were gone. Watson was furious with those otters and I had a good laugh.

Some of the best fishing at the Laurentian Club took place in the spring after the ice on the lake had melted and the trout were ravenous after a winter of fasting. Watson and everyone else fished with streamers, but when I discovered mayflies around the streams, I fished the streams with nymphs or dry flies and had great fun.

There was so much to enjoy at Hauteur. Even the storms were exciting, as long as we were in our cozy cabin, of course. When a nor'wester clashed with a sou'easter, the clouds rumbled and thundered for three days until the nor'wester chased away the sou'easter and the skies cleared.

One evening inside the cabin I spent half the night awake, watching a mayfly dun as it struggled to get out of its case of skin. It never succeeded. Overwhelmed by empathy for the tiny mayfly, I woke up Watson to tell him what had happened. He said I was silly and that we had more important problems to worry out than an incomplete metamorphosis. He was right. Over the radio they announced that Québec had decided to terminate the Laurentian Club's lease and open the fishing and hunting to the public.

We were terribly disappointed, but hardly surprised. Now, our magical wonderland was no longer ours to enjoy. I never returned to Hauteur and not long ago it saddened me to hear from a Canadian member of the Club that there was almost fishing or hunting left in the area, and that he had stopped going there.

After the Canadian Government opened the land up to the pub-lic, no one paid any attention to the law of limits and the Government did not enforce the laws, while poachers took out sacks full of trout on any given day. While I do not blame the Québec Government for opening the Laurentian Club territory to the public, I do blame them for the lack of proper management and enforcement. Such a conservation loss!

CHAPTER NINETEEN

Matane River, Gaspé

"One thing becomes clearer as one gets older and one's fishing experience increases, and that is the paramount importance of one's fishing companions."

—John Ashley-Cooper

In the summer of 1957, I traveled to the Matane River noted in Canada for its large salmon. Beginning its journey at the foot of the Laurentian Mountains, beautifully sculpted and rounded by time and Ice Age glaciers, the Matane is a gentle, grand salmon river that wanders through a lovely Gaspé Valley and finally flows into the south shore of the great St. Lawrence River. Having heard that the Matane was known for its large salmon, I arrived with high hopes.

I found the river easy to fish. Everybody's favorite pool was set near the mouth of the river at the foot of falls the salmon found simple to surmount, and every salmon entering the river stopped in that pool before jumping over the falls. Unfortunately, I never had a chance to fish there and over the years the village of Matane developed around the pool. Despite a law and sign reading "Fly Fishing Only," the pool was seriously degraded as a result of illegal fishing by poachers and logjams.

But then the late Percy Nobbs (1875–1964), a Canadian who probably knew the Matane better than anyone, managed to persuade the Québec government to close the river and launch a program to rebuild the salmon population which he said had showed signs of becoming extinct as early as 1932. The program proved successful and the river was opened once again to fly fishers the year I was there. I also learned that Nobbs, born in Scotland, became a successful Montréal architect and helped bring the arts and crafts movement to Canada. He was also a respected writer and artist and wrote a book in 1934, *Salmon Tactics*, as well as a paper published in 1948, entitled "The Critical Condition of the Atlantic Salmon Industry in Québec." Among his other books was one on design and one on fencing of all things—his passion for fencing propelled him into the London Olympics of 1908, for which he won a silver medal! Nobbs founded the Atlantic Salmon Federation and in 1952, (the year Jack died), he received the Outdoor Life Conservation Award.

When I fished the Matane, I stayed in a small inn near the river called the Metropole that consisted of a line of rustic cabins set behind an old farmhouse; but I was given a room with the family in the main house. My hopes for great fishing were dashed when I learned that every morning at dawn before any of the proprietor's paying guests was out of bed, he sneaked down to the river to check the pool behind his cabins. If he saw a salmon, he fished it out with a metal spinning lure. Needless to say, his guests seldom caught a salmon in that pool.

I learned from my host that a logjam just above the dam at the mouth of the river was blocking salmon from making their way upriver. Nonetheless, I enjoyed my time fishing the Matane and being far away from the heat and hassle of life in New York City, where Watson and I were living at the time (1959). I did not fish every day, however. I had my typewriter with me as it was an ideal environment for writing. And I enjoyed seeing old friends who turned up at the Metropole. One of them was Wes Jordan[21] who traveled to visit and deliver one of his personal rods, a 6'6" impregnated salmon rod, for which I gave him a big hug.

---

21. Wes Jordan was one of the most innovative men to ever work as a rod maker. His influence is still felt today. Throughout his more than fifty year career, Jordan worked at the Cross Rod Company, South Bend Bait Company, & Orvis. In this article we'll look at Jordan's work at the Cross Rod Company. Wes Jordan was born May 13, 1894 in Lynn, Massachusetts. Please see flyrods.weebly.com/1/post/2012/04/wes-jordan-the-cross-rod-co.html. for more information.

A man by the name of Stanley Bogdan[22] arrived with Wes that day. After Wes introduced him to me, he asked Stan to show me the reel he had made. It had a two-to-one ratio and I was astonished when Wes said Stan had never caught a salmon.

Wes and Stan were camping upriver, and toward the end of the week they came to see me while Dr. Fredette was at the Metropole. Dr. Fredette, a young man and ardent local fly fisher, had come to take me fishing. Having grown up in Matane, he was as concerned about the condition of the river as he was about his patients' ailments, and he knew more than any other fisher where and when salmon could be found in certain pools. He offered to take me to a pool in which I knew were salmon. When Wes and Stan appeared, I introduced them and told Dr. Fredette that Stan had never caught a salmon and asked if he would take Stan fishing instead of me. He agreed.

In the end Wes and I went along as well and Dr. Fredette, acting as guide, stationed Stan in the best but most difficult place to cast. A rock wall at his back interfered with the backcast, but Stan, who had mastered fly fishing for trout at an early age, had no trouble. When he hooked into a large salmon, his very first, he played it quietly, expertly, with the dignity Salmo Salar deserves. His eyes and face expressed pure joy beneath the cool demeanor, and thanks to Dr. Fredette's expert guidance, Stan caught his first salmon! Now the custom-made Bogdan reels are treasured by salmon fishers and to this day Stan delights in calling me Gilly.

Another day, I went alone to a fascinating pool where the river rushing into a sheer bank of granite forced the current to make a right-

---

22. Stan built reels in New Hampshire for seventy years, crafting reels by hand to impeccable standards on a one hundred-thirty-year-old Flather lathe and more recently a fifty-year-old Van Norman milling machine. With son Stephen as his partner, Stan constructed the most distinguished and desirable reels for rivers throughout the range of the King of Fish. Stanley Edward Bogdan died in his hometown of Nashua, New Hampshire, on March 27, 2011, at the remarkable age of ninety-two years young. His career is a monument in a regal history of salmon and trout reels with manufacturing roots in the German-American tradition of Edward Vom Hofe and Otto Zwarg. Please see /olsonreels.com/news/chasing-silver-article.html. for more information.

angle turn. Only one fisherman was there when I arrived. Fishing from the shore with a streamer fly, he rolled a salmon beside a boulder in the middle of the current, just below the turn. Standing above the boulder, he cast again, sending the streamer down to the boulder. That time the salmon ignored it.

Realizing that the salmon was not rising to the streamer but was coming up at the side of the boulder as a trout rises when feeding on mayflies, I sat up and watched more intently. Finally, I concluded that since there were no flies in the air or on the water. The old salmon simply felt playful and was rising as it had in its parr days when feeding on flies.

I yearned to wade into the river and fish for it with a dry fly, but my concern about the ethics of good sportsmanship stifled that urge and I remained in my place, sitting on the bank—until finally, the discouraged fisherman trudged out of the river. It took only a second for me to realize my good luck. "Would you mind if I try for that salmon?" I asked. "Well, I'm sure it's hopeless, but go right ahead." He got into his car and drove away.

Standing in the river below the salmon, I cast a dry fly, a large White Wulff, well above the submerged boulder, and I cast a bit of slack in the line so that the leader fell on the water in a curve (good!). As the White Wulff approached the side of the boulder, the salmon rose for it just like a trout! I waited until it turned in a swirl and then struck, lifting the rod to set the hook.

The great salmon displayed the most impressive performance I had ever seen, leaping over and over. Then, bearing down, it swam slowly upriver and stopped in deep water at the foot of the shear granite wall. I tried every trick I knew to get the stubborn salmon to move, but failed. Gradually, when my hand felt that alarming vibration from the taut line, I knew that smart salmon was sawing the nylon leader on a sharp edge of granite beneath the surface. Then minutes later the rod snapped back into place. I retrieved the line and inspected the leader. The salmon had escaped with my fly and left nothing but the frayed ends of the leader.

Another day, a fisherman whose name I cannot recall stopped at the Metropole and offered to take me to a pool he said was full of salmon. Deeply touched by his generosity, I accepted at once, although I must admit I did not believe any pool in the Matane was full of salmon since the logjam was still blocking fish near the mouth of the river.

My new friend drove us to the river in his car and to show me the "hot spots" he fished down the current ahead of me. I waded a good distance behind him and we both fished with wet flies, cast them down the entire run several times with no success. Expressing disappointment, my fishing companion crossed over to the other side of the river to try his luck from there.

The water was too deep for me to wade across, and although I felt sure there were no salmon in the run, I decided to experiment. In my box of salmon dry flies, I had a large Spider, one Jack had tied especially for salmon fishing. I greased it, tied it to the leader, waded back into the river and began fishing down and across the current. Suddenly, as the fluffy fly skated across the surface, the water exploded salmon. Taken aback, I yanked the fly away from them.

There must have been a half-dozen salmon in that spot! Backing up a bit, I blew on the fly to dry it, waited awhile to rest the pool, and began fishing. Again, a shocking display of salmon pyrotechnics almost scared me out of my wits and made me yank the fly away too soon.

My companion on the other side of the river fished for the salmon, too, but they were interested only in the Spider. Finally, I calmed down and hooked one, the sole large salmon in the bunch. Feeling the hook, it leapt into the air, gave my rod a hard jerk, fell back into the water and quickly swam toward the spawning beds. I reeled in the line, the fly was still there, but the heavy salmon had ruined it by straightening out the bend in the very small hook.

My friend waded back across the river and fished down the run with a wet fly. I always took two salmon rods, one with a weight-forward line and one with a floating tip for dry fly fishing, but the salmon had no interest in anything but the Spider. Since I had no more

Spiders, I went back to the Metropole with an empty creel but plenty of cherished memories after my day of fun.

At the Matane that summer, I landed only a few salmon. It was September before a heavy rain dislodged the logjam. Unfortunately, very few salmon in the early run reached the spawning beds. After Percy Nobbs died, the river never had the chance it needed to recover from the continued onslaught of ruthless poachers, commercial fishers and poor river management. I felt no desire to return to such a sad river.

Happily, today the local fishermen are working hard to restore the Matane.

CHAPTER TWENTY
Petite Cascapédia, Québec

The solution to any problem—work, love, money, whatever—is to go fishing, and the worse the problem, the longer
the trip should be.

—John Gierach

A wonderfully mystical atmosphere surrounds rivers that attract
Salmo Salar. In a dreamy mood while en route to Petite Cascapédia,
I was driving my Chevy station wagon around the Gaspe Peninsula,
along the Atlantic, and in my mind I was fishing in a beautiful fairyland river bubbling with salmon.

Arriving late in the afternoon at the Petite Cascapédia, a real
fairyland river, I registered at Camp Melacon, a lodge that used to
belong to a private club of Canadians and was now owned by the
Québec government. The Government had terminated the lease and
opened the river to the public, and I was delighted. In the dining room
that evening, the cook served poached salmon smothered in a smooth
Bearnaise sauce; and later that night, in a comfortable bedroom overlooking the Petite Cascapédia, the river's lapping, like a quiet chuckle,
lulled me into another world of dreams.

In the morning the manager, Steve McWirdor, introduced me to
Dan, an elderly French Canadian—a scrawny, nervous man designated
to guide me that week. It quickly became obvious that he wanted no
part of guiding a woman, particularly an American woman traveling

alone, and I sensed he was hoping to guide the other fisher in camp, an important gentleman from Montréal.

There were only two fishers in camp. It is a small salmon river and already fishers were complaining of a severe drop in the salmon population. The gentleman from Montréal and his guide, Nap, would fish the upper part of the river, while Dan and I would go to the lower half, and the division would be reversed each day, Steve told us.

The first day I fished all day long, caught nothing until sundown, and then hooked into a large salmon just as Nap and his fisherman entered the pool on their way back to camp. Nap anchored his canoe behind me until the big salmon tired, and then when he saw it was in the net, Nap started downriver again. As he paddled past us, Dan asked him if he'd had any luck. Nap shook his head and said he had not caught a fish, not even a Sea trout. Dan, brimming with smug joy, patted me on the back, pulled up the anchor and followed them down to camp with the big salmon lying safely at his feet in the canoe. From that moment on, I belonged to Daniel Leblanc, and woe to any guide there who might try to take me away from him!

I would have liked to hear Dan's report about "his" salmon in the guides' camp that night. The Canadian guides—some of the best in the world—had become a source of amusement to me. It was the custom for them to return to the guides' camp after a day of fishing and boast to each other about the fish they had caught, as though the fishers had nothing to do with the catching.

Of course, we salmon fishers like to boast about the fish we catch as though we did it all by ourselves, and we are notorious for stretching the size of each fish beyond all rhyme or reason; but experienced fishers know that a good guide is just as important to success as the fisher. Also, we know that being with an inexperienced guide can end in calamity, and the guides know that their day with a fisher can be enough to drive anyone crazy.

No more salmon were caught at the Petite Cascapédia that week, but the poor fishing that year (1962) failed to discourage me from returning the following year. Dan greeted me when I arrived at Camp

Melancon, asked me to be ready to go fishing the next morning at eight and was gone before I had a chance to say that eight was too early for me.

The next morning in the dining room, Steve McWirdor greeted me with the news that a really big one had entered the river the night before and Dan was going after it with a vengeance. So, that was it! No wonder he was too preoccupied to notice my existence when I had passed by him on the way to the dining room.

I enjoyed a leisurely breakfast, and when I went outside Dan was there, pacing up and down beside the truck, obviously annoyed, so I hurried over to him. Each morning a truck took the fisher, guide, and canoe upriver. Dan had assembled my rod, put it and my fishing bag inside. When he finally got me into the front seat by the driver, off we went. The driver took us a couple of miles upriver. Dan helped him unload the canoe and then almost upset it—and me—as he pushed us away from the shore and jumped into the stern. Finally, he settled down and began paddling downriver. Not once did he mention what he was going after "with a vengeance." Instead, he began berating the government for giving him such a small net—he was holding a long-handled salmon net, no more than twenty inches in diameter.

Dan worked for the Club and it seemed he was unhappy about the change in management. It occurred to me as he paddled furiously that the main reason for his great hurry was the fear that Nap might sneak down to the big salmon ahead of him.

Nap was the most popular guide at the Petite Cascapédia. He loved "his" river and knew every inch of the riverbed. He had grown up nearby and knew just when and in which pool salmon were inclined to stop overnight; and he knew whenever a salmon entered the mouth of the river, which empties into the Bay of Chaleur, where it was easy to see fish through the clear, shallow water.

This time, Nap was guiding the well-known French Canadian from Québec City. In no mood to get involved in Dan's problems or to let him spoil my day, I sat back in the canoe and gave my entire attention to the wonderful river. The clear, pale green water was covered with patches of sunlight, magnifying the magical riverbed covered in colorful pebbles and gleaming sand. Flanked by underwater ledges, shelves of frosty-green shale, the river provided perfect places for fish to hide and me to cast my fly.

But Dan decided to paddle right through that pool, continuing downriver. My respite from his distractions came to an end when he dropped anchor at the head of a rapid. The Petite Cascapédia, a frisky little river, has numerous wild rapids and keeping a canoe upright in the rapids was tricky. A master of vituperative swearing, Dan expressed his outrage—*en français*—because the club had always hired two guides to get a canoe safely through the rapids, but the government, now in charge, had hired only one.

I tried to pretend I was alone, but Dan was anxious for me to get to work and insisted that I start to fish. He had anchored the canoe at the head of a rapid. Reluctantly, I stood up in the canoe (a sturdy Gaspé craft) and surveyed the pool that had been formed by the long, wide, rapid rushing over a bed of gravel into a granite bank. There, making an abrupt right-angle turn, the river settled into a beautiful salmon pool with a lively energizing brook entering from the left. At once I recognized the potential for hooking a big salmon.

Driven by a sudden spurt of inspiration, I stood up, stripped out line and began fishing. I cast out a wet fly on each side of the canoe, lengthened the line a bit after each cast, fished down to the bend in the river and caught nothing. Dan told me to sit down so he could move the canoe downriver. He dropped the anchor a bit below the turn in the river and from that position I cast my salmon fly, a beautiful Blue Charm, into the current and almost immediately caught a salmon—a female. The twenty pounder performed a great dance of silver leaps accompanied by gorgeous splashes and sprays of white foam, but obviously it was not the fish Dan was looking for. He netted it as quickly as possible, hit it on the head with my priest (an instrument designed for that purpose), and with no more ado tossed the salmon into the stern and asked to see my hook.

I dangled it in front of him and he snipped it from the tapered leader, examined the leader, cut off a piece, shortened it down to fifteen-pounded test, tied a large Black Dose on the end and handed the rod back to me. I refused to fish with that ugly fly. Ignoring me, he insisted I stand up and start fishing, carefully, where I had caught the female—near the submerged boulder at the tail of the pool. Then Dan sat back in the stern and lit a cigarette.

Annoyed, I stood up, stripped out thirty feet of line and cast out all of it, slapped the Black Dose down on the water beside the submerged rock. The instant that fly hit the surface, a great swirl took it underwater and a hard yank almost jerked the rod right out of my hand. Never before had I felt such a heavy weight on the end of a fishing line! Quickly, Dan got us close to shore, stepped into the river and held the canoe steady. The first time that I pumped it up to Dan, he tried to net and in a growing state of alarm realized it was too big for the net.

Both Dan and I watched, spellbound, as the weighty salmon turned and swam slowly across and downriver. I thought it would never stop. Finally, as it reached the boulder, it stopped in the middle of the current, and as it tired I pumped it back slowly, carefully, to Dan. Confused and helpless, he stood over the big salmon shaking his head.

Knowing he could not get it in the net, he dared not try; so again we watched in a state of dismay as the salmon turned and a big wake moved slowly back to the submerged boulder. The third time I pumped it back to Dan, he groaned. If he'd had a gaff, he would have had it the first time, he announced. Gaffs were illegal, thank heavens, but I knew how important that big salmon was to him. He had told me he was seventy that year and would have to retire. He had no interest in retiring, but if he could take that great salmon back to camp, he could at least retreat in a blaze of glory.

I suggested he try to get the net over the salmon's head, but that proved impossible. If Lee Wulff had been there, he would have tailed it. Unfortunately, neither Dan nor I had ever heard of tailing a salmon at that point, and I doubt if Dan's hand was large enough to reach around the wrist at the tail.

Finally, with a fifteen-pound test leader on the end of the line, I decided that I had no other choice but to take a chance and try to beach that huge salmon. It had turned belly up and holding the rod high, I jumped from the canoe to the shore just as the nearly expired salmon righted itself and started across the river. I could hardly believe my eyes. Spellbound, we watched the big wake move slowly across the opposite bank and turn in a feeble swirl. As the enormous tail surfaced above the water, the deep curve in my rod snapped back. The tail had come down on the leader and the great fish was free.

I had the great salmon on the end of my line for one hour and ten minutes—Dan timed it—and up to the net three times before it won its freedom. I felt miserable and at the same time, relieved. I hated playing that valiant fish for such a long time; and while playing it the thought that this hookbill had been with the female salmon we killed made me feel all the more sad. And, of course, I felt sorry for Dan. It took a while to convince him. He simply could not believe the salmon was gone until I reeled in the line and held up the leader for him to examine. A knot had pulled out, he said, and added that I'd had the salmon for an hour and ten minutes. All the way back to Camp Melancon, he mumbled over and over that I'd had it on an hour and ten minutes. Poor Dan. He did not go to the guides' camp that night. He went home.

I did not return to Petite Cascapédia until several years later. It was July and I had just fished the Matapédia. Jean-Paul had warned me that no salmon had been caught all spring at the Petite Cascapédia and as a result fishers had canceled their reservations. I would be the only one there and decided to give it a try.

Nap guided me. We were both deeply concerned about the state of the salmon population in the beautiful little river, but we enjoyed having it all to ourselves. One morning when I met Nap at the truck, he greeted me with a smile and news that two salmon had come into the river last night. Somehow he knew where they would stop and took me there.

He anchored the canoe ahead of the run. I stood up carefully and began fishing with a wet fly, a Green Highlander, which I cast across to the opposite bank and let swing around in the current. Lengthening the line a bit after each cast, I fished down the run, fished its entire length several times, and caught nothing. Finally, I reeled in the line and sat down.

As always after I had finished fishing a run, Nap circled the canoe back to the top and drifted directly over the pool searching for salmon. The time he spotted one! He let the canoe drift a good distance past the pool and then paddled back upriver.

Wearing chest-high waders, I suggested he put me on shore where I could get out of the canoe and wade. The shore sloped into the river where the bottom was sandy, so wading was easy. I went out to the run and began casting about forty feet above the salmon. Sending a wet fly to the opposite bank, I dropped it on a shale shelf, jerked it away and at the same time tossed a loop of slack line upriver—so the fly would sink a bit and swim down along the ledge—and just as the fly started to swing around in the current, a hard yank pulled my rod into a deep arch!

Nap had no problem netting the salmon, a hookbill weighing about twelve pounds, and we decided to keep it. The other salmon had been a female, Nap said. I asked what he thought happened to her and he answered with one word: "Poachers." Such a shame since we planned to return any female we caught to the river.

The next morning we fished a pool that had been one of the best in the river. I fished it carefully but caught nothing. That was hardly surprising given that the settlement had grown up at one side of the pool and generally any fish that stopped there overnight were netted out by poachers before dawn. That, and the sickening fumes from a small mill built nearby just the autumn before, drove us out of the pool.

The salmon we caught was the only one we saw in the Petite Caspedia that week. A new road had been built along the other shore all the way up to the headwaters and spawning beds. What had once been nearly impenetrable wilderness could now be easily reached. The poaching business was booming and the mouth of the river at the Bay of Chaleur was being heavily netted by poachers and commercial fishermen. I was concerned because I had seen no par jumping in the river that week, a sure sign that not enough salmon were getting a chance to spawn.

That was the last time I fished the Petite Cascapédia. In the summer of 1987, my friend Jean-Paul told me that a few years after the Petite Cascapédia had been "fished out," it had been restocked; and seven years later, a good run of mature salmon had returned to spawn. For that success, Québec has the enterprising *Société Cascapédia* to thank. Its excellent river management, protection rules, and enforcement of very strict anti-poaching laws combined with a five-year plan of restocking, saved the river.

CHAPTER TWENTY-ONE
St. Anne River, Gaspé

More than half the intense enjoyment of fly-fishing is derived from the beautiful surroundings, the satisfaction felt from being in the open air, the new lease of life secured thereby, and the many, many pleasant recollections of all one has seen, heard, and done.

—Charles F. Orvis

In all of my travels, I have never found any small river as unique and wonderful as the salmon rivers in Québec's Gaspesian Park. I first fished there during the year 1961 (just before my daughter, Mary, gave birth in Paris to my first grandchild, Catherine) when the Gaspé Peninsula was still sweetly quaint and virtually untouched by modern civilization. The first continuous road around the Peninsula had been built only a few years earlier and tourists were just beginning to discover the charm of the Gaspé.

The rivers are fairly small and were favored by large salmon—and sea trout, too. My good friend, Jean-Paul Dubé, then director of the Gaspé District Park Service, reserved water for me. He introduced me to the Petite Cascapédia, the Matapédia, The St. Jean, the St. Anne, and the Cap Chat. The government of Québec had terminated the leases of these rivers and opened them to all. In 1965, I went back to St. Anne and fished ten government pools, all of which had previously been leased by an American couple for many years and produced

203

the best fishing in St. Anne. The couple had employed two excellent guides, local men who had accomplished wonders by protecting the St. Anne River from poachers and illegal fishing, and allowing Nature's perfectly designed pools to remain pristine.

Jean-Paul made a reservation for me to fish there for a full week. I lodged at the Gite du Mont Albert, an inn consisting of a group of buildings beside the main lodge. The kitchen and large dining room were in a separate building, and the Gite was noted for having the best chef on the Gaspé. All the buildings, including a group of small alpine chalets for guests, were clustered together at the food of Mont Albert with the dramatic backdrop of ancient rock mountains—dark, bald-topped, scoured and rounded by time and the Ice Age. It was a fascinating place to rest after a day of fishing.

The Gite catered to mountain climbers and salmon fishers and sat near the headwaters of the St. Anne River. The Grand Fosse Pool, just across the road, was a main attraction. One could stand on a high bank and look down to see salmon lying in the pool's translucent, pale green depths. Some fish were huge, but it was a holding pool and the salmon had no interest in our flies. The guide suggested I fish a bit above the pool at the inlet, in fast water.

There I could stand at the shore and hooked into a salmon, but I was with a guide who was not a guide as much as a gentle guardian with no net. I tried to beach the salmon, but the bank was too steep and the thick brush behind us left no space in which to back up. Finally, the salmon "threw the hook" and the poor guide seemed on the verge of tears.

I fished the rest of the pools from canoes with two guides. The wild little river flowed through dense woodland or raced through a narrow riverbed of sheer rock. Its bumpy rapids required two guides to keep the canoe upright. The stretch of ten pools, several miles long, was well managed by Québec's Park Service. Only two fishers per day were permitted to fish that stretch. One fished the first half, the other the second half, and they rotated the following day.

So we fished from canoes, each with two guides. I was on the upper half, leaving a fisher from Québec City to the lower half. From the start there was tension with the head guide who (as I had experienced before), it seemed, very much wanted to guide the French Canadian but he was stuck with me. When the guide and I met, he greeted me with a grunt and made a remark about there being no salmon in the river. When I started to question him, this tall, cadaverous-looking man mumbled, "Je ne comprends pas bien l'anglais." How convenient.

On the way downriver, he and the second guide (a small unassuming man) paddled through pool after pool without stopping to fish, and from the few French words I could understand, I gathered they could see no signs of salmon in the pool. Every time I tried to get them to stop, the head guide mumbled, "Je ne comprends pas, madame." He was right, though. No one had caught a fish there in the past week. It was terribly frustrating to be on such a wonderful salmon river without having a chance to fish, and when we came to a little waterfall—low but fierce—the head guide motioned for me to get out of the canoe, walk down the trail and wait for them at the bottom of the waterfall. Having been told that shooting over the low waterfall in a canoe was great fun, I refused to get out; but he paddled to shore and pulled me out.

At the end of the trail we found a camp overlooking the river. It had belonged to the American couple but now belonged to the Québec government. The guides prepared lunch in its kitchen and served me in its dining room. I tried to move into the kitchen, but the head guide's emphatic no scared me back to my table alone in the dining room.

After lunch, he led me down to the river and showed me where to fish. There were no fish in the pool, but I wanted to fish anyway and waded in, making my way to the little waterfall, and began fishing at the head of a run. My guide stretched out on the shore and promptly fell asleep. The other guide was sitting in the background shade when I hooked into a large salmon. Leaping into the air, it began cavorting over the pool. I was having a wonderful time when two long arms encircled me and then grabbed my rod. The head guide held me captive in his grip, clutching the line close to the rod, while the salmon leaped one more time into the air, dove back into the river and . . . the rod snapped back into place. Glaring at me, the guide began shouting—in English—that it was all my fault.

Dumbfounded, I stared at him, mouth open, unable to utter a word in my defense. On the other hand, that quiet, the other guide who had been so quiet until then surprised me by exploding into a burst of rage. I didn't understand one word of his French, but was pleased to know he was defending me. Our villain looked subdued after, but still refused to admit that it was his fault we lost the salmon. I fished another pool that day but had no luck. None of us spoke and the silence became embarrassing. I felt relieved when the truck came to take us and the canoe back to the Gite.

The man who supervised the guides apologized to me for the head guide's shocking behavior. The other guide had reported it. No one was available the replace the head guide who had literally fallen asleep on the job, so the next day the three of us fished together again. The guides behaved as though nothing unusual had happened. I caught no fish. That night the weather brought in a heavy rain and we awoke to a clear sun in the sky. The head guide seemed more optimistic as he announced, "We will fish the upper stretch again," and paddled down the St. Anne a short distance from the Grand Fosse Pool where he anchored the canoe in a side brook.

The second guide sat in the stern while I stood in the canoe alongside the head guide, who kept the canoe close to the bank with a paddle. He told me to cast my fly across to the other side of the river and, stripping out line from the reel, I was pleased to note that the guides had positioned the canoe so I would have no problem with my backcast. The only opening in the dense foliage behind me was over the brook. Thanking them with a nod and a smile, I faced the river and surveyed the fascinating pool.

The force of the brook's current into the river had dug out an ideal salmon pool on the St. Anne's opposite shore. The river was no more than thirty feet wide and the night's storm had turned the water to clear amber. The guides called it alder water and the head guide insisted the salmon never took a fly in alder water, but encouraged me to give it a try anyway. I could see everything in the pool, now aglow with sunlight, and on the bank a rock wall of ledges dropping into the river disappeared into its own jet black shadow. The guide whispered that I should cast over to the overhanging ledge.

I chose a Lady Atherton, a wet fly Charlie De Feo had designed and named after me. I told the guide that the three long strands of bear hair gave its tail a sexy come-on wiggle that lured big salmon out from under ledges. Looking at me as though I were crazy, he pointed a finger over to the ledge, so I cast the fly over there again, and again, with no success. If there was a salmon lurking there, we would be standing almost on top of it and it would see us, so I suggested we get out of the canoe and cast from shore.

Ignoring my suggestion, the guide looked straight through me and motioned to the ledge. Having no desire to argue, I cast the fly across the river once more and this time it fell on the ledge; so I jerked it into the water and watched, spellbound, as not one but two large salmon swam out from the black shadow and cautiously followed the fly until it began to drag in the current! Turning, both salmon disappeared into the shadows. The guide was silent, staring into my face, still as a statue. When the second guide asked if we had seen a salmon, the first whispered "Oui, deux" and motioned for me to cast again.

That time I deliberately cast the fly on top of the ledge and jerked it once again into the water. It worked! Two salmon, a hookbill and a female, swam out from the black, followed the fly again, and then vanished into the shadows. I waited awhile and then cast to the ledge, jerked it away, and that time the hookbill swam out alone. His nose nearly touched the fly and then suddenly he turned in a swirl and disappeared.

Unaware of what was going on in the pool's black shadows behind the clear amber-tinted waters lit by the sun's golden glow, I waited. Then I cast the fly back to the ledge, jerked it into the water and watched, entranced, as the two large salmon with a golden sheen swam out of the black and cautiously followed the fly. The hookbill darted ahead and she could not resist the competition. Racing past, she nabbed the fly, pulled a deep arch in my supple salmon rod, moved a few feet upriver and stopped.

Immediately I tightened the reel brake a bit and jumped from the canoe to the shore. The guide followed and had the salmon in his net twenty minutes later. Everyone congratulated everyone, and that lucky day I was allowed to ride in the canoe when the guides took it skillfully over the little waterfall.

Several years passed before I returned to the St. Anne. Once, after a week of fishing at the Matapédia, Jean-Paul asked if I would like to have a few days of fishing on the St. Anne. Of course! The fishing had been poor that summer, so reservations for that week had been cancelled and there were no other fishers. It was wonderful to be with different guides and we had ten beautiful pools to ourselves, but there were no fish that week. Everyone at the Gîte complained about the alarming decrease in the St. Anne salmon population and not until my last day there did I understand why.

As we drifted down to the last pool where the truck was waiting to drive us and the canoe back to the Gîte, I noticed a man standing at the back of the truck wrapping a salmon in paper. Seeing us, he quickly dropped the salmon on top of a pile at his feet, pushed the pile to the back of the truck, and covered it with a tarp.

"Poaching!" I exclaimed loudly. The two guides were silent, but their concern was visible. Of course they knew the man. He drove the truck for the government. Instead of stopping to fish the pool as planned, the guides paddled to shore and helped me out of the canoe. The driver helped the guides load the canoe into the truck and then helped me get up to the front seat. The guides climbed into the back and as we started up the main road, two men arrived by car. Their faces expressed surprise and alarm. What they had come for was in the truck and its driver, a trusted government employee, dared not stop to give them the salmon.

It was clear that the driver had set out a net in the dark of the night and come back early to the pool to retrieve the salmon, netted and ready for the men in the car. We had arrived earlier than expected because, having lost interest in fishing empty pools, I had suggested we let the canoe drift over the pools to see if any salmon were visible. There had been no salmon in any of the pools so we had arrived at the last pool early.

The late Francois Gourdeau, director of the Park Service before Jean-Paul, was at the Gite that week; and when I reported what I'd seen, his brow furrowed with concern. They had suspected the driver of poaching, he told me, but had never found concrete evidence. He asked me to report it. "It won't do any good," I said. "I'm an American."

Poaching had become rampant in all the rivers around the Gaspé, where it seemed everyone was related; and nothing was being done to stem the illegal fishing because no one wanted to testify against a relative or neighbor. As a result, very few salmon were making it up to the spawning beds.

On the other side of the mountain, the Cap-Chat, a marvelous little river noted for large salmon and many ideal pools, could be fished easily from the shore but once discovered, was doomed. Children fishing for trout where the river spread out in the village before entering the St. Lawrence killed too many parr; and although the Cap-Chat had been leased by a Canadian for many years, he employed no guardian and poachers were able to take over the river. After the man died, Québec's government opened the Cap-Chat to the public but by then, between commercial nets and poachers, there was no salmon fishing for sportfishers.

When I fished the Cap-Chat, I saw no sign of any salmon. The following year I was surprised to see two salmon in a pool. I was the only one fishing the river that day and tried to tempt the salmon with a dozen different flies, both wet and dry, before finally realizing it was hopeless. I could see them in the clear water and they could see me. The guide admitted there were no salmon in the river. Later that day a disgruntled fisherman at a restaurant admitted that he and every fisherman on the Gaspé had fished for those two salmon and had paid the Québec government and guide a good price to do so.

The Grand Cascapédia, always noted for its exceptionally large salmon, was one of the most stunning rivers I had ever encountered. Clear and pale green, it wound through the Gaspesian Park's serene and dramatic beauty. When I finally had a chance to fish there almost twenty years later in the summer of 1980, almost no one was catching salmon. Lack of river management caused pools to fill with gravel and commercial nets in the Atlantic were capturing too many Grand Cascapédia salmon before they could reach the spawning beds. Even more distressing, I found evidence of furunculosis disease in a large salmon I examined that had been caught by another fisher.

By 1987, after finding furunculosis in the salmon of the Matapédia, I told an old friend and resident of the Gaspé, that I was going to revisit all the other rivers I had fished to check for furunculosis. Shaking his head sadly, he whispered, "All dead . . . "

CHAPTER TWENTY-TWO
Matapédia River, Québec

The angler forgets most of the fish he catches, but he does
not forget the streams and lakes in which they are caught.

—Charles K. Fox

Of all the salmon rivers I have had the privilege of fishing, Canada's
Matapédia was my favorite. I fished it for the first time in 1962 and it
was well managed and protected for many years by the International
Paper Company[23] in New Brunswick. A guide who worked for the
company told me it had employed thirty guardians and stationed them
day and night in log cabins by the best salmon pools.

A mighty but fairly short river, the Matapédia flows out of Lake
Matapédia into the Restigouche River near the village of Matapédia.
After the Québec government took over the paper company's water
and opened it to the public, I went to the river each year, making
reservations through Jean-Paul Dubé. Once the government opened
fishing to the public, the Matapédia continued to produce a healthy
population of large salmon as a result of good river management prac-
tices—but only for a while. When the separatist government came

---

23. The Canadian International Paper Company (CIP) was a Montréal-based
    forest products company, a former subsidiary of International Paper. It was
    originally formed as the St. Maurice Lumber Company in 1919 but was
    renamed in 1925. It was sold to Canadian Pacific Forest Products in the early
    1980s, which became Avenor Inc. in 1994; this company was then bought by
    Bowater in 1998.

into power in Québec, poaching increased as the number of guardians dwindled, and drag net use increased. Meanwhile, Jean-Paul was relieved of his job as director of the Gaspé Salmon Rivers.

Before that happened, I remember a time Jean-Paul and I fished together in turn, sharing a canoe. He fished in the morning and caught a large salmon. And that afternoon, I caught a large salmon from the same pool. We were overjoyed with our luck, but it was not all luck. We had an excellent guide and I was especially excited, experiencing for the first time the thrill that accompanies success from perfect teamwork between an expert guide and fisher. The Matapédia had to be fished from a canoe, which required a different technique than wading. The guide dropped the anchor well above the tail of a pool and, fishing the current with a wet fly, I would cast out only a few feet of line, retrieve the fly slowly, and add more line with each cast until I had about thirty feet of line on the water. If no fish rose for the fly, the guide dropped the canoe downriver again, anchored again, and started my casting and line lengthening again.

All of the Matapédia guides were well trained, having worked with experienced fly fishers. I especially enjoyed being with Henry Lyons, a guide I still revere. A large, healthy young man, he had gone off to World War II and returned to Matapédia weighing less than a hundred pounds. He had been held prisoner in a Japanese camp, a grim experience from which his health never fully recovered. His love for the Matapédia and guiding proved the best therapy possible. I knew him as a good-natured guide with an elastic imagination that always added length and pounds to every fish I caught.

Howard Firth was another Matapédia guide. One day at Richard's Pool when he was sitting in the stern and I was at the center of the canoe standing and reeling in line, a fish took the fly quietly, not in the current but in deep still water no more than ten feet away. There had been no disturbance on the surface and, wondering whether I had hooked into a salmon or a sea trout, I sat down and started stripping in line when suddenly a heavy weight pulled my rod into a deep arch. Quickly, I released pressure, the line moved slowly toward the canoe and then underneath, and everything stopped. But not Howard. In one great leap he shot over my head to the stern where he released the line that had become tangled in the motor's rudder; and before realizing what was happening, I was playing a huge salmon. Howard finally netted the impressive salmon with great aplomb, as only an expert nets such a royal fish.

Yes, guides should and do play an important role in the sport of fly fishing, but not always. I laugh now, thinking of the time I fished from a canoe for lake trout with a streamer fly and the guide was the most exasperating I had ever encountered. I learned that the dynamic between inexperienced guide and fisher can end in nothing less than scathing frustration. My streamer had raised a trout along the bank of the lake, but the guide was paddling the canoe so fast, the trout never stood a chance of grabbing the hook. The French Canadian, an excitable man who claimed, "I'd rather fish than do anything else in the world," had never heard of fly fishing and was guiding for the very first time. Since he spoke no English and I spoke no French, every time my streamer fly raised a trout, he would have a fit of joy and shoot the canoe past the fish. Nonetheless, he was a kind young man who desperately wanted to please me, and when I reprimanded him, insisting he slow down, he looked so terribly woebegone I mustered up a reassuring smile. We returned to camp after a day of strenuous fishing in a lake filled with trout completely empty-handed.

The guides at the Restigouche river in Québec worked for themselves or clubs, and one day a freelancer took me fishing. Standing up in the canoe—one of those sturdy Gaspé creations—he said he would show me exactly where to cast. There were three grilse in the pool, but after paying him a fairly serious fee to act as guide, he caught every single one and I was helpless to stop him. Was I furious? Yes, I was!

Another time at the Restigouche in New Brunswick where the Kedgwick enters the river, I was lucky to be in the company of an experienced guide who worked for an outfitter. There were seven fishers in camp that week and we fished a series of pools made famous by Edward Hewitt. He had written about the large numbers of salmon he'd caught there when the Restigouche had the reputation of being the most productive river of large Atlantic salmon in Canada. The week I was there, however, only two salmon were caught by seven rods in seven pools. The pools had been filled with gravel, and my last day there and many unsuccessful hours the guide suggested we stop fishing and go upriver. He wanted to show me why the pools we had fished that week had produced no more than two salmon.

His canoe had a motor, so the trip was easy, and on the way he stopped several times to show me long stretches of shores cleared of trees. They had been cut too close to the shore, so there were no longer any roots to hold the soil and gravel in place. So the pools Edward Hewitt had so praised were now filled with gravel.

I never fished the Restigouche again, but went to the Matapédia every year. I stayed at the Hotel Restigouche, where the Matapédia joins the Restigouche. Generations of salmon fishers had lodged at that hotel, now a motel, and for us it felt more like a club. The same fishers returned each year and I looked forward to the social life and seeing old friends.

Even the logging industry could not ruin the beauty of Matapédia's wonderfully unique pools, banked with sheer rocks and great boulders that could not be washed away. Richard's Pool was one of my favorite fishing spots. Local lore had it that Richard Adams, a handsome white-haired guide, with a reputation as a ladies' man, once carried a lady fisher who had no waders piggyback across the stream between the road and the pool—much to the delight of the other guides. After that, that fabulous pool became known by Richard's name.

Richard's Pool sat at the top of a remarkable double waterfall, with one fall just above another. We fished from the shore and nine out of every ten salmon hooked turned and went over the falls and back down to the river. To get down we had to climb and jump over huge boulders along the bank, not an easy task—particularly while holding a rod with a fish at the end of the line. I was already in my sixties when one day I hooked into a large salmon in Richard's Pool. The guide wanted me to give him the rod but I refused. I scrambled, slipped, fell, stumbled, and nearly broke a leg, but I held onto the rod. The guide tried hard to get it away from me, afraid we would lose the salmon. "Even if it kills me, I am not letting go of this rod or the salmon," I declared.

I was lucky. Once I made it down to the river, the salmon was still on the end of my line. But it had stopped at the top of the lower fall and refused to budge. The guide paced the shore, pleading with me to give him the rod, insisting I was going to lose the salmon. Sensing in my bones that the salmon was well hooked, I ignored him and finally got the stubborn fish to move down to the river where the guide could net it.

Once it was netted, I made my way back to Richard's Pool with a great deal of help from the guide, and hooked into another large salmon. That fish shot straight down the river, over the falls, pulling out yards of line, and stopped at the base of the falls. Again, the guide tried to get me to hand over the rod. Pushing him out of my way, I slipped on a boulder and fell hard. Instead of coming to my aid, the guide grabbed my rod and ran it down to the river. I was furious, but I was even more anxious about saving the salmon; and now with both hands free, I managed to slide down the treacherous boulder to the river without mishap. The guide handed the rod back to me and in no time at all, he had the second salmon in the net. We had our limit and packed up.

The Pool's namesake, Richard Adams, had the reputation of being the luckiest guide at the Matapédia. One day, it was his turn to go to Jim's Rock Pool, another marvelous salmon gathering spot in the Matapédia. Fishers liked to stand on top of Jim's Rock, a tall boulder, and fish with dry flies. The holding pool at the base was noted for attracting extra large salmon; but they were seldom if ever caught in the deep water there. Generally, fishers caught them at the side of the boulder near an inlet where the bubbling current picked up oxygen. A fisher could go to Jim's Rock Pool day after day and not see or raise a salmon, but occasionally around sundown, a big one would find a hook and the excitement would ripple down the river.

I tried my luck above and around the inlet with a wet fly, from a canoe, to no avail. So Richard paddled us down to the end of the exceptionally long pool. Before I even started to fish, he cut my tapered leader down to fifteen-pound test, and on it he tied a large Jock Scott. Tossing it into the river, he sat back in the canoe and watched me with a quiet grin on his face.

Our timing was perfect. With the third cast, I hooked into a salmon. Richard pulled up anchor and started after it. "I can keep it in the pool," I told him, but having seen the size of the tail, decided that was not a good idea. He went after the salmon as it started down a wide rapid. To keep the canoe in the deep current, Richard had to paddle it close to the bank while I did my best to hold onto the rod and substantial salmon as it seemed the overhanging brush and tree branches on the bank might sweep me away. Squeezing my eyes shut, I held onto the rod with one hand and Pete, my Springer Spaniel, with the other. Finally, the salmon stopped in a pool and, happy to still be safely sitting in the canoe, breathed a sigh of relief and quickly reeled in the slack line.

The salmon had decided to stop in the middle of the current. As Richard got the canoe below it, I managed to keep the fish fighting the current until it tired. Finally, Richard paddled to shore, stepped into the river while keeping the canoe steady with one hand and I pumped the heavy salmon up to the net. Pete, who thought he knew more about catching salmon than anyone else, jumped in the water to "help." Despite the splattering distraction, Richard had no trouble getting the huge salmon inside the extra large net.

As the years passed, I found fewer salmon in the Matapédia, and more fishers. I caught my last salmon there in 1978 when I was fishing a long, wide pool close to the highway. Sitting in a canoe, I hooked into a magnificent silvery salmon that startled me by darting straight downriver, but it stopped when my line ran and some of the backing ran out. My guide quickly paddled to shore and stood in the river next to the canoe while I played the salmon. Slowly, deliberately, I pumped the heavy salmon up to the net, but when the guide tried to net it, the salmon swirled in one big motion and took my fly back across the river to the tail of the pool. Again, I pumped that salmon back to the guide, this time with great difficulty, since I had left the detachable butt of my rod at the hotel, and with the reel anchored against my belly, it was difficult for me to turn its handle. Somehow I managed to get the salmon back up to the net where it turned and once again swam downriver. The guide insisted over and over that I hand him the rod. "No," I snapped. "I've been fighting this big guy for at least twenty minutes and I am not giving up now." My arm and hand ached, but I held on tight.

Suddenly, when the salmon turned and started back across the river once again, it no longer seemed like a beautiful silvery trophy, but a monster I no longer wanted. "Damn you!" I shouted. A burst of laughter from the highway across the water surprised me. I looked up and saw that several cars had pulled up and along the river bank was a captivated audience. I had been on the verge of handing my rod to the guide, but now I had no intention of backing down. So I went back to work and carefully pumped the salmon one more time up to the guide. Finally, he had it securely in the net and our audience clapped and cheered, and my ears rang happily from the loud applause. (Years later at an annual dinner of the Atlantic Salmon Federation, a stranger introduced himself to me as a man who had stood on the bank of the Matapédia watching me struggle and laughing as he heard me curse that big salmon. I wish I could recall his name!)

Another season in 1978, I fished the Matapédia for a week and caught one grilse, but no salmon. No one had good fishing that season—except for the poachers. They fished the pools in reserved water early each morning before sportfishers who had paid a fair fee had a chance. And outside of the Matapédia, commercial nets, particularly driftnets, were killing too many spawners. That was the year I discovered that the deadly disease, furunculosis, was killing fish in the Matapédia, and in the Miramichi, too. No one wanted to talk about the disease, but after fifteen years of studying its symptoms in various river populations, I concluded that whole schools of fish were infected with the bacteria.

Meanwhile, it had become almost impossible for an American to get a reservation at the Matapédia, so I gave up and began traveling abroad to fish for salmon.

Max with guide, salmon, and Springer Spaniel, Pete. c. 1979.

CHAPTER TWENTY-THREE
Chalk Streams, Ireland

When you are on the river, ocean or in the woods, you are the closest to the truth you'll ever get.

—Jack Leonard

It was 1963 when I felt a yearning to fish for Atlantic salmon in Norway and could find no one who could go with me. A fellow fisher suggested I write to captain Norman-Bracy, a former officer in the British army during World War II. After the war, with nothing better to do, the Captain became an agent for sportfishing, it seems. I wrote, asking him to reserve water for me in Norway and, as an afterthought, also asked him to make reservation for me to fish a chalk stream in England.

A week later I received a letter confirming a reservation had been made for me at the Driva in Norway, but that it was impossible to get a reservation at a chalk stream in England since the Englishmen reserved beats years in advance. He asked if I would consider traveling to Ireland where he had a new representative who would take me to chalk streams around Dundalk in County Lough, a part of the country rich in beds of limestone.

I agreed, It was the summer of 1963 when I flew from Montréal to the Dublin airport. The new representative—I'll call him Sean—met me there in a great state of excitement. Less than an hour before, President Kennedy's plane had landed. Thousands of people had gathered to greet him. Indeed, Sean wanted to talk of nothing else, while I had been looking forward to this fishing trip for weeks and was anxious to hear about the rivers I was going to fish.

In Canada, "fish talk" had been the order of the day, all day, every day. That was not to be in Ireland. The instant we got into Sean's car, he turned on the radio and we learned all about the American president's visit. Of course, Ireland was proud, having produced the forefather of the United States president; and no doubt Sean and everyone else in Ireland thought that as an American I wanted nothing more than to hear them gush about Kennedy's visit. I listened patiently and dreamed of fishing Irish rivers.

It seemed I would be staying at Castle Bellingham, a fair fortress converted into a hotel, and I learned that Sean's mother and Lady Bellingham had been close friends—and that his mother had been pregnant when they drove her from her home. I gathered that "they" were members of one of the Irish revolutions, and that Sean's parents were Irish aristocrats. Like Captain Norman-Bracy, Sean had been an officer during World War II, giving his most productive years to the war; and when it was all over, he earned a living as a race car driver.

It also turned out that I was one of Sean's first customers in his new venture as a sportfishing agent. Not having made any detailed advance arrangements, I had no idea what to expect. The morning I arrived in Ireland, the morning was sunny and sweet, and when the car radio began playing gentle Celtic tunes, I sat back in the seat and turned my attention to the rolling countryside. Bathed in sunlight, the lush vegetation met the moist air leaving a mellow fragrance that still lingers when I remember that trip. A small island nation, Ireland was noted for its rich fertile soil, and Sean proudly boasted that the farmers were masters at making every inch of dirt produce the maximum in crops.

It was a fairly fast drive to Castle Bellingham, a bit south of Dundalk. The three hundred-year old castle was all that a fabled fortress should be—surrounded by a hundred acres of parkland and gardens, somewhat neglected but beautiful in its rough natural state. From the window of my room I could see the Clyde, a fairytale chalk stream flowing through the castle grounds. The brochure lying on the table in my room explained that the fishing was free and that one could fish for salmon and trout in the three miles of fishing grounds for which the owners held rights. What more could one want?

That afternoon I fished the Clyde, only to discover that it had everything a chalk stream should have except fish! Sean explained that there was an effort in progress to rehabilitate the Clyde and bring back both salmon and trout, both of which were fished out during the way; and then he drove me to a pool near the castle and parked by an ancient stone bridge, arched gracefully over the water. Above it, a weir had formed a beautiful pool, banked with luxurious clutches of yellow iris and brown cattails. The pool's water lilies were in bloom and I was surprised to see several small but active salmon at the foot of the weir which was closed. I reached for my rod, but Sean said I couldn't fish there. "The brochure in my room says I can fish anywhere on the castle grounds," I pointed out, but Sean shook his head and announced that it was time to return to the castle.

That night in my four poster bed I dreamed I was Lady Bellingham, back in the time when salmon in the Clyde were plentiful and no one could stop the lady of the castle from fishing that beautiful pool filled with salmon. I had a wonderful time catching salmon that night, all night long.

Each day Sean drove the guide, Burty, and me to a different chalk stream, all in the vicinity of Dundalk. During the week I spent in Ireland I fished four rivers: the Clyde, Castledown, Fane, and Dee. Yes, Ireland has a Dee, too, and Sean said it was known for its exceptionally large salmon. All were lovely chalk streams, and each one flowed into the Irish Sea at Dundalk Bay.

Sean drove and stayed with us all day. He refrained from fishing but Burty fished, and that was a problem. Burty was a master fly fisher and knew exactly where there would be trout in every river and demonstrated by catching the trout himself.

He tied his own flies, and tied flies for me—perfect Black Gnats, "a wee bit of black hackle wound around the shank of a week hook."

At the Fane, where brown trout were splashing enthusiastically at the sight of black gnats, I caught and released several wee trout. All the trout in that pool were wee, and I was fairly certain that they had been recently planted for the American visitor.

Sean belonged to a club that had bought the commercial netting rights for salmon at the mouth of the Fane and then stopped all commercial netting. Sean took us there and Burty went directly to where the stream turned and the current passed beneath willow branches hanging over the water. Standing beside Sean, I watched a perfect performance as Burty fished with a dry fly and caught a huge brown troutbrown trout. Sean said I could fish if I wanted, but figuring that the trout Burty caught was a loner, I moved up to where he was now fishing at the foot of the weir.

Sean took Burty's rod from him and handed it to me. It was much heavier than my trout rod and after taking one look at the large red and orange salmon fly tied on a short heavy leader, I gave the rod back to Burty. In a pleading voice, Sean turned to me. "Please, do give it a try. You won't be sorry!" So I acquiesced and hooked almost immediately into a large salmon. What a thrill! It ran out line, jumped, fell back into the water, and was gone. So was the fly. I glanced down at the reel. There were no more than thirty feet of line left on the reel and no backing.

Both men seemed embarrassed, but that didn't stop Sean from taking the rod out of my hands and giving it back to Burty who promptly tied another fly on the leader and cast it into the current. The same thing that had just happened to me, happened to him. We had lost the only two salmon in the pool. "One must never stop the run of a salmon," I half-muttered. I had one hundred yards of backing and a full length of line on my trout reel, and if I had been fishing with it instead of Burty's rod, I could have had the salmon in the net. Glancing at Burty's net, I shook my head. It was a trout net, and the bank was too high for anyone to beach a salmon. Burty and Sean, masters at avoiding trouble with an angry American woman, remained resolutely silent.

I realized that they undoubtedly knew when they took me there that the weir had been closed and salmon were in the pool. Also, I had not been told I needed a license. As soon as we got back to the castle I bought a salmon license. It cost only $7.50 and was good for a week, but I never had a chance to use it.

The next day was Saturday and Sean announced in the car that we would not be going fishing that day. Instead we were heading north on a sightseeing tour. I had little desire to sightsee, but we were already on our way and I did not protest. There was no doubt that Sean was bored since a woman whose primary interest was fishing was not exciting to him. Burty, on the hand, had been able to fish productive waters he never would have fished without me, so I imagine he was pleased with the arrangement.

The three of us drove north over a scenic mountain range to a tavern near the Northern Ireland border. A couple Sean knew owned the tavern. He had been an army officer and his Canadian wife had been a nurse in the war. She was the one who let me know that our trio would be spending the night at the tavern.

Wearing slacks that I usually wore under my fishing waders, with a sloppy sweater, I felt uncomfortable in the dining room that evening—an evening that remains vivid in my mind. The room was full of noisy men sitting at tables, singing and shouting at each other while a few couples danced around the small dance floor. As I sat talking with the couple who owned the tavern, John and Ellen, a rosy-cheeked Irishman with a warm smile and a sweater even sloppier than mine, strolled confidently up to greet me and invited me to dance.

I stood up and as my partner, jolly from a bit too much ale, bounced me around the small dance floor, the loud hooting and clapping was deafening. Several minutes later when I was delivered back to Sean and the tavern keepers, I knew from the look on Sean's face that I had done something somehow very wrong. Later that night when I was alone with our hostess I learned what my companions were thinking.

I had accidently become an instrument in the fight between Northern and Southern Ireland. Ellen explained that their tavern was near the border and that every Saturday night their pub was crowded with men from both sides of the border. Tempers generally ran high and the least disturbance could set off a brawl, or worse. She warned me to be careful. Americans were popular now that President Kennedy was in Ireland, and by dancing with an Irishman from the North, I had inadvertently insulted the Irishmen from the other side of the border.

I had no desire to enter into that fight but I felt the need to defend my behavior. "Sean, if you had told me before we left the castle that we were going north to sightsee and spend the night in a quaint tavern, I wouldn't have worn my fishing clothes—I could have worn a proper dress and been more careful of my behavior." Sean's lilting reply rang true as he pointed out, "If I'd told you we weren't going fishing, you would have refused to come along on the sightseein' trip, now wouldn' ya?"

The next morning, a Sunday, Sean suggested at breakfast that we go to church. I had no interest in a church service, nor did Burty, and Sean's sudden tongue-lashing against Protestants and heathens surprised me. As a native of Southern Ireland, Sean was Catholic, while Burty, from Northern Ireland, was Protestant. So I guess that made me the heathen.

Burty, quiet by nature, remained silent during Sean's outburst. Nevertheless, I sensed a strong bond between these two men. Burty was older and had worked for Sean's parents. At one point Sean explained that Burty, a fervent lifelong fly fisher, had taught Sean how to fish when he was a young child and taken him fishing countless times.

As it happened, no one went to church that morning and I wondered if Burty, in his understated way, was perhaps a stronger force than I had imagined. I felt sorry for Sean's friends, John and Ellen, as they were living in turmoil of the violent tensions between north and south, as well as the aftermath of World World II. After spending the prime of his youth fighting for an elusive patriotism, John found it difficult to earn a decent living. As for his Canadian wife, Ellen hated life as a tavern keeper on the simmering border.

As a whole, the Irish people were friendly and kind to me, and I received special attention during my time there because my American status lifted me almost to the level of their idol, President Kennedy; but in the end, I was disappointed in the fishing. Too many salmon and trout had been killed before spawning. In the area where I fished, the only chance of hooking salmon was to fish water in which a private club had purchased the lease from commercial fishermen and guarded every inch of the river, all the way to the spawning beds.

On my last day in Ireland, Sean drove me to the Dublin airport and I flew to London, where I stopped for a couple of days and enjoyed the city as a tourist. I joined a sightseeing tour by bus and stayed in my seat when the bus stopped to allow passengers to visit the Tower of London and the crown jewels. I was allergic to crowds, especially after time in the quiet open space of Ireland's countryside, and remained on the bus.

I dozed until the passengers returned and the woman who sat down beside me said I was the only wise one on the bus. She had stood in a long line, waiting for more than a half an hour before getting to see the jewels, and once there, she was pushed past them so fast she barely had a moment to see them. And the poor woman had come to London especially to feast her eyes on these royal jewels.

The next morning before boarding a plane bound for Norway, I called for a taxi and asked to be driven to Hardy's. The driver took me downtown, but as we got close to Hardy's, the street was blocked by a large crowd. I had a hard time pushing my way through, and when I finally go out onto the empty street, a Bobby rushed out and pushed me back into the crowd. Bystanders looked at me as though I was crazy, but of course they had no idea how determined this fanatical fly fisher was to make her way to Hardy's.

And I had no idea what the crowd was waiting for until the Queen of England herself, riding in a horse-drawn open carriage with Constantine II, King of Greece, followed by Prince Philip in another carriage with the Queen Anne-Marie of Greece, passed by en route to Buckingham Palace. I was too intent on admiring the perfectly matched magnificent horses pulling the carriages to get much of a look at the royal figures riding by. Once they had passed and

the crowd began to disperse, I found a Bobby and explained that if I didn't get to Hardy's soon, I would miss my plane. He took me by the arm, led me to a subway entrance, and instructed me to walk underground to the exit that would lead me to my destination.

Hardy's, just across the street from Buckingham Palace, was empty when I arrived. I was surprised to find no one was guarding these true treasures, and when a salesman came into the shop from the street, he seemed surprised that I was not outside with everyone else. My interest was elsewhere and I quickly bout a line and backing for Burty's reel, arranged for Hardy's to mail it to Burty, and then hailed a cab to catch my flight to Oslo.

CHAPTER TWENTY-FOUR

The Driva, Norway

The charm of fishing is that it is the pursuit of what is elusive but attainable, a perpetual series of occasions for hope.

—John Buchan

Norman-Bracy, knowing that I fished only with flies, commented that the Driva was ideal for fly fishing in low water, which was its present condition after a dry spring. He made the reservations through Erik Myhre, and once I landed in Oslo, I went directly to Erik for instructions.

Erik arranged for me to go to Fahle Farm, a working farm on the bank of the Driva that for generations had catered to mountain climbers and sportfishers. I boarded a train in Oslo and then a bus to Opdal. I asked the bus driver to stop at Fahle Farm, but he forgot and when I stepped out in Opda, I phoned Fahle Farm. Egil Hagen, a tall and handsome young man, came to get me in his car.

Egil drove along a road that followed the Driva. It was one of the most exciting introductions to a river I had ever experienced. Surrounded by the vital stark beauty of the Sunndalen Valley, a narrow passage walled in by sheer stone cliffs offered a series of slender waterfalls. They resembled streamers of white gauze cascading down hundreds of feet to the base of snow-capped peaks and into the Driva. There, strong, clear green waters tore, swirled and pushed their way between backs of solid rock. Egil told me, "The Driva attracts many large salmon from the North Atlantic."

In charge of the fishing for a seven-mile stretch of the Driva that included two and-a-half miles of Fahle Farm pools, Egil spoke English fluently. He assured me that I would have no problem in Norway because English was taught in all Norwegian schools from the start. I learned that he had trained as a pilot in Canada before Norway got involved in World War II and then, while in the United States for university studies, he trained American pilots.

Soon after arriving at Fahle Farm, I changed into fishing clothes and Egil and I went to his favorite salmon poll in the Driva. Several guests were fishing there, from the shore using prawns, and although I wore waders, the river was too deep and swift to wade, so I was forced to fish from the shore. Realizing there was virtually no chance of catching fish with a salmon fly amid a bevy of picked prawns, I soon lost interest.

But the salmon also seemed to have no appetite for prawns. The other fishers soon became discouraged and one of them told me Egil was the only guide there and they could not fish unless he was with me, so I began feeling discouraged as well. This was the beginning of a frustrating week. I had expected I would be able to fish the Driva all day, each day, as I had fished salmon rivers in Canada. But that week I spent more time waiting in the farmhouse for Egil than with a rod and reel in hand. And it was difficult to adjust to the change in routine since the summer months brought sunlight-covered mountaintops until 11 p.m. The twilight period followed, with the darkest twilight around 1am, and some guests fished until then.

Day and night a long table in the spacious dining room offered us a smorgasbord of nourishing cheeses, smoked fish, meats, a variety of fresh breads, hot tea, and coffee. One hot meal was served daily at 4pm. As a rule, guests ate breakfast and lunch at the smorgasbord when they wanted, went to the river, and returned at 4 p.m. to enjoy a hot meal, then rested for a couple of hours, fished some more and returned to the farm and more smorgasbord around 1 a.m. An exhausting schedule. At least it was for me.

There were four businessmen from Oslo staying at Fahle Farm. They had their own cars and drove to the upper pools, fishing without a guide, but each morning Egil had to make a show of pointing out the pools that were allotted to them. It seems we five were the only fishers at the farm who had made reservations long in advance and Egil took care of us first.

He seemed to have little time for sleep. Each day, as more fishers arrived, he rushed around frantically finding places for them to fish; and although he was expected to accomplish the impossible, he remained cheerful. I suspected that the overbooking took place in Oslo at the main office where reservations were handled.

As a whole, the Norwegians are a friendly people, and the four guests from Oslo were quite wonderful to me. They wanted the little American lady to catch a salmon and were concerned that I was fishing with flies rather than bait. I was the only one fly fishing, and what they considered a short rod. Of course, my nine-foot Gillum salmon rod by American standards was not too short at all by American standards.

One day as we stood outside in the front yard, one of the men, Rolphe, kindly insisted that I use one of his rods. "It is a short rod, good for you," he said handing the rod to me. It was short by Norwegian standards, but it was a stiff fourteen-foot bait casting rod that in my petite palms felt like a telephone pole. Keeping that thought to myself, I thanked him and explained that my small hand and wrist would have fewer problems with my lighter-weight rod.

I added that I was disappointed I couldn't fish without Egil and when Egil joined us and instructed me to wait until he had showed the men where to fish, Rolphe offered to take me fishing. Was that possible? Rolphe suggested he take me to the river and act as guide, and Egil agreed, and off we went to the best salmon pool in the river, the one I had fished the first time. But this time I was the only fisher there and I fished from a rowboat with Rolphe at the helm.

The pool was quite long and Rolphe rowed backwards until we were stationary in the swift current. I must admit I was too concerned about his being able to row to really enjoy fishing. He was not a big, strong man and he had to row backwards with all his might; but he managed to keep us in place until I had cast a few lines off the side of the boat and then he let the boat drop down the length of my line, then got us into position again while I fished.

On the second drop a large salmon took the fly, a Silver Grey, and suddenly leapt high into the air. It put on a spectacular performance, dancing and splashing in the river. Suddenly, it began swimming downriver, took out all of the line of the reel and just as unexpectedly, turned back upriver again, leaving the length of backing and line on the water. Alarmed, I glanced down at the rod. I was using my new Bogdan reel which had a two-to-one ratio that could reel in a fish in a jiffy. It was the first time it had a chance to show me what it could do and I was delighted. Blowing a kiss into the air for Stan Bogdan, I settled down and focused on the business of playing the big salmon.

Poor Rolphe was still rowing backwards, valiantly, when a man appeared opposite us and began yelling at him. Rolphe said he was a farmer who lived on the other side of the river and was noted for being the best sportfisher in the area. It seems he was advising Rolphe to take me across the river to a short stretch of gravel shore where he could beach the boat. Following the salmon while my guide was paddling to the opposite shore would be a tricky maneuver, since changing direction could loosen the hook in the fish's jaw; but to the left of us where the farmer was standing there was a high bank, so Rolphe followed the farmer's instructions.

It wasn't easy. We were fighting a powerful fish and current, but we got lucky and Rolphe finally beached the boat. Keeping a curve in the rod, I stepped out and stood on the shore. Rolphe stayed in the river and I gradually managed to pump and maneuver the heavy fish up to him. Finally, he gaffed the salmon as there were no nets at Fahle Farm.

Egil and everyone else at Fahle Farm seemed to appear out of nowhere. The word had gotten out. After congratulating me, Egil explained that the farmer across the river had jumped on his bicycle and rushed down to tell Egil that a little woman fishing with a little rod and fly had caught a big one.

As it happened, I was the only one who caught a salmon that day. The conditions were ideal for fly fishing. Fishing had been poor that week and everyone was blaming the Driva. The water was too low and clear they said. For metal lures and prawns, yes; but not for salmon flies cast by a perfectly balanced custom-made split-bamboo rod with a Bogdan reel!

That evening Rolphe and Egil planned a surprise party for me on the bank of the river. We sat around a blazing bonfire while Rolphe barbequed spareribs. Egil played the guitar and a waitress at the Farm sang a Norwegian folk song—a song about a woman who loved to fish the Driva for its mighty salmon day and night. The pretty singer motioned to me. Everybody clapped and then Egil explained that the song was about a real woman who had lived in the

Rolphe and Max with her Driva catch.

valley long ago at a time when almost no women fished. She had become famous for her love of the Driva.

At the end of the night of twilight we were still standing around the glowing embers of a bonfire drinking toasts to each other. Holding cans of beer high in the air, the Norwegians drank a toast to me and then to America. In return I drank a toast to them, to their beautiful country, to the Driva and to its mighty salmon.

The next morning Egil took me to a pool with no other fishers in sight, a pool where I could wade and really make use of a fly. Almost at once I hooked into a large one! The silvery salmon leapt high, fell back into the river, and made its way upriver to spawn. My line had caught on the handle of my reel and while I was tying another fly on the leader Egil cast a prawn into the run, hooked another great salmon, and it too skyrocketed into the air, splashed back into the river and continued on its way to the spawning beds.

I was thankful to have the chance more often, but fished only in the mornings. In the afternoon I sat inside with other guests obviously disgruntled as they waited to be taken to the river. Egil worked hard, but he had been given an impossible task. More fishermen without reservations arrived each day, so I decided it was time to leave. I had caught only a few salmon, but there comparatively few in the Driva. This didn't surprise me because when I had been in Oslo with Erik Hyher, an enthusiastic young assistant boasting about the Driva made the mistake of telling me that over five thousand salmon had been caught at the mouth of the Driva that morning. Erik had groaned and reprimanded him, but I knew the young man was talking about driftnets.

None of this stopped me from loving the Driva and fishing there, particularly the pools I could wade. That was more than twenty years ago and the last report I got said that driftnets were preventing all but a few salmon from making it up to the spawning grounds, and almost no sportfishers were going to the Driva anymore.

Of course Egil Hagen loved the Driva always and was concerned about what was happening to its salmon population. And I was concerned about what the war had done to Egil. His plane had been shot down while he was flying over Bergen, and although he survived, the emotional scars from being shot down in his home skies never fully healed.

Rolphe, Max, and Egil after a day on the Driva in Norway. c. 1963

CHAPTER TWENTY-FIVE

Rivers and Reveries, Canada's Arctic

Whatever befalls the earth befalls the sons of the earth. Man did not weave the web of life. He is merely a strand in it. What he does to the web, he does to himself. This we know.

—Chief Sealth, 1854

At midnight in the Canadian Arctic, the summer twilight's fading aurora borealis cast a ghostly glow over the landscape, where ancient glaciers had strewn moraines of rocks and boulders across the vast tundra. Huddled in a folding canvas chair, I found myself in Barren Lands, home of the rockpile Inuit graves. Everyone else had gone to bed and finally, when a small threatening cloud of huge mosquitoes hovered close to my head, I crawled into my small tent. That night as I slept a ghost chased me over the tundra all night long. There was no place to hide! When I emerged to meet the day, I was exhausted.

We were at the mouth of the Wilson River in the Keewattin District where the river enters Hudson Bay on its northwest coast, just south of the Arctic Circle. I was one of five members of a small expedition that Canada's Department of Northern Affairs had organized as part of a plan to open its Arctic to sportfishers and develop more employment for Inuit citizens. Norman Ferrier was the government biologist in charge and I was the only woman in the group.

Max holding skull and rifle in Inuit grave site. Canadian Arctic, c. 1963.

The night before we had arrived in sturdy canoes propelled by powerful motors, and that morning after I crawled out of my tent, I was surprised to find that everything had changed. Sunlight flooded over the tundra and the clearest of clear water rushed over a riverbed of rock that transformed the Wilson into a most exciting river, where its fast, splashing rapids had dug out ideal pools for fish. Even the granite boulders on the tundra seemed to have changed. Each was tinted by its own mineral. Some were a tawny pink, others pale blue or creamy yellow, all pastel hues covered with a decorative floral pattern of lichen moss that had dried into a dark green or black with time.

Norman explained that we were going after Arctic char and that all of the rivers emptying into Hudson Bay were fairly short and frozen solid during the winter months, so the char (no salmon ventured that far north) returned to the Bay after spawning, and if fishers were not there during a run of char upriver, they would catch none. Norman could sense our nervousness and reassured the group. "Our trip has been carefully planned around the char's spawning schedule, so you will find there is char in the river."

Before starting on this fishing expedition, I spent some time exploring the tundra and its unfamiliar base of permafrost—a few inches of soil spread over a base of hard ice hundreds of feet deep. It kept the soil moist at all times and tucked beneath shelves of rock in this damp dirt I found single clumps of wild flowers. They were exquisite, tiny, and few and far between, but all the more precious and exciting in their contract to the barren landscape.

An Inuit guide called to me. It was time to go fishing. We were heading to see what we could find in the Wilson River. An unassuming and dull name for such an exotic and faraway body of water. Everyone in the group seemed to think that Arctic char would not take flies. The

Department of Northern Affairs was anxious to know if they would, and I hoped to help prove they were right. The Inuit, who netted the river for char, had told the guides where to find the best fishing and the guides took us to marvelous natural pools. But I had a problem. The guide in my canoe, Angangai, knew nothing about fly fishing or where to place the canoe in a river when fishing with flies, and he fished with a metal spinning lure while I used a Streamer fly. He anchored the canoe in an ideal position for metal lures and at once caught char. Although there were more char in the pool, no one caught any.

Finally, getting exasperated, I asked Angagai to pull up anchor and drop down to another pool. No one followed us. As we came to what looked like a good pool, I asked Angangai to stop and told him where to put the canoe. He was about to start fishing and I asked him to let me fish first. He complied graciously and when my Streamer had no competition with spinning lures, I caught char.

They averaged ten to twelve pounds, and I caught a beautiful pale pink female, spotted with silvery grey dots the size of a dime. The hookbills were brilliantly colored, like male brook trout, and the Arctic graylings loved my dry flies.

The expedition's main purpose was to train the three Inuit guides, particularly for sportfishing, and I was very impressed by the good humor and intelligence of those young men. It was a joy to be with them. At the end of the week, I went on to the Meliodine, another river that runs into Hudson Bay. We were only there a day and it wasn't enough time to explore the river's treasures.

From my perspective the most important part of the expedition was a flight we took over northern Hudson Bay on my way back to Churchill. I had been booked on a flight from Rankin Inlet to Churchill, but missed it. So the Department of Northern Affairs arranged for me to return to Churchill by freight plane, routed to the east coast of Southhampton Island, to deliver supplies to an army base and then fly down to Churchill.

The pilot was instructed by flight controllers to fly over Marble Island, somewhat out of his way; and as I stood behind him as we came down low, I had a view of two harbors, an inner and outer harbor connected by a narrow channel. Just outside one harbor, the noise of the plane had stirred up several white whale, gorgeous in the clear blue water. About twelve miles long, the island was adorned with pink marble mountains and pink lakes in a pink valley scoured clean of till and polished by weather.

I could detect the island's lakes only as I looked back and saw the sheen of sunlight on rippling water. The copilot commented, "That water comes from melted snow. The lakes have no real inlets or outlets, and there is no dirt, vegetation or habitation of any kind on the whole island." I couldn't help thinking that Marble Island was one of Nature's greatest works of art.

Gaining altitude as we reached the tip of the island, the plane headed north. Dazed from the magnificence of it all, I dropped down into the bucket seat and looked out the window. It took more time than I thought it would to reach Southampton Island, but finally the copilot announced, "We are approaching the west shore of the island now." Standing again behind the pilot, I could see it clearly. And I noticed there was a sparkling, solid white line of floating ice in the distance. The pilot explained that it was part of a massive, perpetual ice floe at the Arctic Circle, forever drifting and kept in line by the wind and currents.

Flying over the southern shore of Southampton Island was thrilling, too. Marshes of limestone lowlands had formed extensive summer breeding grounds for water birds, and the plane noise scared up flock after flock of geese, festoons of pearly white snow geese, swinging out in rhythmic unison over the mouth of the Kerchoffer River and over to the deep blue water of Hudson Bay.

After that dramatic introduction to Southampton Island, the 180 miles across the island's vast floor of green lichen seemed dull by comparison, so I returned to my seat where I could watch from a side window. The terrain I saw, part of the Laurentian Shield, bore evidence of a recent elevation of land, or withdrawal of the sea, as part of the Keewattin rock system which, according to my pilots, included the oldest known rock in North America.

Finally, after an hour or more, the plane dropped altitude and passed over some of the most spectacular scenery on Earth: lakes and ponds, each a different color. Quickly, I jumped up to look though the cockpit window. The pilot remarked, "You're lucky to get a view of this—only a handful of folks have ever seen Southampton from the air." In winter the island was covered with snow and in the summer fog or clouds covered the island as it met the Hudson Bay's icy cold waters.

The rise of the continental shelf had exposed the colorful lakes and ponds in newly established land along the coast, and through the clear water I could see where the land began. The lakes, knows as eskers—temporary lakes occupying pond or lake-sized rock hollows— were the results of glaciations. Each hollow, a different hue, was laminated by a couple inches of hardened glacial sediment and colored by its own ore mineral. The feldspar group of minerals, for instance, constitutes almost half of the Earth's crust and imparts grey or pink rock with vitreous or pearly luster—like the rock on Marble Island.

The flight over Southampton was all the more exciting since it came as an unexpected surprise. I had been told we would fly over some interesting scenery, but I had no idea what to expect. From the air, I could see what appeared to be a stream of dark lavender lava that was actually molten lava that millions of years ago had hardened upon hitting the air. To the right of it was an undulating line of pure white forms—lime deposits—and between that and the coast was a cluster of lakes, all creating a superb symphony of colors as only Nature could compose. What a colorist!

Looking out of the plane, I felt as if I had flown back to The Beginning, to the emergence of flora and fauna, while my existentialist imagination took flight through some time-and-space continuum, back, back, back, whizzing still further back in time until the roaring freight plane suddenly landed on the army base tarmac, bringing me back to the jolting reality that always breaks one's flights of fancy.

CHAPTER TWENTY-SIX

Back to the Miramichi

The least movement is of importance to all nature. The
entire ocean is affected by a pebble.

—Blaise Pascal, *Pensées*, 1670

In my final years of fishing, on my own again after my marriage to
Watson, I was drawn back to my beloved Miramichi River where Jack
and I had spent some of our happiest days. My camp, a comfortable
cabin set above the river outside of Doaktown, New Brunswick (population less than five hundred) seemed like a speck of real estate amid
a vast spread of fragrant pines. I relished the peace and quiet—aside
from the cacophony of bird song and the chatter of smaller creatures
ranging from chipmunks and raccoons to foxes and coyotes. I enjoyed
occasional visits from a moose or mother bear, but for the most part I
had this world on the banks of the Miramichi to myself.

There was one notable human neighbor with a camp downriver—a great fisherman and devoted conservationist, and generous man
despite his reputation for gruffness. He was known to millions as one
of major league baseball's great hitters: Ted Williams. When he stopped
by my camp one day to introduce himself, I couldn't get over how
handsome he was, and how he towered over me. I was in my seventies
then and Ted was in his late fifties. We talked about the fishing in the
Miramichi, our latest projects, and conservation. Like me, he was very
concerned about the future of rivers and the salmon and other wildlife

that depended on thriving streams; and we traded articles and magazines on the latest scientific discoveries and conservation strategies.

Ted Williams had a rarely seen side that revealed a kind heart at the core of his sometimes brusque style. Perhaps it was the "coach" in him. People I knew around Doaktown would tell me about the salmon rods Ted gave away to teenagers down his way, telling them to be good boys and go fishing instead of poaching or looking for trouble. He let them fish his pool—one of the best in the Miramichi.

One summer when I was savoring a morning of angling at Ted's pool, I mentioned that I wanted a graphite rod but couldn't find one that suited me. Each one I tried seemed too stiff. The next time Ted came to see me he brought one of his graphite rods for me to try. It was wonderfully lightweight, but too stiff from butt to tip. When I said as much, Ted said, "Can you describe the rod you want, Max, and I'll see what I can do."

I had some idea of what I wanted but wasn't quite sure how to express what I could see so clearly in my imagination. Having several split-bamboo fly rods that Pinkie Gillum made for me, I explained to Ted that I wanted a graphite rod with the same action. Pinkie was extremely particular about the bamboo he used, and the fly rods he made for me have stiff butts and limber tips. He had died a few years earlier and his rods became collector's items. He and Jack used to spend hours discussing just where the break between the unmoving and limber should be in a fly rod, and just how stable the butt should be and just how flexible the tip should be.

When Pinkie handed me the first salmon rod he'd produced for me, a nine-foot split-bamboo, he explained its action. "The rod is designed to do the work for you," he said. Given my small hands and wrists, and the lack the arm-length leverage and strength to shoot a fishing line out a long distance, Pinkie designed the rod so that as I gave it that last drive at the end of the forward cast, the limber tip took over and whipped the line out further than I had ever cast on any other rod.

After Pinkie's death I began to fish with fiberglass rods. They were lighter than the bamboo; although I did find a hollow fiberglass Fenwick rod at Wallace Doak's shop in Doaktown that came fairly close to Pinkies'. The Fenwich was lighter weight, of course, but its handgrip was too large to suit me; and yet, it was my favorite salmon rod until I developed a bit of arthritis at the base of my right thumb. Then even the fiberglass seemed too heavy, so I began my search for a graphite alternative.

I had trouble explaining to Ted exactly what I had in mind. I knew when a rod was right for me, but couldn't articulate exactly what made it right. But Ted understood. He knew more about what I wanted than I did. He promised to have one made and said he'd bring it to me the following summer.

In the meantime I tried out a variety of makes and styles of graphite rods. They were all too unbending from butt to tip. Such a rod was really meant for tournament casting and just didn't perform well until has a fairly long length of line in the air. I wanted a rod that would cast a short line, too. In the Matapédia, fishing from a canoe, I always started with a very short line and lengthened it after each cast, covering every foot of water from the canoe to the end of the last cast. I stripped in line slowly, since I had seen more than one salmon follow the fly right up to the canoe.

Tournament casters cover only the water at the end of his cast. He or she don't cast for fish, but for distance. I suppose rod makers design stiff rods because so many young fishers want them. They can cast an astonishing length of line and the stiff graphites can pick up that super length of line from the water. But that was never my idea of the best way to catch fish. I liked to strip in line and then shoot it out again on the forward cast, seldom casting more than sixty feet of line. My best teachers—Jack Atherton, Edward Hewitt, Charles de Feo and many other masters of the art of fly fishing– taught me that a fish is easier to catch and control with a short line. I discovered that a salmon generally prefers a fly sent out between forty and sixty feet.

I found that when a salmon would strike at eighty or ninety feet, it usually spit out the hook before I could reel in the slack. When I picked up too long a line, it splashed the surface; and when I cast out too long a line, it slapped the surface and required a great deal of awkward effort on my part.

Time and time again I sat on the bank of the Miramichi and watched a young angler casting a long line into a pool I knew well. Each time the fly hit the water beyond the "hot spot." Never anywhere near the lie of a salmon. One day, I watched a young man become so fascinated by the feat of casting a fly ninety feet to the opposite shore he forgot he was fishing for salmon. Finally, he stamped out of the river, muttering angrily, "There are no salmon in the Miramichi, anyway." Right after he left, an old-timer waded into the river, cast a short line to a "hot spot" in the pool, and hooked a salmon on his first cast.

Since my camp was by the Miramichi, I wasn't required to have a guide to fish my pool. Pete, my Springer Spaniel and devoted companion, known by almost everyone around Doaktown, helped me net my catches. When I hooked a salmon or grilse, I gave Pete the command to sit. Once the fish was ready to net, I called out, "Pete, go get it!" Happy to comply, he would jump into the river and chase the fish right into the net. Now how many guides would be willing to do that for me?!

Ted Williams did return the following summer, graphite rod in hand. He presented it to me looking rather serious, and I quickly understood that he was nervous about how I would like the rod. Gripping my new present, I felt touched by Ted's generous desire to help me, an outspoken, seventy-something fly fisherwoman. It didn't take more than a few moments for me to know that this rod was different from all the others I had tried. "I love it!" I exclaimed. And I did.

My river neighbor's furrowed brow relaxed into a proud smile as I gave him a big hug to thank him for the wonderful gift. Only Ted Williams and Steve Trewhella, president of the Shakespeare Fishing Tackle Company, knew the exact specifications that made my graphite rod perform so magically. A nine-foot rod with a fairly stiff butt and limber tip, it had a smallish handgrip and felt light as a fly. It cast a long line with very little effort; and when I stepped into the Miramichi and sent out my line with that delicate but powerful rod, I felt as graceful as Anna Pavlova in those San Francisco ballet performances Jack and I had enjoyed fifty years earlier—although I resembled anything but a ballerina in my baggy waders and floppy Orvis sun hat!

That happy day I went down to the Miramichi with my new graphite rod and christened it with two grilse. As I walked up the hill away from the water, the evening breeze smelled like warm dirt and wild flowers. I turned for a moment, delivered a silent thank-you to the river for all of her gifts to me over the years and smiled knowing that all my worries—about rods, about my advancing years, about the future of salmon and their waterways—had floated downstream and out of sight. I felt like the luckiest woman in the world.

Ted Williams and Max discussing rods, fishing, and conservation during summer. c. 1979.

Afterword

Catherine Varchaver

Ultimately, Max was as much a true environmentalist—and observer of human nature—as she was an avid fly fisher. Permeating most of Max's conversations with all who would listen (and some who wouldn't) were her latest readings about the devastating decline in the health of salmon and their rivers. Max also saw human overpopulation as a terrible ecological burden to the Earth—one she believed contributed to the ruin of natural landscapes everywhere as the planet struggled to adapt to the increasing lack of balance between human beings and the natural world.

In the years that followed my grandfather's death in 1952, Max became more acutely aware of the imminent path to extinction for both Atlantic and Pacific salmon. In her many decades of fly fishing, Max watched the state of Atlantic and Pacific salmon deteriorate dramatically. She recognized human caused impacts to oceans and rivers, from net fishing and poaching to industrial and runoff pollution, destructive land development and poor natural resources management, even when many other sportfishers preferred to remain in denial about the environmental degradation affecting more and more of the waterways they cherished. Today, she would be horrified—

although hardly surprised—to add climate change to the top of the list of threats. I have no doubt that if Max were with us now, she would give much of her considerable energies to raising awareness about the impacts of global warming on the planet's oceans, icebergs and rivers, along with the flora and fauna so dependent on healthy waters, landscapes, and intersecting ecosystems.

Over the last twenty or so years of her life, Max expressed her environmental concerns in articles that appeared in the *Atlantic Salmon Journal* and other publications. In one piece, *Restoration and Management of Ruined Salmon Rivers*, Max bemoaned the fact that she received requests for funding to save seals, whales, elephants, and many threatened wildlife species, but never, outside of the Atlantic Salmon Federation, did she find organizations asking for support to work on behalf of Atlantic and Pacific salmon. (Today there are a handful, but they remain small and more locally focused.) Max recognized that the plight of salmon and their rivers was a microcosm of larger ecological pattern across the planet. She was adamant that "the whole truth must be told to the public and governments" about what was happening to the salmon population so that legal regulations could be put in place to manage this precious resource. "To save the salmon from becoming extinct, governments are going to have to outlaw all nets, as Franco did in Spain," she noted. "If they don't, I fear the entire, already badly depleted salmon population will drop to a point of extinction, as did the Atlantic salmon population in the United States by the year 1953."

Max went on to recall that as far back as "the year 1952, when John and I, on our way to Canada, stopped by Maine's famous Bangor Pool in the Ponobscot River; it saddened us to see the pool spotted with foam caused by a poisonous chemical pouring into the river from a mill on the bank. One lonely fisherman was there. A very sad man, indeed, and he said that every year Maine had sent a salmon to the president of the United States, but there was no salmon to send the president that year—no salmon left in any of our salmon rivers."

Max's article closed with a plea to all Atlantic salmon fishers to "go back to your favorite salmon river, and even if it is bereft of salmon, stay and work with the Atlantic Salmon Federation. Do everything in your power to bring back the salmon in the river you love, and try to get the United States Government to work with the Canadian government on a plan to form an international organization of governments [that supports the restoration of] rivers in which salmon spawn."

As it turns out, my grandmother's deep concerns regarding the planet's dwindling populations of wild salmon and fishing rivers have since proved all too well-founded despite certain successes in terms of reducing river pollution and developing healthier salmon farming methods, for instance. Yet, even in light of the worrisome environmental picture overall, there is no doubt that Max would have wanted us to hold onto an overriding sense of hope and forward-looking vision. As much of a truthsayer as she was about the human contribution to overfishing, environmental and industrial misdeeds, Max believed ultimately in the power and resilience of the human will—and heart—to do right. So, even as she feared for the ecological future of salmon, their rivers, and the natural world at large, Max experienced the world through a multifaceted lens of hope, self-determination, and faith in the creative ingenuity of people to find solutions. More than problems, she saw possibilities. More than suffering, she felt passion. She believed in the power of Nature.

Max Atherton was herself a force of Nature. As her granddaughter, I happily carry in my heart and in my cells the soulful sound of Max's mildly irreverent laugh, her high-energy telling of time spent on one river or another, and her passionate treatises on conservation concerns. I hope I also carry Max's profound appreciation for the Earth's endless gifts and a grasp of the responsibility we bear to act on our awareness of the natural world's true value and to take any steps we can to safeguard its future.

May all who knew my grandmother, or who come to know her through these pages, including my son, Sasha, be inspired to revel in the artistic canvas of the natural world. And may the magic of the rivers that nourish majestic salmon as they strive to keep their place in the wild. And may we ensure that our children and all generations beyond the digital age find easy refuge in endless varieties of land and water scapes—and in them, the possibility of satisfying surrender to the joyful lure of fly fishing.

And now, as I close my eyes and travel back to Max's lifetime, it is easy to see the way she made herself at home in fishing camps and rocky streams, rod in hand, at a time when few women ventured there so regularly or artfully. And it is heartening to watch as my grandmother steps eagerly and expertly into hip-high waters to cast ever careful yet carefree lines across life's rivers, intent under a generous summer sun.